Bula

ISBN: 978-0-9817575-1-3

Maps used are public domain

Manufactured in Puerto Rico

*Dedicated to my mom and dad,
and to those of you who have given up
everything to seek out your dream.*

This is a true story,
well mostly.

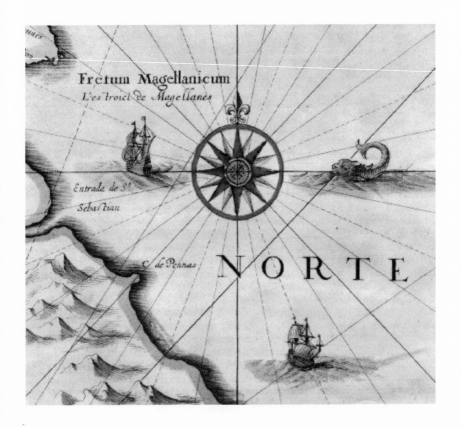

The Dream

Day after day, I sat in my cubicle plotting my escape. I was a caged animal. I was twenty-nine years old, living in San Diego. I worked for a corporation selling commercial real estate. I hated this job.

Most days when I arrived at work, I would fall asleep within the first two hours of sitting in my chair looking at the computer screen. I thought that I might have a physical condition and decided to go see a doctor.

They took blood samples and looked for something that might give me an answer, but nothing availed. I realized that I just lacked the motivation to work for the corporate world. I had to get out. Somehow.

In the winter of '99 I sat at work, bored, with the sound of the clock ticking into my brain. All my coworkers dreamed of buying big homes and flashy cars. I dreamed about the incredible countries and cultures I had visited in my travels around the world. I reminisced over the days I spent in the Arctic Circle, unable to sleep under the midnight sun. I thought about my trip to Turkey, riding on the back of a camel through the valley of the fairy chimneys. Everest will last in my memory forever.

I had been a world traveler, not meant to sit in a cubicle. I just couldn't focus on the present. My direction was uncertain. I wanted to put myself in the hands of fate, so I decided to buy a boat and sail across the Pacific.

However, I didn't have a lot of sailing experience. I learned how to sail on my roommate Thorly's sailing-wreck called the *Wasted*. It was a thirty-foot something and always sinking. It washed ashore in San Diego Bay two separate times, gaining publicity in the local papers to add to its infamy, and ours.

Thorly had one rule onboard the *Wasted*; the boat never leaves the dock without two cases of beer. Most of the time, it was just the two of us.

I once questioned him, "Why do you have this stupid rule? We'll never be able to drink all this beer."

With a fake Viking accent, he said, "They will be drank sooner or later matey."

He had a point.

Therefore, my experience of sailing consisted of drunken cavorting aboard a salty sea wreck on the occasional weekend in college.

I sat in my diminutive square at the office and began searching the newspapers for sailboats. I tried to keep the crinkling noise of the newspaper to a minimum, because it only meant I wasn't working. All the boats that looked interesting were out of my price range.

I found a website that listed boats all over the world and I began looking online at thousands of options. I focused on the ones close to home. Southern California had many boats for sale. San Francisco also had a few that were interesting. I could make a trip up north if I found something that was worthwhile. I searched websites for days.

I narrowed my search to boats within my budget. I realized the only ones I could afford were less than 40 feet in length. I locked into a few around San Diego that intrigued me and decided to take a drive down to the docks to have a look on my day off.

I first drove down to Shelter Island and marveled at all the beautiful boats packed into the marinas. I walked the docks with the seagulls flying overhead and breathed in the crisp fall air. I studied the many different makes and models.

I stepped inside one of the elaborate offices of a big-name boat broker. A stout man with an air of overconfidence was smoking a cigar sitting behind a desk. He was wearing a loud Hawaiian t-shirt and white pants. There were multiple photos of boats for sale in glass cases on the wall behind him.

He said, "Can I help you?"

I didn't want to do business with a guy who looked like a used car salesman. I kindly asked, "I'm just wondering if you have any printed listings of boats that I could take with me?"

His demeanor changed as he pointed to a stack of listings near the door. He went back to smoking his cigar and reading his newspaper. I grabbed the listings and stepped out the door, never to return.

I walked the stretch of boat brokerages and slipped in and out without too much attention, procuring as many listings as possible. I got back in my car and drove around to Harbor Island to have a look at the boats on that side.

As I entered the island, I glanced at various signs of private marinas. I came upon a small boat broker's sign that was unpretentious and pulled into the parking lot. I parked and walked down to the marina but couldn't find the office. I turned and began to leave when I spotted a door with the broker's name in small print. I stepped inside.

There were two guys inside chatting. I overheard their conversation about sailing in Mexico. They were wearing surf trunks and didn't appear to work there. I asked, "Do you guys know who works here?"

One of them had a genuine smile and said, "I guess I kind of do in between sailing trips. Can I help you?"

I said, "Well, I'm looking to buy a sailboat. I don't have a ton of money to spend, but I need some guidance on finding the right one."

"What do you plan on using the boat for?"

"I want to sail across the Pacific."

He looked at me trying to judge whether I was serious. "By the way, my name is Mike."

"I'm Bryan, nice to meet you."

Mike didn't seem like a salesman. He had a glowing smile and hair too long to be a businessman. He wore Birkenstock sandals and a t-shirt.

We chatted for awhile. He told me about his sailing adventures through Mexico. He voiced his disinterest in sitting idle on his boat in the city. He told me he just wanted to make enough money to head back south of the border to freedom.

I told him I only had thirty grand to spend—my whole life's savings. Thirty grand was barely enough to find a boat that was worthy to venture out into the deep sea.

Mike told me about the type of designs that were good for sailing offshore. He showed me all the listings that would be of interest to me. I asked a barrage of questions and he happily answered all of them.

He said, "What are you doing right now?"

"Not much really."

"Want to go take a look at some boats?"

"Sure."

We hopped in his borrowed truck and cruised down the road to a marina nearby to view some possibilities. He seemed happy to help me find my first boat.

After parking, we strolled up to one of the sailboats he had mentioned in the office. I looked at it as if it could be the one. He told me the good qualities and some of the bad. He wasn't trying to sell me on the first boat.

Walking over to another dock, Mike said, "How many crewmembers do you plan on taking with you on your trip?"

"As few as possible," I said. He raised an eyebrow, probably thinking I was irrational, or smart. Less crew meant fewer headaches.

The second boat seemed a little more practical. He again pointed out the many features, never pressuring to sell. After the third boat, I had a better idea of what I was looking for and what I could afford.

I said, "Mike, I appreciate you spending so much time with me. I truthfully didn't want to use a broker after my first experience." After a short pause, I said, "I'd like for you to help me find the right boat."

He said, "I may not be the best of resources, because like you, I just want to be out there in the deep blue. But I'd be glad to help you. With a little luck we might find what you're looking for, even at your price."

"I like your honesty." I gave him my phone number and he explained that he would continue searching.

"Something could pop up at a moments notice," he said, "and if you're ready, maybe we can get a deal on a good boat."

We parted in the parking lot of his office, and I walked back to my car. My emotions were vibrating. I went home, dreaming about the adventure.

Over the next two weeks, I received calls from Mike about certain boats and I looked at them online. I wasn't overly impressed with any of them, until one day, he called me at my office.

"Bryan, hey it's Mike. I found something that just came up today."

"What did you find?"

"Just take a look at it on the internet and call me back. It's a Crelock design built in California. It's a solid boat and a great price. They're asking thirty-five thousand, but we can probably talk them down. We should go down and look at it before someone else snaps it up."

"Ok, I'll give you a call back as soon as I check it out."

I dashed to the computer and pulled it up online. I got butterflies in my stomach as I stared at the photos. It seemed too good for that price.

I called him back, "Hey Mike."

"Did you see it?"

"Yeah, can you call and find out whether it's still available?"

"I'll call right now and call you back."

I was pacing around the office trying to look busy. My cell phone rang. It was Mike. "What did you find out?" I said.

"It's still available and there have been two offers on it."

"Two offers! Today was the first day it came on the market."

"Good deals don't last my friend. Listen, the boat is located down in the Chula Vista Marina. Do you have any time to look at it today?"

"I can get off work early and I'll meet you down there in hour and a half."

"Call me when you are ten minutes away. I'll meet you at the private gate to get us through to the docks."

"See ya there." I had to make up some excuse to get out of the office to view my little secret.

At ten past three, I managed to get out of the office unscathed and sped down to the south bay before late afternoon traffic. I called Mike and told him I would be arriving soon.

I met him at the gate, and we walked down together. I had a premonition that the boat was going to be a hoax or something unmentioned in the ad was wrong with it.

We walked up to the slip E14 and there it was. It looked more impressive than the photos. I was shocked that it could be mine if we negotiated the price down. Mike thoroughly looked it over and I dreamed of sailing the South Pacific.

"Wow," Mike said, "nice boat."

"No kidding."

Mike pulled out a piece of paper with the combination to the lock. He unlocked it and we entered the cabin to view the interior. It was impeccably clean and new inside.

"What year is it?" I said.

"68."

"The interior looks brand new."

"The previous owner intended to sail it around the world, but his wife became ill and they had to sell it."

"I feel sorry for them. Maybe the boat will still get its chance."

"I might be interested in buying it myself," he said.

"Hang on, you're the broker, you're trying to find *me* a boat." I thought for a second that he could be making some slick sales tactic. However, he seemed genuinely interested in the boat.

He said, "You're right, you're right. If you decide to pass on it, I might sell my boat and buy this one."

My excitement was taking hold. I tried to contain my emotions and think rationally. After discussing the important aspects of the boat and its pros and cons, I made my decision.

"Let's make an offer," I said, staring at Mike with wild eyes.

"I think this could be the one."

"Alright!"

He closed everything and locked up the cabin. We walked back to the parking lot and he discussed the broker's fees. He also informed me of the logistics of making a first offer and counter offers. I told him to call me with any details. I got in my car and slowly drove home with a warm feeling inside. It felt right.

Over the next few days, Mike and I conversed about the counter offers from the owners. He told me I would also need to have the boat surveyed by a professional. We finally locked into a bid.

I arranged to have the boat hauled out of the water and surveyed on land. The boat was pulled out in the Chula Vista Marina boat yard and a surveyor spent an hour inspecting the vessel. The results were good, and I made the final offer. The owner accepted at $30,500.

The owner came down to Mike's office and we both filled out all the paperwork. I handed him the largest check I've ever written and we shook hands. I was the proud owner of my first sailboat.

My new sailboat was a Columbia made in 1968 when fiberglass boats were just evolving and they made the hulls thick. Thick was good considering the journey. I had no idea what I was going to encounter crossing the Pacific. The sailing books I had read inspired me to go, but they also left questions in my head over the reality of battling storms in the deep sea. I could be enveloped by the waves and disappear forever. This frightened me, but it also sparked the allure of danger that I incorporate into most of my sports. If a game doesn't entail some element of doom, I lose interest.

The boat was a mono-hull sloop, 36 feet from bow to stern. She had a 42-foot mast and a fin keel. I would've felt safer with a full keel, considering the challenge. Beefy is better when it comes to getting beat up in the deep sea. However, the fin keel gave me one advantage, speed. In times of bad weather, I could get to my destination maybe one day sooner and escape the evil sea.

She was white with navy-blue sail covers. I outfitted all the deck hardware and the varnished wood with navy canvas attachments to protect them from the damaging sun. There wasn't a lot of varnished wood on deck, which provided me with another advantage, less work.

Well kept in a meticulous manner, the interior had beautiful varnished mahogany and navy-blue upholstery. The galley was very spacious for ease of making meals. She had two double-births and two quarter-births that would allow six to sleep semi-comfortably. She was equipped with a small 23-horse diesel and some outdated navigation devices including a Loran. A Loran is a navigation receiver used for offshore vessels. It picks up signals from transmitters along the coastline. It only works close to shore and has become obsolete for decades since the government created GPS.

I had to install new equipment for the trip, but kept the Loran on the boat just in case. Every little bit of electronics could help in a pinch. I could "McGuyver" something together and make a transmitting device. But knowing my little knowledge of electronics, I would probably start a fire in the process.

I changed the name of the boat, which is taboo according to ancient sea lore. *Sharon* was the previous name. Boats are referred to as female and often named after a lover. I changed the name to *Bula*. It's a Fijian word meaning "hello", "goodbye", "cheers" and "thank you". It doesn't seem as if you would need any other words when visiting a foreign country. This word is the "aloha" of Fiji. I also found other meanings of the word. In Borneo, it means "crazy". Once I found that out, I knew it was right for the boat.

Get on the Boat

After three long months of outfitting the boat, I finally reached the last day before departure at midnight. I invited two of my friends to be my crewmembers, Ryder Watson and "Big Daddy Dawkins".

Big Daddy was six-two, 200-plus with blonde hair and blue eyes. I had met him in San Diego after college. We had traveled on many surf trips together down to Mexico. He was going to sail with me as far as Costa Rica.

Ryder and I grew up in Texas. He was from Dallas, and I was from Fort Worth. Though we attended different schools, we met my senior year in high school.

Most of our friends called each other by their last names or some stupid nickname. Everyone called me by my last name, Carson, and he was just Ryder.

Built like a redwood, he had the arms of Popeye and the calves of a German grape-masher. Take the head off George Michael and put it on Fred Flintstone's body and there you have him. Not that he resembles George Michael, but he's definitely better looking than Fred.

He was a sailor and one of those friends I seemed to have known forever. When considering my lack of experience on the high seas, I couldn't have thought of a better friend to invite on the journey south.

Ryder had sailed from Florida out to the Bahamas on a lake sailboat back in college. It's only a two-day sail but they missed the island. His roommate Zupanski, the so-called captain, forgot to calculate in the Gulf Stream, a rapid current that runs north along the coast of Florida. Zupanski realized his mistake and they finally found land after being lost at sea for days.

Ryder and I were speeding around San Diego in a mad frenzy. We were trying to get everything we thought we needed to sail across the deep sea. We had transformed into something similar to the insane survivalists moments before the Y2K dilemma.

Our last stop was at the local Costco, the gargantuan food warehouse where everything is bigger than Texas with Mexican prices. We grabbed a couple of huge carts and headed off in two different directions without any plan. I was speeding through the crowded isles grabbing nearly everything I saw. I'm five-foot-ten, one hundred and sixty pounds, but I eat more than most humans who are my size.

I rounded a corner with my shopping cart and ran into him. He looked at my cart full of beer and junk food*.

"So that's your beer?" he said, pointing at the two cases in my stuffed cart.

"Well I figured one case for you and one for me," I said. We were only sailing from San Diego to Cabo San Lucas together, roughly a two-week trip into Mexico.

"That's your beer, I'll get mine."

I shrugged and continued, thinking it was excessive to get any more. The trip to Cabo wasn't exactly going to be a pleasure cruise.

Ten minutes later, I rounded a corner and ran into him again. He had five cases of Coors Light and no food.

---

* junk food = 1 : sugar coated, greasy, processed, polyunsaturated, partially hydrogenated, nutrition-less, ass-building, belly-bulging, stomach-wrenching, thigh-swelling, gluttonous pile of plastic food evilly produced by satanic companies who manipulatively draw you into their clutches for their own selfish monetary gains 2 : those who don't call it junk food, which is most of America, just call it food, which is scary

"Five cases?" I said. "You're only on the boat for two weeks. Let's see, that's about 14 days—5 cases at 24 a case—you got yourself about nine beers a day there buddy."

"Beautiful." he said.

"Alrighty then."

We paid and drove back to the boat to drop off our supplies from Costco and other important stuff like . . . surfboards, guitars, sunglasses, silly hats, loud Hawaiian t-shirts, sun butter, and we couldn't forget the dirty magazines to keep us straight. To eat, we had cases of corned-beef hash, roast-beef hash, spam, beef-jerky, stacks of sticky buns, pop-tarts, brownies, chocolate chip cookies, and vitamin C gummy-bears for good health. For the good and the bad times we had whiskey, vodka, rum, tequila, gin (I hate gin), and seven cases of beer—oh, and some sails for the boat.

I needed fishing gear for the trip and asked my buddies Casey and Big Daddy to take me to their favorite fishing store Squidco. They were both avid anglers. I told them I had plenty of loot and needed the right stuff.

Casey is a Canadian—short with blonde hair that was too long about a decade too late. He weighed around one-forty. He was nicknamed "Figman". The name derived from this growth of yellow-reddish hair he purposefully grew on his chin, resembling a fig. He isn't a very big fellow either, about the size of a Fig Newton. The name stuck. He was going to join the *Bula* on the Mexico-Tahiti leg. I had commissioned him to find some used rods and reels for the trip.

Four hundred bucks later, he got me *five* rods and *two* reels. That didn't make much sense to me. I figured that you must catch such big fish out there that you snap a few rods. Four hundred bucks and I hadn't even been to the tackle shop for the lures.

Back to the bank and off to the tackle shop Squidco. I had Big Daddy and Figman personally escort me in there to utilize their experience. As we walked into the store, their eyes lit up. They introduced me to this big Hawaiian guy behind the counter. They seemed to know him well. These two, probably lived in this store similar to a couple of old Italian ladies in their favorite shoe store in Rome.

Figman said to the guy, "Our buddy here is sailing across the Pacific. We wanna help him find everything he's gonna need."

"Ok bradda, let's get 'em stah-ted," the Hawaiian said with a pigeon accent.

Big Daddy and Figman pushed me out of the way and began pointing and firing requests. Plastic fish started pilling up on the counter and the two of them gained momentum with every new order. Figman grabbed me and began furiously firing fish-jargon off my forehead.

Big Daddy nearly had me in a headlock and said, "You gotta have some of these. Ohhh, these are unreal. Maybe a couple of those suckers. And this here . . . this is da bomb."

Figman dragged me around a corner and pointed at more stupid-looking fake fish.

He said, "Do you know how many doe-does I've picked up on these babies?" I felt dumb enough already, I didn't want to ask him what a "doe-doe" was.

Then he pulled me down to the coveted glass-case that showed those things that are too expensive for someone to steal, or even buy. He was pointing in there with lost eyes of an old soothsayer. He began turning the glass case salivating over the sparkling reels. "Carson, you gotta have yourself a Four-O."

"What the hell's a Four-O?" I said.

"Bro, a Four-O is a midsize reel for catching your bait fish, in order to catch the monsters."

Acting as if I knew what he was talking about, I said, "Ohhh, a four-ooo . . . ah huh. I guess I better get me one of those."

With a flash, the Hawaiian guy unlocked the case and put the reel into my hands. I nodded, "Yep, just throw this in the pile over there."

I finally gave the cut signal with the hand-slicing-the-throat motion. They were satisfied. I said to the Hawaiian guy, "What's the damage?"

It took him ten minutes to tally it up with a calculator that had buttons big enough to hit with your fist. His fingers were about the size of my whole hand. He finally said, "Four-ninety-five-sixty-five."

"WHAT?" I said. There were too many numbers.

He didn't repeat the price, but said he had already given me a 20% discount. I tried to rationalize that it was a good investment for a return in fish for years. I paid the man.

I eventually learned that fishing is not an investment. It's an expensive past time unless you have a huge fishing net.

Driving away from Squidco, I said, "Five hundred bucks on fake fish. I should've gone to Costco and spent the money on fish sticks. At least I could've *eaten* them."

The Mexican fishing license was another pain in the wallet. I drove down to the Semarnap office. It was located in some dilapidated building in downtown San Diego.

The Hispanic woman behind the counter was old and partially deaf. Her hair was metallic-blue cotton candy. It was huge and never moved. It was a tumbleweed-fusion-bomb attracting fuzz balls through static electricity. How do you take someone serious with such an enigmatic coif?

With shot-out-English, she said, "Con I hep yew?"

"Yes, I need a fishing license for Mexico. I'm sailing there next week," I said.

"Is it yewr yacht?"

"Yes ma'am."

"Ok, fill out d's forms for yewrself, and d's for yewr yacht. And do you have small inflammable boat?"

"You mean in-*flat*-able?"

"Yes."

"Ok, you need license for yewrself, yewr yacht, yewr inflammable, and everyone onboard need license."

Maybe I'd just skip fishing in Mexico. But I just spent nearly a grand on all the equipment, what was another 40 or 50 bucks.

After I filled out enough paperwork to become a diplomat for Mexico, I handed her the pile. She gave me a look as though I was wasting her precious time to type up another stinking fishing license. She said, "Comb back in un hour."

Looking at my watch, I said, "Aren't you closed at that time?"

Without a flinch, she said, "Comb back in turdy minute."

I left the particleboard office and milled around outside on the sidewalk with nothing better to do.

I returned in *turdy* minute. She was handing a sailing couple their paperwork. They also had the look of indignation.

She handed me my licenses and said, "Dat will be one hundred and turdy tree dollar."

"Excuse me."

She deftly pointed out the breakdown. "Forty dollar for yewr license, sixty for yewr yacht, and turdy tree for yewr dingy."

I wasn't even going to fish off the damn dingy. Turdy tree bucks my ass. I paid the cotton-candy-haired lady and stormed out of the office.

I drove back to the boat to finish the last minute preparations. Big Daddy came down to the docks with an incredulous look on his face. I was diligently mounting the wind-vane, the *day* of departure. I had no clue how to operate the intricate device. Through the years, I've discovered the wind-vane is one of the most important devices for sailing across an ocean. It's similar to an autopilot that steers the boat about 99 percent of the time.

Big Daddy helped me for awhile, but I sensed that something was simmering in his head. Like every project I undertake, I was missing half the parts for completion. I asked him if he wanted to join me in a quick run to the marine store. He reluctantly agreed.

As we were walking down the docks towards the borrowed Plymouth Valiant, he finally broke down and said, "Carson, I've got to tell you something."

"OK," I said, stopping to listen.

He looked around, trying to find the words. Finally, he stealthily pulled out a folded-up piece of paper from inside his jacket pocket. "Check this out."

He unfolded the paper and flattened it down on a dock bench. It was a weather printout showing a large storm in the North Pacific. Big Daddy said it was coming down the coast of California towards San Diego. Granted it was the middle of winter, and all the prudent sailors had already left for Mexico on their pleasure cruise three months prior in the easy weather.

Big Daddy had a salty background on the Alaskan fishing boats. He'd seen his fair share of dangerous seas. I'm sure he was questioning my experience as a captain and the state of my boat with all the necessary equipment being installed, hours before departure. Big Daddy also got himself married a few weeks prior. The reality of responsibility was kicking in.

"Carson," he said. "I don't want to miss an opportunity like this to sail and surf all the way to Costa Rica, but I've gotta tell you something."

I could see the consternation on his face. He said, "Man, I'm waking up in the middle of the night with these terrible nightmares." Embarrassed, yet honest, he threw the truth right at me.

In most cases, I would've waited for the storm to pass. However, I was on a tight schedule to get out of town fast. I bought the boat under an offshore-delivery premise. I had to vacate the country with the boat in less than 90 days, or pay the California state sales tax. I had to raise the sails and head south of the border, or forfeit three grand in tax. Big Daddy knew I had the impending dilemma and I was at the end of my 90 days.

Feeling disconsolate, I continued looking at the weather printout. It claimed 25-foot seas all the way into Mexico. However, the winds were only 25 knots, which didn't seem too bad. Besides, we were heading south, and it was coming from the north. It would boot us right in the ass all the way to Mexico.

Downwind in 25 knots of wind and 25-foot seas wasn't a great way to start a trip. I kept weighing out the weather and the cash, the weather and the cash. It was a manic ping-pong match in my head.

Then from out of the depths of some cheesy sea novel, it hit me. If I was going to be a sailor, I had to step up. I said, "Well Big

Daddy, I'm going! Ryder and I can hopefully handle it, and if you change your mind, you're more than welcome to go."

He was relieved that I didn't give him a hard time. I said, "You mind if I keep that weather printout?"

"Yeah, sure," he said. He handed me the crumpled printout. I quickly hid the evidence.

If Ryder found that paper, I'd be crewless.

10:01 pm . . . Ryder and I were driving around town in the old Valiant at a highly illegal pace. We were frantically picking up all the last-minute supplies we could get our sweaty hands on. We zigzagged through town, back and forth to the boat, stacking up a pile on the dock as Big Daddy kindly sat watch.

I was afraid to inform Ryder that our crewmember, with the most experience of big seas, had backed out because of the storm brewing in the North Pacific. I was diligently working on the right wording to make it sound advantageous. There was no way I could make it sound better to have less crew with the recent storm factor. However, I was still wickedly hatching an infallible plan. I finally locked into what I thought was a benign formula.

I said, "So, I was just informed that Big Daddy decided that it might be a little cramped on the boat with three guys and is going to stay. I think he's right. That means more food and beer for us."

The plan failed miserably. He turned to me with a look as if people were dropping out of the race and things were turning from bad to worse.

"You know, I'm not sure about this now," he said. "I think I want out as well."

I back-pedaled, stuttered, and tried to regain a positive direction. "Wait a minute bro, you know I gotta get out of here tonight and you're . . . you're my last crew member left. Everything's gonna be fine. What about all the food that's gonna spoil, and the beer?"

I kept throwing out the "food and beer" tactic, hoping he would see the light at the end of the Pringles can. He formulated a quick plan in his head.

He said, "I think we should just check out of the country and tuck back into a hidden part of San Diego Bay. The Coast Guard will never find us. This will buy us a few days to get organized and wait the storm out in safety."

I considered it. However, I knew the Coast Guard had an obligation to stick their noses up everyone's arse, due to the amount of navel warships in the bay.

I felt as though I was sitting at the craps table in Las Vegas with three grand in chips, all riding. Any minute I could crap out. I didn't want to take the risk. I'd rather face the storm and gamble my luck at sea. That didn't sound good either, because I'd opted to forgo the boat insurance.

I confided with Ryder. "The storm ain't gonna be that bad. It's probably all hype, as most threats are."

I wasn't about to show him the weather printout that I had surreptitiously tucked deep into my coat pocket. He came around at last. For the moment, I still had one crewmember.

11:32 pm . . . We came flying into the harbor parking lot with the wild-haired Ryder at the wheel. We had to get out before midnight.

We came to a skidding halt, parked sideways and shot out of the car, grabbing bags, boxes, and random things—throwing them all into a dock cart. We frantically carted everything down to the boat with junk falling out of the speeding cart.

We got to the boat, and there was Big Daddy and his new wife. They were comfortably lounging on all the boxes to pack onto the boat. I began stowing everything as quickly as possible with no organization.

11:44 pm . . . We began throwing things onto the boat. With fifteen minutes to spare, we ran out of room and left the unimportant crap on the dock. Big Daddy handed me a bottle of champagne.

He said, "Crack this mother open when you cross the equator."

"Thanks, but that's the last place I'm thinking of. I just want to get out of the harbor."

His wife handed us more sticky buns and they said their "bon voyage". We now had enough sticky buns to patch a gaping hole in the vessel. They stick to your teeth like glue. They just might work as a quick fix.

11:52 pm . . . We untied the dock lines, as if they were our souls chained to reality. In three months, I had bought a boat; put ten-grand into her; worked four jobs; broke up with my poor girlfriend; sold everything I owned; and gave the rest away.

11:58 pm . . . We pulled out of the quiet harbor two minutes before midnight. Ryder and I began howling at the tops of our lungs across the windless bay. We could hear the echoes bounce back from the skyscrapers lining the downtown San Diego waterfront. The blissful serenity of floating free in the clouds enveloped me as we motored out of the calm bay into another world.

Going Deep

The lights of Tijuana glimmered across the ocean as we got further out to sea. A large ship passed by us in the darkness. Seagulls circled the boat squawking in search of food. It was a moonless night with a few stars twinkling through the patchy fog. We were three miles out with no wind, motoring southbound.

My mind dwelled on all the things we forgot to get for the trip. No matter how prepared you think you are, once you leave is when you remember what you forgot.

Five miles off the coast, in between San Diego and Tijuana, the cold wind began to blow. I knew the storm was out there somewhere, ready to pounce on us like a pit-bull on a kitten.

Here I was embarking on a dangerous journey across the Pacific and the furthest I had sailed offshore was to Catalina Island. You can *see* Catalina from Los Angeles.

Finally, we had enough wind to sail. I turned the boat into the wind, turned on the overhead deck lights and raised the mainsail. I tightened the main halyard with the winch and returned to the cockpit. I unfurled the headsail from the cockpit by releasing the furling line and pulling on the port jib-sheet. I secured them and steered back onto our southern course. The wind filled the sails, and I trimmed them for the best speed. I turned off the lights and killed the engine.

"Ah, mother nature," I said.

"Yep, hopefully we won't need that engine for awhile." Ryder stared up at the faint white sails in the darkness.

With the noise of the engine gone, the only thing we could hear was the ocean breeze. Small waves gently splashed on the hull of the boat as we gained speed. I reclined on the bench seat of the cockpit and put my hands around the back of my head. I stared into space through the gaps in the clouds. I was embarking on my dream.

We crossed into Mexican waters sometime around two in the morning. It's not like there was a sign out there casually floating, saying something like, "Welcome to Mexico, please beware of unmarked vessels harboring dangerous banditos, corrupt boating officials, outlandish port fees, and fishing licenses more expensive than all your fishing equipment combined, so have a nice trip, and sail at your own risk."

We gazed at the lights of Tijuana. I had visions of the helter-skelter taking place in that dangerous town at that moment. I actually felt safer at sea with the Devil storm about to descend upon us.

Ryder was reaching his daily limit of cold beers. I hadn't touched one yet. I needed to stay sober. He cashed another can and ripped it in half. He chucked it over the side and looked at me with eyes like cherry-filled donuts. Twitching in a state of frazzled fatigue, he said, "I'm going down."

"No worries mate, get some zzz's. I'll keep 'er headed south."

He was off to hibernate as if he was the last remaining bear before the long winter nap. Ryder also had another nickname, "Good Night Ryder". He gained the name because by six o'clock, he has usually smoked himself into oblivion, cashed a twelve-pack, forked down half-a-dozen sausages, and passes out.

I kept her on course through the night. I got my second wind as I watched the sunrise over the town of Ensenada. A beautiful red and orange hue filled the sky from the rays of the sun bouncing off a circle of clouds near the horizon. Caught in a dream state, I breathed in the moment as we drifted through a living painting. It was the first sunrise of the trip in another country.

I got out the fishing rod and tied on a lure made of a cedar plug named "The Morning Wood". They work best at sunrise. I let out 50 feet of line, envisioning fish tacos for lunch. We had enough canned food to last us two months, but I had spent so much dough on fishing tackle and licenses, it was time for a serious payback.

Rising out of hibernation, Ryder said he was getting hungry after his winter nap.

"Yeah I'm famished," I said. "Why don't you cook up some oatmeal?"

"Aye aye Captain," he said.

That was the first time someone had called me captain, and it felt pretty cool, even though it was probably blatant sarcasm.

I glanced behind the boat and saw something dragging on the surface attached to the fishing lure. I thought it must have been some seaweed. I went back and started reeling in the line. As it got closer, the seaweed resembled a fish. I thought there was no way it could be an actual fish. I didn't hear the drag on the reel and the object appeared as dead driftwood skipping along the surface.

I pulled the slimy fish into the cockpit. It wasn't even big enough to fill a tuna can. I wondered how many miles we had been dragging that poor sap. Strangely enough, it was still alive and only slightly larger than the lure.

I yelled, "ONE THOUSAND DOLLARS AND ALL I GET IS THIS PISS-ANT SARDINE! Look at it. It's all bones. It's a living X-RAY!" I was mumbling a make-believe episode to myself, "Ahhh, yes ma'am. I would like to order the fish-bone sandwich please, with not a lot of meat."

Ryder looked at it from the galley and said, "You can't keep that thing."

I got defensive, squeezing it to see if there was any meat. "Hang on man, we might be able to make this sucker into an hors d'oeuvres."

"That wouldn't fill one cracker."

"Yes it would, maybe two."

I chucked it back into the sea to grow. Big fish probably didn't want to eat it either; figured they'd hurt their mouth.

The prodigious bowl of oats finally arrived. "Have you got a shovel?" I said.

"I've got a funnel," he said with the voice of a lumberjack.

I just looked at him funny. We sat in the cockpit eating our bowl of oats as the late morning sunshine broke through the fog. We were sailing by the little island Todos Santos, off the coast of Ensenada. The inhospitable shoreline was rocky with sheer cliffs rising sixty feet above the ocean. The tops of the cliffs were vibrant green. The long green grass at the top intertwined with large sunflowers swaying with the onshore breeze. A thick sea fog hung over the island. Only a tenth of a mile long, this tiny island gets some of the biggest surf in the world. We were hoping to catch a few waves that morning.

There was no place to anchor. We decided that we would take turns sitting on the boat under idle while the other surfed. There was only one problem . . . there was no surf.

After circling the surf break "Killers", we sadly gave up and continued our journey south. We sailed on down the coast until we reached the grandiose sand dunes of La Bufadora. Large sand dunes rose hundreds of feet above the glistening blue sea. We glided downwind, deeper into the land of the Aztec.

We picked up some wind off the desert coast. The waves quickly increased in size. Throughout the day, the ocean swell tripled in size and the cold winter-wind blew 25 knots from the north. We were flying downwind under full sail. Waves were breaking behind us. The bigger waves rolled over the top of the transom into the cockpit. We were running wing-and-wing with the mainsail and headsail on opposite sides of the boat. It was a precarious sail pattern in such winds. I tightened down the boom-vang, a block and tackle system that keeps the boom from flying dangerously upward.

A wave crashed into the stern, spinning the boat sideways. I ducked as the boom whipped to the opposite side. *BAMM*! The boom-vang ripped out of the mast. The mainsheet traveler shot across the transom and took a huge chunk of wood out of the cockpit combing.

Ryder flew out of the galley to see what happened. I stood there desperate and yelled, "THE BOOM-VANG RIPPED OUT OF THE MAST, WE'VE GOT TO TAKE THE MAINSAIL DOWN."

Together we frantically pulled the mainsail down, tugging on the tight canvas. I shot back to the cockpit and reefed the roller-furling unit on the headsail, decreasing the size of the sail for safety. The wind and seas were gaining power by the minute. I was hand steering because the autopilot was useless in that weather. The winds increased to 40 knots with full-breaking seas, pushing us closer to land.

I said, "Ryder, find out our position by GPS and sort out the closest anchorage to duck into along the coast." He found a small curved peninsula on the chart near a town called San Carlos. It would provide a decent shelter from the north wind. We could pull in for the night and let the storm pass. Our mental state became more relaxed once we had a plan. However, the weather was rapidly deteriorating.

I continued hand steering. I was having a frightening time with the bigger waves. Ryder gave me some good advice that I still use to this day, "Act like your boat is a giant long-board and surf the waves, don't battle them."

Everything became clear and easy. I surfed down the face of the waves and turned the 36-foot long-board at an angle for more speed and longer rides. It was the same as surfing just on a larger scale. The detriment of wiping out would be slightly more severe. I concentrated on reaching our destination safely.

We pulled into San Carlos that evening in the middle of the storm. We sailed around the peninsula to calmer waters. The big seas were blocked, but the winds continued to howl across the cove. It was going to be a rough night.

I put two anchors out for reassurance. We were just on the outside of the shore break. There was a small fishing village onshore at the base of a barren mesa. It looked barely inhabited. There were some oddly constructed houses. The houses had fishing nets rotting away in the front yards of sand and cobblestone. Sun-bleached debris and car tires dotted the beach. A lack of concern seemed to hang over the dismal village. We were not looking for a welcoming parade, but maybe a lit cerveza sign. Any form of movement would have provoked us to venture ashore to the cactus wasteland. We saw nothing and stayed on the boat.

That night the wind and seas had their way with the boat. We pinned ourselves into separate corners to avoid rolling onto the cabin floor. I looked out the window with the wind screaming over the peninsula. I saw a huge bonfire. It was blowing thirty-five knots with sideways rain and four Mexican men were out there standing around a bonfire on the exposed finger of land. They were probably tanking a couple cases of Tecate and blasting that obnoxious Mexican music.

Traditional Mexican music is a conglomeration of various-sized Spanish guitars, indigenous Indian drumming, the accordion, German tuba, and a unique vocal style over that rumpus. It reminds me of being at the circus. You can't listen to it sober. I used to hate it, but now that I've figured it out, I love it. I never understood the German polka influence until I remembered their presence in Mexico in WWII.

The men out there didn't look like they were having fun, and I didn't hear any circus music. We heard a long buzzing noise escalate from the darkness. We then spotted a small fishing boat coming back to land from the wicked sea.

"That fire was a homemade lighthouse," I said.

Ryder stared out the window in disbelief and muttered, "Whoa."

We sat back and contemplated how many poor souls had been lost at sea over the years. I passed out from exhaustion. I hadn't slept in three days.

Trapped

I woke up from a nightmare that the little town where we were anchored was an outpost for aliens who disguised themselves as Mexican fisherman. They were creeping in to suck the meat out of my head to have themselves a plate of brain biscuits for breakfast.

The howling winds gained velocity throughout the night. The ocean swell had also increased in size. The boat was spinning in circles from the waves and currents. We were rocking back and forth wildly. Items not tied down on deck could easily slide into the ocean.

I got out of my bunk and went up top-deck to have a look around. I placed a third anchor astern to keep the boat in one place. Ryder was awake in the galley heating up some breakfast for us.

We sat inside the cabin salon eating garlic soup in the mid-morning gloom. I had caught a cold from the freezing wind and lack of sleep. I tried to boost my immune system by eating garlic and vitamin C gummy bears. Ryder and I were competing to see how many cloves of garlic we could eat straight. It wasn't easy. Those little suckers are almost as tough to eat as jalapeños. The cabin started reeking from all the garlic gas and we sat around laughing—eating more garlic.

The wind picked up to forty knots. Waves were breaking on both sides of the boat. It was time to anchor further out before we got a breaker on the bow in the impact zone.

This time I dropped four anchors out, one in each direction to keep the boat stable. It didn't work. All the anchor lines twisted up among themselves and actually became a hazard. How was I to know—I figured more was better. The weather was pounding us down. This was no vacation and the days wore on us. I was not thinking clearly. My mind was chewing on itself like a mangy dog nibbling on its own tail.

The storm finally passed. We pulled in the four anchor lines that were knotted-up and headed south. We stayed five miles off the inhospitable coast of monolithic stone mountains. There were sparse settlements. The small villages we saw could not possibly have any roads leading to them. Surrounded by huge mountain ridges, the only means of transportation could have been by boat, plane, helicopter or UFO.

We gradually moved further away from the Baja coast. We were heading towards Guerrero Negro where the land juts out into the Pacific in the shape of a shark fin.

"I'll take the watch," Ryder said. "Why don't you pass out for a few?"

He got himself a foldout beach-chair and sunk down into the cockpit behind the wheel. He was wearing five layers of winter clothes, plus gloves and a beanie.

He asked me for two Coors Lights. He said. "I need two at a time to save myself a trip to the fridge."

I began to think he might actually cash those five cases by the time we reached Cabo, if not before. I tossed him a couple of cold beers and went forward to catch some sleep.

The forward cabin was crammed with surfboards, backpacks, crates of canned food and cases of that cheap beer he was rapidly consuming. I dove underneath the surfboard bags and everything else for extra warmth. I was out before I stopped moving.

A couple of hours passed and I faintly heard someone yelling at me from a hazy nightmare, "CARSON . . . CARSON!"

I exploded upward and banged my head on the low ceiling. I woke up thinking we were sinking. Trapped in the bow of the boat, I was fighting to get free from whatever was holding me down. I frantically inched out of there and scrambled towards the cockpit. I stuck my head out and yelled, "WHAT HAPPENED?"

"Oh nothing, I was just getting tired and figured it was your turn for a shift."

"You scared the living lizards out of me. I was having a nightmare we were sinking and coincidentally you started yelling my name."

"Oh, sorry buddy. I've been yelling down at you for some time now."

My heartbeat slowed down. I nodded and moved back into the cabin out of the cold wind. I put on my usual five layers of tops and two pairs of pants. I then put on my raingear over my clothes and climbed out into the cockpit for my shift.

We were peacefully speeding downwind under a starry sky with neon green wind-waves across the horizon. Ten minutes ago, I thought we were sinking and now I thought I was on the moon. Baja has one of the largest conglomerations of phosphorescent plankton in the world. This microscopic sea-life reacts when afflicted with any movement in the water to create a bright neon glow.

Ryder headed for the aft bunk we named the coffin for two reasons: it was the same size as a coffin, and it kept it humorous given our volatile situation.

The wind and seas died down to a light gentle breeze. Tiny waves lapped at the sides of the boat as we moved through the moonless night on an electric sea.

Ryder woke up hours later, and came up top-deck to see me leaning over the side staring into the water. "Man, I don't know what these things are. I'm seeing tiny green-glowing eyes in the surface of the water."

"Well, let's just get ourselves a flashlight and get to the bottom of this here bizarre mystery."

He walked away to the cabin shaking his head.

"That's not going to help. It's probably that microscopic plankton playing tricks on me."

He returned with a flashlight. We got down on our hands and knees near the side of the boat. He shined the light on one of the many glowing eyes. It was a tiny crab floating in the water. He shined the light around and there were thousands of small red crabs with neon-green eyes floating near the surface.

"We're forty miles out to sea," I said. "What the hell are these things doing out here?"

Ryder just looked at me and shrugged. It was one more unexplained incident of the deep sea that we knew little about.

The following day was a monumental mark. I said to Ryder, "Take a look around buddy. Nothing but water in all directions. No land in sight. This is crazy."

We looked in every direction of the horizon. The intense feeling of freedom had a touch of apprehension. Without any coastal obstacles, it puts navigational skills at ease, but it puts a squeeze on the conscious that we may really, truly, be fucking lost.

BUZZZZZZ. My favorite sound hit. "FISH ON," I yelled and grabbed the fishing pole. The fish was peeling off more line than I could reel in. The boat was sailing too fast. We had to slow down.

"RYDER, SLOW THE BOAT DOWN!" I shouted.

He jumped behind the wheel. He switched off the autopilot and steered the boat into the wind. We began slowing down, and I started reeling in that mother.

Exhausted, I finally got it next to the boat. Ryder gaffed the fish and pulled it into the cockpit. It was thrashing about on the deck. I thought it was going to break something. In order to stop the thrashing I grabbed the winch-handle and began bashing it over the head. It did its last death-dance.

I was covered in blood surveying the mess. Ryder grabbed the camera and I held it up for a photo. A forty-pound . . . ok ok, a thirty-five-pound yellow-fin tuna. I filleted it and stocked the freezer.

We were nearing Turtle Bay on the mainland, around the point from Guerrero Negro. We rounded the point and sailed into this perfectly protected bay. It was barren of all plant or tree life. There was a run-down fishing village with tiny, dusty houses.

We anchored near the small village and launched the inflatable dingy off the deck. We named the inflatable the "donkey". It got the name because it wasn't very fast, but it would get you where you wanted to go.

We motored to shore with the small Nissan two-and-a-half-horse outboard. It came with the sale of the boat and we gave it a nickname as well. It was called the "sidewinder", because it never motored in a straight line, always side to side like a rattlesnake.

We were on our first mission to land in Mexico. There was no need for checking into the country. There wasn't a customs office for five hundred miles.

We were approaching the beach when we spotted a shady looking Mexican man in tattered clothes quickly walking down to us with a fake smile on his face. He was waving an arm at us in greeting and yelling out to us before we got to shore.

"Hello, hello, how are you my friends?" he said.

Ryder and I looked at each other without responding back to the man. I hardly got both of my feet on the ground when he said, "Welcome, welcome, can I help you guys find anything?"

This guy has everything that you don't need or want. He was probably the only one who spoke some English and thrived on gullible Americans sailing in there on expensive yachts. I supposed we fit the description, except for the *expensive* yacht.

He was helping us pull the inflatable up on the beach. After we had the boat high enough on the beach, he put his arm around my neck.

He said, "Hey, you guy's want to get some . . ." He paused and looked at me with crazy bloodshot eyes and said, "Marijuana?"

His act was amusing, yet sad. We wanted no part of this villain.

"No thanks, we are just fine." I said prying his arm off me, though trying to be polite. Ryder was trying to keep his distance, though the guy had glommed onto me.

We tried to flee from him hoping to see other people, but there were none. Was he the last one in this dying town? Had he evilly eliminated all of his neighbors? Or was it another unsolved mystery of the chupacabra*?

We found a store and bought many supplies of canned food and vegetables. We fled back to the inflatable before some other freak, cretin, or clown latched onto us. We quickly put our supplies in the donkey and pushed it back into the water before our friend accosted us. He was probably waiting around for us to return.

We motored back to the boat safe and stowed our provisions. We cooked up a fresh meal with our new food supplies and retired early with intent to head out in the morning.

We sailed out the next day, into the beautiful freedom of the high seas drifting along by the wind and currents of Mother Nature to some mysterious foreign land. I could sail anywhere in the world, as long as there was water. The possibilities were vast. I could sail straight into a wildly exotic port in Papua New Guinea or some quaint villa in the French Riviera. I could be involved in an ancient headhunting ritual in the lost jungles, or sipping Campari cocktails in a swanky resort. It's daunting when the sea's the limit. Presently, we were off the lawless land of Baja, now spotting whales on the horizon.

As we moved further away from the coast, a whale breached a hundred feet behind the boat, startling us. We ran astern to see an entire pod of whales all around us swimming in the same direction. Ryder was concerned, babbling something about whales

---

* chupacabra = 1 : the name translates literally from Spanish as "goat sucker" 2 : it comes from the creature's reported habit of attacking and sucking the blood of livestock, especially goats 3 : physical descriptions of the creature vary 4 : associated particularly with Puerto Rico, Mexico and the US 5 : some people in the island of Puerto Rico believe that the chupacabras were a genetic experiment from some United States' government agency, which escaped from a secret laboratory in El Yunque, a mountain in the east part of the island, when the laboratory was damaged during a hurricane in the early 1990s

sinking ships. The whales purposefully bash into their hulls, mistaking them for other threatening whales.

We heard another whale spout just in front of us. Ryder dashed to the bow while I clicked off the autopilot and began hand steering to maneuver out of danger. Ryder was looking to the left and right of the boat. He said, "They're everywhere."

I looked on both sides of the boat to see multiple, white-bellied monsters, peacefully cruising at our same speed. I spotted at least five of them, no more than 50 feet away on both sides.

Ryder was on the bow directing me with hand signals of a traffic cop. He was pointing to starboard then back to port as we weaved our way through the whales. We were slowly overtaking them and trying to avoid running the boat straight up one's ass. They didn't seem too threatening to me, but Ryder was adamant about steering us clear. We eventually overtook them, seeing fewer and fewer spouts.

Ryder took another nap while I sat in the cockpit watching the inhospitable desert slowly creep by us. All sailboats are snail-boats. I could jog around the world faster than I could sail around it.

Our next destination was Santa Maria. It's a half-moon shaped bay north of Bahia Magdalena. I began veering back towards the coast trolling for fish with two lines off the back. I dozed off in the cockpit.

I felt the boat losing its inertia, slowing down to a near stall. I woke up to see the coast about a half-a-mile off the port side. The sails were filled with wind but the boat was stalled. Was it a current ripping northward up the coast?

I stepped out on deck in a sleepwalking stupor to look around. We were completely surrounded on all sides by a giant kelp patch. We had sailed straight into a floating seaweed island.

I remembered seeing something on the charts about this bog swamp, but I didn't know what to make of the chart markings. It didn't resemble anything I had seen on any charts before, like shallow sandbars, rocks, or reef. It just looked like squiggly lines on the chart.

I didn't dare wake up Ryder. I would've never heard the end of it. I simply lowered the sails and contemplated my next move. I couldn't use the engine with the propeller wrapped up in kelp. I couldn't tack and sail out of there either.

I spotted a fishing boat working the kelp beds. They were surveying my situation. I tried to flag them down with my arms flailing about. They saw me and motored in my direction. I just stood there on deck with the look of . . . I'm a jackass standing in quicksand, do you think you could be so kind and toss me a line?

Two Mexican fishermen were in the small wooden panga boat. They were wearing tattered yellow rain-gear, covered in blood. They looked menacing. They weaved their way into the kelp bed, lifting their outboard prop every few feet to avoid the kelp. Once they were close enough, I noticed their smiles.

"Hola," I said, "Buenos dias."

"Buenos dias," they both responded together. Those were the only words spoken between us. One tossed me a line, while the other fished the kelp out from around my prop and rudder with his gaff. They began towing the boat out of there. Once we were free of the main patch, I raised the mainsail and sailed away.

The *Bula* picked up enough speed and I tossed the towline back to the fisherman. I said, "Muchas gracias amigos."

"De nada," they said in unison. They turned and got back to work. I could only imagine the comments, once I was out of earshot. It was probably, "Pinche Americano cabron". Ryder snoozed through the entire episode.

We pulled into Santa Maria Bay and I peeled off four out of five layers of tops. The weather was getting warmer as we neared Cabo San Lucas. After anchoring, we dove in for a swim. We didn't stay in for long. The water was cold. We got out and dried off.

We sat in the cockpit under the midday sun drinking beer on the bobbing boat. I was looking at the foreign land wondering if there were any inhabitants. Santa Maria was another desolate bay with that lunar landscape that's prevalent throughout Baja. Sand, rock, and cactus.

It was a two-day sail to Cabo and Ryder was about a case-and-a-half away from killing his stockpile. Maybe he felt he had to get his money's worth before he left the boat in Cabo. I turned to him and said, "Two days till mayhem."

Mystery of the White Zombie

We were a few hours away from sailing into Cabo San Lucas. It was time for a shower. It had been two weeks. I grabbed a large bucket with a long rope attached, a bar of soap, and a towel. I headed for the bow for a saltwater shower.

The first bucket I threw into the ocean nearly pulled me overboard. It's not easy heaving buckets of water onboard, sailing along at six knots, naked. I heaved it onboard and dumped it on my head.

"Warm water," I said to myself. That was my first feeling of the tropics. It was an amazing change, just from Santa Maria. I sat on the bow, soaping up, with the sun beating down on my pale skin the color of low fat milk.

I tossed the bucket over the side to rinse and it almost yanked me into the sea again. There I was buck naked, bent over, covered in soapsuds and straining to haul that five-gallon bucket of seawater back on deck. I got it back on deck and doused it on my head.

After drying off, Ryder came up top-deck and stared at me strangely. He said, "What the heck have you got all over you?"

"What?" I said, surveying myself. At first glance, it seemed as though I had a bad case of albinism. This white muck covered my entire body. It looked like someone had dipped me in corn-dog batter. Then I realized the soap never washed off. I didn't understand. I had dumped multiple buckets of water on my body. I found out the hard way that bar soap is not soluble in saltwater. I couldn't shower with my precious supply of fresh water. I may never be able soap up again. No wonder sailors were such a salty lot.

I didn't find out until later, after chatting with another sailor who taught me the trick. The only soap that is soluble in salt water is liquid soap. Joy seemed to be the preference for most sailors. I began theorizing that liquid detergent couldn't be good for you. Human skin isn't anything like kitchenware. I was reassured it was fine. I thought about the state of sailors. Most were old wrinkled goats. Maybe "Joy" did it to them. It's a paradox that too much joy could make one wrinkled and old.

Sailing into Cabo is rather majestic with the colossal rock outcropping called "Lands End" at the tip of the Baja peninsula. We sailed past the trademark rock arch that extends from land into the water. We anchored in front of the resort-lined beach. The boat rolled back and forth. We would have to get drunk in order to sleep. We had just completed a successful run to Cabo during the worst time of the year for sailing. It was time to celebrate.

Tourists crowded the beach, sunning themselves on towels and beach chairs. They were sipping cocktails through straws in pineapples. People were parasailing, windsurfing, and playing volleyball. Mexican venders had everything from Chiclets to talking parrots. Being the captain, I had to overlook the beach candy and go straight to customs to check into the country. It would be the first port of call since San Diego. I then realized it was the weekend. We couldn't check in until Monday. We were free to do anything we wanted, except go to shore legally. I thought I would have a beer and maybe a shot of tequila.

I cracked a beer and took a swill of tequila off the bottle. I snorted fire. I handed it over to Ryder and said, "Here ya go buddy." I tried to come up with some meaningful phrase after our strenuous plight from California. "This will bring strength in times of war, and fertility in times of peace."

He looked at me for a couple of seconds and shook his head in defiance. I continued holding the bottle out for him. He finally gave in and grabbed it. He said, "What the heck, we made it alive."

Ryder, not known for drinking alcohol straight, because of his weak stomach, took a large pull off that crazy fuel and snarled.

Five shots and eight beers later, I didn't seem so worried about the illegality of entering the country. The authorities might throw me in the pokey*, but I didn't care.

I shaved the wooly beard off my face. I looked a little less like a pirate, though it didn't tame my harbored feelings of pillaging and plundering. I put on a pair of loud plaid pants and a guayabera also known as a Mexican wedding shirt. Ryder was wearing a Hawaiian print t-shirt and an old pair of blue jeans with a shark belt buckle that had a bottle opener. We left the boat heading deep into the heart of madness.

We were marauding down the sidewalk ready to take on anything. I'm generally a passive person, but for the first time I sort of knew what it was like to feel like a pirate and come into port to pillage anything in our paths, including Chihuahuas, if we could catch the little bastards.

We stormed into some club called "El Squid Row", whatever that meant. It was three stories high, with balconies full of young punks, sexy college girls, and seedy locals. We nodded at each other in approval and charged straight up to the closest bar. There was a gaggle of sweaty drunks rushing a young bartender.

We jumped into the crowd and pushed our way to the bar. I was behind Ryder who parted the sea of people. We fought for a couple of cocktails.

We then moved to the center of the Saturday-night-Sodom-and-Gomorra. Letting young Americans loose on vacation in a foreign country is like feeding chili to a baby; something bad is going to happen.

We kept doing laps between the dance floor and the bar. Everyone there seemed to be under age, including the cheap booze.

---

* pokey = 1 : jail, clink, slammer, the big house, county lock up, cross-bar Hilton, room without a view 2 : reference to being poked in the rear; being someone's bitch

Sunburned teenyboppers from the States wearing nearly nothing wobbled through the bar carrying small buckets of Coronitas.

I lost track of time and I lost Ryder. I felt as though it was getting late due to my condition. I hadn't sipped more than a few beers in two weeks and that cactus kool-aid[*] was swelling up my head. My eyes were on a merry-go-round and my brain was under demolition. I had to get out of there fast before I took a dive and passed out in some dark corner, where people were pissing.

I was in the blackout stage. I was still functioning but I would never remember it the next day. It was a timeless twilight zone where every minute was carefully erased from my memory.

Ryder found me and dragged me out of the club. We staggered along the sidewalk and passed someone cooking up the enticing hog dogs (hot dogs wrapped in bacon). When you enter a club in Mexico, you'll maybe see one of these mobile red-and-white-stripped carts parked out front. By closing time, they will have multiplied, coming out of every crack and crevice from the darkest parts of town.

In the past, I have fallen for these succulent-smelling hand-grenades. Afterwards I needed a stomach pump. I would've saved money and felt the same if I would've sprinkled some salsa on the back of a toad and gobbled it down. I had learned my lesson and safely escaped. The hog dogs won't kill you but they could maim you for life.

We meandered off to a more reputable eatery and found one that had picture frames on the walls. I said, "Ah ha, high class joint. This place will be safe."

We entered and sat down at a table.

---

[*] cactus kool-aid = 1 : that dangerous rotgut made in Mexico from fermented cactus; tequila 2 : the word tequila is derived from two Nahuatl Indian words meaning "lava hill" 3 : anybody who puts a worm in their bottle is crazy, and that's not saying much for the one who drinks it

(The rest of the night was erased from my memory.)

I woke up the next day in a galaxy of pain. I felt as though someone had constructed a voodoo doll of me, tying me into a pretzel with my head on a hot plate. I could already see the Mexican hospital report: Paralysis de Tequila.

I overheard Ryder giggling.

I said, "My head is killing me and my nose feels broken for some reason. What are you laughing at?"

"Don't you remember what happened?"

"The last thing I remember is you pulling me out of that club"

He said, "Well, after that we found a taco shop and sat down at a table. The waiter came and took our order. When the food came, you turned into a rowdy five-year-old. You were throwing slices of tomatoes on my head and so forth. I took it for a while, trying to enjoy my fish tacos. Then it was one tomato too many and I busted you in the nose by accident. I didn't mean to actually hit you; I just wanted to come close enough to get you to stop."

"That's why my nose hurts you asshole. I think it's broken."

"I seriously didn't mean to hit you that hard."

"Yeah right."

"Well, you kind of deserved it."

"I don't know about that."

Ryder had to catch a bus back to San Diego that day. They could stow him in a body bag down below with the luggage. He'd sleep better *and* save money. Ryder cracked a Coors light to kill the hangover and I cringed. I had to focus on sobering up and getting supplies. I also had to find a crewmember to sail with me to Puerto Vallarta. Ryder didn't have anything to worry about but a 30-hour bus ride.

He got as many beers down as possible, including multiple shots of vodka. He couldn't touch the tequila. I came out into the cockpit and there he was sunning himself. He was sweating from the mid-morning sun that was frying his skin.

"Well, I'm ready to go," he said.

"Where, to A.A.?"

He began fumbling around, grabbing his bags. He lethargically tossed them into the donkey. We motored to shore and tied up to the closest dock. We started walking to the bus station. My feet had concrete slabs tied to them. Ryder was swerving, but he moved in a more eased manner.

"Hey man," he stopped and said, "You don't have to walk me all the way up there. It's a long-assed way." We stopped and looked at each other as two parting brothers.

"You know what bro," he said in an edifying manner. "You're becoming a damn good sailor. I had a good time with you. As far as crew, you don't need any. You can handle it yourself. You know you can."

Those words sank deep and nearly brought tears of accomplishment to my eyes. "Well man," I said, "I couldn't have had a better crew member onboard than you. Thanks for everything." We gave each other a bear hug. As he walked off, we looked at each other and both smiled, happily nodding in unison over the incredible experience we shared.

The Devil knows when you're Alone

My good friend had just left and I felt lonely in a strange world. I was feeling insecure and was second-guessing his comment about my abilities to sail the boat alone. I didn't know the boat well enough. I had only encountered one tough storm with an extra hand on deck. I needed a crewmember.

I phoned various friends in San Diego, though nobody could get off work. I tried to find a friend that was living in Cabo, but he had gone back home for a couple of months. No luck. I decided I would do it alone. It was only 300 miles, a two or three day sail.

Sailing across the Sea of Cortez posed one threat, the fierce local winds known as the "Chubascos". It sounded too much like Tabasco, bringing thoughts of getting burned.

I would monitor the forecast and leave when the weather was inviting. The entrance to Bahia de Banderas in Puerto Vallarta also posed a navigational threat. There are uncharted submerged rocks in the area. I had to chance it.

To go to sea and battle the odds was frightening enough, but to do it alone threw in a new monkey-wrench into the game.

Once I took on the commitment, the idea of single-handing seemed prodigious and noble. The more I thought about it, the stronger I felt. The idea was encompassing my entire being. I was ready to take on the new challenge.

The next morning I woke up and listened to the local weather report on the VHF radio. It claimed 15 knots of wind out of the northwest for the next two days. I could sail a beam-reach, the fastest point of sail, all the way to Puerto Vallarta.

I looked out to sea and took a deep breath. I pulled in the anchor, motored out past the famous Lands End arch and raised the sails. I was nervous but I felt an autonomous strength.

The winds were light, yet the sky was overcast, which meant a new weather system could be moving into the area and could change things for the worse. However, I had enough confidence in myself to remain calm and positive.

I sailed onward with the northeast trade winds pushing the boat at a nice clip. The day went smoothly, and the night was approaching. How was I going to stay awake through the night? I could safely sleep for fifteen-minute intervals and no more. The real threat of sailing in a coastal environment is other ships. There are many accounts of cargo ships plowing over small vessels. One tanker showed up to its destination with a small sailboat wrapped around the bow and no one onboard.

It takes about 20 minutes from the time you spot a ship on the horizon to the point it could reach your vessel and dice you up like sushi. Most single-handed sailors are known to sleep in 15 minute intervals, get up and check the horizon, then go back to sleep for another 15 minutes. I knew a single-hander who wore a bulky cooking timer tied around his neck and reset it every 15 minutes. All I had was a tiny wristwatch with an alarm. I didn't feel like sleeping that night anyway. I was too nervous about the tankers. I stayed up all night and watched the sunrise the next morning.

The next day I figured it was safer to sleep in the daylight. I decided to take my first 15-minute catnap. I set my wristwatch alarm and put my head down. The alarm rang as soon as I got comfortable. I got up and checked the horizon.

The second one seemed even shorter. I repeated the process for over an hour. One particular time, I woke up and my watch alarm wasn't beeping. Something seemed different. I quickly looked at my watch. I had slept for, "TWO HOURS, OH SHIT!" I yelled and scrambled to my feet to check the horizon, and . . . nothing. I had been out of sight of land since the previous day. I was relying on my instruments, the location of the sun, and the direction of the wind for a bearing.

I was standing there half-asleep, alarmed, and a bit confused. The wind was now coming out of the southeast. How could the wind have changed 180 degrees while I was asleep, unless? I quickly glanced at the compass and realized I was sailing . . . *backwards*. The exact direction from where I had come from. I wondered how long I had been sailing back to Cabo, and how the boat had turned around. I was using the autopilot and it had been acting suspicious. It must've been over-stressed in that storm near San Carlos in the heavy winds.

"Great," I said to myself. I was out there alone with another night ahead of me with no trust in my autopilot. I had tried to operate the wind-vane, my other self-steering device, and couldn't seem to manipulate it to keep a steady course. I didn't feel so confident anymore. I was a floating duck. I was destined to be ship shrapnel during my next nap.

I spun the boat around and got back on course for Puerto Vallarta. I trimmed the sails to create the least amount of weather helm so she would sail herself.

Night was approaching. I needed something to keep me awake. I started power slamming that toxic energy drink Red Bull, one after another. Don't ever drink more than five of those at a time. My stomach was eating itself from the inside out. Feeling as if I was on cocaine, I was ready to tackle another night.

A quarter moon rose to a cloudless sky with a nice breeze of ten knots. If I could just make it through the night alive, I would be home free and pull into Puerto Vallarta around noon.

Time was creeping into the single digits. I was trolling a fishing line for any possible entertainment. My eyes were becoming astigmatic, unable to focus on anything without seeing strange lights or faint blips that weren't there.

I heard a big splash, looked up and saw a pod of dolphins rushing towards the stern of the boat. They were speeding towards me, leaping out of the water under the moonlight. *BUZZZZZZ.* Something big hit the lure. "Oh hell," I said, thinking it was a dolphin.

I grabbed the rod and tried to feel the weight of the fish to judge if it was actually a dolphin. It didn't seem that big, so I tightened down the drag.

After a few seconds, the drag stopped buzzing and I began reeling in the fish. I realized it was definitely not a dolphin, besides they were smart creatures.

I reeled it in and got the fish next to the boat. "Big-eye tuna," I said to myself with elation. These pelagic fish are one of the few that feed at night. I hauled it in, admiring the shiny gem under the glowing moonlight. I would be pulling into Puerto Vallarta with a load of fish and ready to get into a bottle of brain damage.

The sun rose over the first visible land I had seen in three days. I was honing in on the bay. I took the safest path through the entrance to avoid any submerged reef. There are still reports of uncharted reefs that occasionally unveil themselves to unsuspecting vessels.

I made it through without sinking her. I was only a couple of hours away from my destination. There was a nice wave peeling off the point to my left, whales breaching to my right and the bay was full of day-sailors.

I felt the change of temperature from Cabo. It was beginning to feel and smell more like the tropics. One rubs-on the tropics like suntan oil.

Baggy Wrinkle and a Bottle of Bust-Head

I pulled into Marina Vallarta around noon. I had a challenging time anchoring the boat. I had to anchor "Med-mooring" style in 15 knots of wind by myself. Med-mooring is a style of anchoring that entails dropping your anchor 100 feet offshore and butting the stern up to land by tying two long lines to shore at an angle. This is necessary when there are too many boats in one area. It's like parking your boat in a crowded lot.

A young skinny sailor paddled over in his canoe to help me set my stern lines. He tied one line to a small tree and the other haphazardly to a big bush. I envisioned a huge gust of wind uprooting them and my boat drifting out to sea, trolling a tree and a bush.

"Thanks a lot. Care for a beer?" I said.

"Sure, names Jay," he said.

"Carson, good to meet ya."

He was a tall sailor, with blond hair and small spectacles. He and his girlfriend were on their 24-foot, wooden gaff-rigged sailboat named *Baggy Wrinkle*.

A few beers in and we were laughing like old friends. He and his girlfriend had sailed all the way from Alaska. He told me about another boat anchored nearby, named *Boread*, was also from Alaska. They were young sailing cruisers as well. "Cruisers" are sailors traveling around the world's oceans in search of adventure. Some are nihilists, ex-pats, sea gypsies, or retired couples who have forgone the Winnebago idea to be a Blackbeard. We were all in our late twenties. Most people our age were just starting their careers, or getting married. They weren't living on the high seas.

In Puerto Vallarta, I planned to make the boat repairs, get food supplies, and sail to Costa Rica. From Costa Rica, I planned to cross the Pacific to Tahiti. I knew I had a massive amount of repairs to complete on the boat. I hadn't even figured out how to operate the wind-vane yet. I needed to sort that out before I embarked, because the autopilot had me sailing backwards.

I began working on a list of repairs. Once the list got longer than a kid's wish list for Christmas, I knew I was in deep.

After talking to other cruisers, I found out various sailboats were leaving from Puerto Vallarta to Tahiti in two months time. They claimed the distance was the shortest from there. That didn't make sense to me. Costa Rica was much further south and closer to the southern latitude.

I didn't believe it until I pulled out the chart. It's actually a few days shorter. If I pushed on to Costa Rica, plus crossing the deadly Gulf of Tehuantepec in southern Mexico, the boat would be in shambles. I probably wouldn't be able to make it to Tahiti that year.

I decided to stay in Puerto Vallarta, make the repairs, test all the systems and become more familiar with the boat before I embarked on the month long crossing to Tahiti.

It was time to kick back and soak in the suds. I would start working on all that nonsense later. I told Jay from *Baggy Wrinkle* to grab his friends off that *Boread* boat, and come over for some free beer. He scrambled into his canoe and speed-paddled over to their boat. They were anchored a few boats away. When Jay got over there, all I could hear was, "FREE BEER?"

I heard knocking on the side of my boat. "Come aboard," I said.

They jumped aboard and introduced themselves. Their names were Darren and Amber. They had sailed from Alaska in a tiny boat that was a mere 30 feet long. I had come to realize, the smaller the boat, the crazier the sailor.

They were a quirky couple turned on to life at sea. Darren was of Czech decent with a good build—five-ten, and sandy blond hair. He retained a look in his sky-blue eyes as though he had just arrived to this planet.

Amber was the Mona Lisa. She was of Italian descent, five-two, with a thick-boned structure and a sarcastic smirk. She had dark hair, cut short like a boy. She had a comical edge about her, but I could sense she had the heart of Mother Teresa.

We started cracking beers and Darren pulled out the Mexican dirt pot. He had a bag of grass that looked more like hay.

I pulled out a bottle of bust-head*. Beer, booze, and pot after two sleepless nights is enough to send anyone into a coma. However, I had a nervous energy buzz from the completion of another perilous challenge.

I discovered that Darren and Amber were also sailing to Tahiti. We began scheming over our intrepid journey at hand. Jay secretly wanted to sail *Baggy Wrinkle* to Tahiti as well, but he said, "The miss' doesn't like to get out of sight of land, so that makes it a little difficult."

I muttered, "Why don't you just put pictures of land in the windows." Jay looked off into space as though he was working on his own absurd plan. The conversations merged into one-on-ones in various corners of the boat and the music continued to play.

I asked everyone with a slur in my voice, "Co' beer?" The question seemed redundant. Sauce to a sailor is like steak to a Rottweiler.

After a couple hours, the party on the *Bula* was getting enjoyably undomesticated. Although, it seemed we were missing someone. I looked around and didn't see Jay. "Hey, what happened to Jay?" I said.

Amber said, "Last time I saw him, he was going to take a leak over the side of the boat." This is a concern on a boat. If someone was drunk enough, they could slip overboard.

I said, "I didn't hear a splash, but you never know. Let's go check."

---

* bust-head = any bottle of booze that gives more pain than pleasure

We went up top-deck and didn't have to scout far. There was my new buddy Jay passed out in the starboard gunwale next to a trail of puke.

Jay rolled over and mumbled, "Ooohhh . . . heyyy. I was just taking a nap."

"Looks more like a crap," I said. "What happened over the side there, sailor?"

"Ooohhh . . . nothing, nothing."

Amber said, "Well if you're going to roll off the side, try and make a loud splash so we'll know to fish you out." Jay garbled something that sounded like he was chewing on hamsters.

Darren said, "Maybe we should call it a night anyway."

"That's probably a good idea," I said. "We should let the other boats around us get some sleep too. Hey, will you grab that heap and make sure he gets back to his boat before his miss' comes after me with an oar."

"No problem brother," Darren said.

They stumbled off the boat, climbing into their tiny dingy, trying not to fall overboard, and motored away.

The Figman

I got to know Darren and Amber over the next week. Darren was diligently outfitting *Boread* for a sail across the Pacific. I was doing the same to the *Bula*. Darren was an eccentric who was slightly more introverted than extroverted. He didn't open up until I got to know him. He wasn't xenophobic; he simply chose to be around people when he wanted.

This was a guy who drove from his hometown in New York City to Alaska in his van and gave everything away to go and live in the bush for months . . . naked. The locals found out there was a man living out in the woods that refused to wear clothes. He spent the summer out there and when the weather began to change in the fall, the local people tried to bring him clothes. They convinced him to come back to civilization.

Amber was the exact opposite from Darren. She was the funny Italian extrovert who liked to entertain people. They would invite me over to their boat and Amber would be telling me silly stories while Darren was building something new in the cabin.

I continued working on the boat everyday and stayed in contact with my friend Figman in San Diego. He was supposed to sail with me across the Pacific to Tahiti. I could use an extra hand and some comic relief.

His emails were getting more and more skeptical. One message he sent, claimed he might just meet me once I got to Tahiti. I had only single-handed for three days and wasn't ready to take on an entire month at sea, solo.

I returned his email:

> Listen bro, there's no pressure to go. I can probably find another crewmember down here. Granted, they'd be a stranger, and it's better to know someone before you decide to spend a month at sea together. I'm not looking for an experienced sailor. It's good to know something, but it's tough when they think they know everything. Congeniality and mental stability is everything out there. I consider you like a brother. If I can't find a good crewmember, then I'm going alone. This is *not* about feeling responsible to help me. This is about whether you want to do this for yourself. It'd be great to have ya.

> *Your amigo-*

My conscience would be at ease if he came, but if he didn't, I was going alone. This had a venomous though seductive appeal, like Adam and the apple. But I had more important things to worry about, namely the boat. If it wasn't ready, then nobody was going.

I found a spare belt for the autopilot. I installed it and tested it at anchor, but I needed to test it under sail. I asked Darren if he could help me sort out my wind-vane. I had been operating it backwards. We tuned it up and it was ready to test under sail. The autopilot was for light winds, the wind-vane for heavy winds.

I needed three hundred feet of anchor chain to anchor safely in the dangerous coral reefs of the South Pacific. I bought what I needed from a sailor who was selling his boat. It was a sufficient length at 350 feet.

I spent the entire two months focused on the boat and discussing weather patterns and storm tactics with other sailors. *Bula* was getting bullet proof. My brain was getting pregnant.

Towards the end of the two months, my Mom flew in for a quick visit before I set sail. She usually does this before I head-off into the deep.

She always says the same thing with her sweet Tennessee accent, "Well, I wasn't sure whether I'd get to see my baby again."

I smiled and reassured her, "Mom, everything is going to be fine." However, I didn't have a clue what was going to happen.

She is always concerned about me having new socks and underwear. No matter where I'm located in the world, I'll get a package from her. I could be traveling through the lost outreaches of the Sahara desert and a foreign messenger will show up on the back of a tortoise and hand me a sandblasted package with my name on it. Confused, I'll open the hermetically-sealed package to reveal those ethereal white socks and fresh underwear a size too small. It'll be garnished with a decretive note from my dear mother. She will have paid outlandish mailing charges to get them to me safely, as if they don't have clean white socks and underwear elsewhere in the world. Everything is safe in her mind if I'm wearing them, as if they were little angels protecting me in the middle of some third world turmoil—those brilliant fluffy garments, the savior of her beloved son.

We had a great time reminiscing and eating at all the restaurants that I could only lust at from the outside. She also took me to the Costco in Puerto Vallarta. It reminded me of the college days. Every time my folks showed up, they would leave me with a full cupboard. Once my folks left, all my kleptomaniac roommates would slither in like ravenous reptiles and devour the stocks.

Figman finally dropped his resistance. He claimed a force was drawing him to do it. He would be flying in soon. The tension and excitement was rising between all the cruisers gearing up for the South Pacific. Jay from *Baggy Wrinkle* was jealous. He acted like he didn't care and claimed he and his girl were sailing to Costa Rica, where he'd be surfing spots all the way there and back.

"Yeah right Jay," I said. "You'll be battling banditos on land and Floridians in the surf, all the way to Panama." He had no comment.

Figman flew into the airport, and I was there to meet him. I helped him get his luggage and we began making our way to the boat. We were hollering, giving each other cheap shots in the ribs and just laughing for no apparent reason. Now I know why foreigners think Americans are so loud and obnoxious, BECAUSE WE ARE!

He sounded skeptical about his full commitment to do the trip. He said, "Well, I haven't even sailed on the boat yet. I'm just here to see whether the boat is worthy, and you're ah . . . you're able to pull it off."

"What?" I retorted.

"Take it easy, I'm coming around. I just want to ease into it. You know, do some day-sailing and get to know the boat, before I fully commit."

"Alright whatever." He tried to get me to laugh, by changing the subject.

We got back to the boat, and I began showing him everything that I had done in the past two months. He seemed satisfied and the tension faded. Figman changed from an F.B.I. interrogator to "Vacation Man".

"Isn't it spring break?" he said.

"You are correct," I said.

All the young, college kids from the states were descending upon the hot destinations in Mexico. Puerto Vallarta was definitely on the juvenile-party-pirate's treasure map. It was time to forget about boat projects and make a reconnaissance mission into town to weigh the college education.

The Curse

We commenced to cannonball tequila from the bottle. I said, "You've got to meet these sailors I've been hanging out with."

"Oh yeah, where they at?" Figman said.

"I'll go roust 'em." I buzzed over to *Baggy Wrinkle* and *Boread* and invited them over. They said they'd love to come over. Probably just for the free beer.

Within half-an-hour, we had everyone piled on my boat. I put on some swanky Brazilian music and said, "The *Bula* Lounge is now open for cocktails."

I passed everyone a beer and then rifled through the cabinets looking for all the booze, but all I could find was tequila. So tequila it was, straight with no lime.

After we cashed the beers, Figman and I decided it was time to go wreak havoc on the town. I said to the two couples, "We're going to hit the town, are you in?" They both claimed they were out.

Couples will come to your house, boat or trailer and drink everything you have. They'll get drunk and even slightly disorderly, but when it comes to going out, they're out. It's not as if they haven't shagged each other a million times. I guess half the fun of going out is the possibility of running into the right person, or wrong. This leaves you with only half a reason if you already have that person. Half a reason isn't enough to motivate most.

Figman and I threw on some silly outfits and disembarked the boat heading for chaos.

As we were walking through the harbor, I said, "Hey Fig, let's stop in this shop here, I'd like to introduce you to this cute girl I met."

Figman said, "Oh yeah, what do you got?"

"I got a little something."

We walked into this imported art shop and I introduced Figman to this blond Mexican girl named Carmen. She had been pursuing me and I was passively conversing with her from time to time to sharpen up my Spanish. More or less, I was running from her because of her young age, but running with a limp.

Figman was staring at her with his mouth slightly agape as if she was the first woman he'd ever seen. I conversed with Carmen in my irregular Spanish until I began fumbling with my words. I told her that we were going out on the town and wondering where we should go. She grinned and with a sexy accent, she said in English, "Meet me at the Acme bar at ten o'clock."

"The Acme at ten o'clock," I said. "Ok, we'll find it."

We stepped out of the shop and walked out to the main road to hail a cab. There were two cabs sitting out in front of the Marina. An older Mexican man in the closest cab waved us over. We walked over and jumped into the back seat of his cab.

We shut our doors and I spoke to the driver in some riddling Spamish*. I continued for a few sentences, thinking I had a good grasp on the language, after too much tequila. The cabbie had one arm draped over the passenger seat, staring at me with painful confusion on his face. I finished my cave-like argot and confidently waited to see if it worked.

A few uncomfortable seconds passed, and he said, "Como?"

Feeling like a bungling jackass, I gave up and phonetically said, "Ac-me Bar?"

---

* Spamish = 1 : spam + Spanish 2 : A mutated and desperate version of Spanish that is closely comparable to spam

In perfect collegiate English, he said, "Oh the Acme Bar. No problem mister." He punched it. The disheveled cab began picking up speed down the unlit road. He began shooting through stop signs, red lights, taking the shoulder on the opposite side, avoiding traffic by going the wrong way down one-ways, and only pausing for scared pedestrians hopping out of his way. It was a perilous carnival ride. These cabbies are carnies of the streets. I think they believe the closer to death they get you, the more you'll tip. Anyone whose profession involves driving in Mexico has a death wish.

He pulled up to the bar and we fumbled for some pesos. I felt inclined to tip the man.

We hopped out of his cab, looked down the sidewalk both ways and confidently walked into the bar. The whole place stopped to stare at a couple of nickel-necks* barging into their establishment as if we owned it. We were thrown off-guard because we expected the normal swashbuckling Mexican hoedown with drunk college kids blindly frolicking about to cheesy disco music.

The bar was fashionably contemporary with a neo-avant-garde appeal. High-class Mexican yuppie's sipped martinis, wearing slick gear, with a DJ pumping the latest deep-house.

"What the . . . ?" I said.

Figman turned to me with a confused look and no verbiage. They had moved from outdated disco to modern day decadence. I felt like I was back in La Jolla, California trying to mingle with the upper echelon, but always doing a bad job of it. We sat down at the plush bar and ordered a couple of margaritas, just because.

After a few cocktails, Carmen walked in wearing something very different from what she wore in the shop—scandalous. I bought her an expensive cocktail and we talked about how much we liked her choice of bars. After a little Spanish, I ran out of words. The conversation stalled.

---

* nickel-neck = pinhead, kook, derelict, dumb ass, idiot

After few more cocktails, I turned to the Figman and began telling him about some ancient sea-lore. As legend states, it is taboo to change the name of a boat. However, in the event the name is changed, there is a remedy. That is to have a virgin maiden pee on the bow of the boat. I motioned my head towards Carmen sitting behind me at the bar and winked at Figman.

We were about to embark on a month-long journey on the high seas. We didn't need any taboos working against us after changing the name of the boat. I was going to try and ask a young foreign girl in broken Spanish to pee on the bow of my boat without sounding perverted.

(Translated for ease of the reader):

"Carmen can I ask you a personal question?" She nodded and I continued, "Have you ever slept with anyone before?"

Embarrassed, she smiled and said, "Why?"

"You don't have to tell me, but I was just wondering."

"No I haven't."

"Yes of course and that's perfectly normal. Carmen, I don't want to offend you in any way, but can I ask you for an unusual favor?"

"I don't know it depends."

(The next statement is what I thought I asked her in Spanish after an overabundance of cocktails)

I said, "I changed the name of my boat and according to ancient sea lore I need you, a virgin, to pee on the bow of my boat to reverse the curse."

The translation was probably gravely different from what I wanted to say. She gave me a look as if I had shit my britches in a crowded elevator. I wasn't sure whether she wanted to kick me, kiss me, or call the cops. She sat there with her mouth wide-open, eyes squinting, and hands on her hips. She was leaning back and shaking her head.

"You can think about it," I said and walked to the dance floor.

A little later, I ran into Carmen in another part of the bar and we calmly chatted. She wasn't avoiding me, but the subject never came up again. I resolved that the beautiful, young Carmen was "under my league". I covertly shied away from her for the rest of the evening.

Figman and I left the bar and much to our amazement, we didn't see any of those hog-dog carts on the sidewalk in front of the establishment. It must have been *high class*.

I woke up the next morning sweating from the heat with a bad hangover. Hair-of-the-dog was out of the question. I had too many things to finish on the boat. Figman got up and looked like someone had sent him through a car wash on a tricycle. We were to set sail around the beginning of April. It was the end of March. It was time to get serious, no more nonsense like trying to get under-aged girls to pee on the boat. Figman agreed, claiming he wanted to help.

After two days of work, Figman began to complain about the monotonous rigmarole. He felt as though he was working on the boat all day and not enjoying his vacation. He wanted to surf, party, meet girls and bring-on the good times. I had just spent the last two months doing repairs. He did a couple easy days of work and started bitching. Did he think he was crossing on a luxury-liner with a maid and room service? I tried to explain to him that the trip wasn't going to be a night at Chuck E. Cheese playing video games. However, he never takes me seriously.

The spring trade winds were kicking in and the weather was looking favorable. A couple of boats had already left Puerto Vallarta, starting their journey into the deep blue. We were receiving reports that they were catching the trade winds about 200 miles off the coast. They claimed it was blowing 20 knots from the Northeast. Perfect. It was time to hop into the big bathtub.

We decided on April 5th for the official departure date for two reasons: it wasn't the *first* of April and it wasn't a Friday. It's taboo for sailors to embark on a long journey on a Friday. Why Friday? Did they reserve it for celebrating the end of the workweek? I never understood this one, but for some superstitious reason I tried to uphold yet another rule of the high seas. Trying to uphold the last one with the virgin could have got me thrown in jail.

We spent the next week focusing on the boat and any problems we could encounter out there. You have to be ready for the worst, from patching a gapping hole in your boat, to extracting a tooth or amputating an arm. When you're at sea for over a month, anything could happen. It's hard to imagine the amount of pre-emptive thought and supplies that go into such a journey.

The final day was nearing and the weather specialists were seeing a good window of opportunity. The *Bula* was ready to set sail. A few other boats were planning to leave the same day, including our friends on *Boread*. It's nice to know there will be a few other boats out there when you are at the mercy of God.

We made all the last minute checks to make sure everything was in working order. We provisioned-up with enough food for a hundred days at sea. If you figure it will take you a month to complete an ocean passage, bring enough food for three. You never know what could happen out there. The excitement and fear were rising like the fur on the back of a cat. We were to set sail the following day.

Into the Unknown

We listened to the weather report during breakfast. It sounded good. I turned to Figman with wide eyes and said, "It's on!"

"Wait a minute," he said. "What the hell am I getting myself into?"

"Too late now buddy."

He shook his head. "Oh god, here we go."

We made our way down to the customs office that morning and checked out of the country. They stamped our passports and we took a cab back to the marina.

We said our farewells to all the sailor friends we had made in Mexico. Then we made phone calls to family members who began praying for us immediately. Never deny extra help. We had enough good luck charms and talisman to rival a witch doctor. We had rabbit's feet, crosses, the Holy Bible, Tibetan prayer flags, a wooden Tiki, Semper Fi, Jah Rastafari, Chinese incense, and Saint Christopher hanging on my necklace. Best of all was my plastic lizard that my friend gave me years ago for good luck before I flew off to Papua New Guinea. The lizard goes everywhere.

We were a mobile shrine. I secretly wished the cute Mexican virgin had peed on the bow of the boat, but it was too late now.

After boarding the boat, we pulled the anchor and motored out to catch the wind. *Boread* had already been out for half an hour. The winds were light in the bay and we crept along slowly. It would take us all year at that pace.

We sailed out past the Marieta Islands, near the entrance of the bay. Something large burst through the surface of the water from out of the depths, about 50 feet away. It came out of the surface a second time. It was a giant manta ray doing back-flips out of the water. It had a wingspan of eight feet. Shooting straight out of the ocean towards the sky, it spun in the air landing on its back.

"Marco . . . Polo . . . fish out of water," I said.

What makes these fish do such tricks? Is it for personal enjoyment? Or are they just sick of being slimy fish and trying to reach the other side? The grass is always greener. The sky is always bluer.

We spotted a pod of whales swimming near *Boread*. The whales swam past them moving in our direction. As we watched, one came flying out of the water. It spun in the air landing on its side. I was clicking away on the Canon, ready for its next move. Another one rocketed out of the water. When it landed, it sent spray fifty feet in every direction. They were dangerously close and heading straight for us. I was getting a little nervous.

They kept up the display with a baby whale trying it's best to get as high as it could, but the poor little thing was only getting its nose or tail out of the water. It became apparent that this was your typical mom, pop and baby whale family. They were not threatening—only out for some high-flying stunts. Figman and I were babbling about the best whale show we had ever seen. We decided it was in our honor as a farewell party.

Boread had turned completely around, sailing straight towards us. Why would they be coming back in this direction? Did they want to see more of the whales or was something wrong? I grabbed the VHF microphone and hailed them, "*Boread, Boread* this is *Bula*. Do you copy?"

Darren replied on channel 16, "This is *Boread*. You wanna pick another channel?"

"How about 69?"

"Sure, meet you on 69."

I switched the channel to 69. *"Boread . . . Bula."*

"Yeah, hey *Bula*. We got ourselves a little problem. Our rudderpost is leaking. It's not that bad, but I don't want to chance it before we set off on a month-long passage."

"Roger. That doesn't sound good. What's your game plan?"

"I'm not sure right now, since we've already checked out of the country. Maybe we will anchor in the Marieta Islands, away from town and take a look at it while at anchor."

"That sounds like a better idea than having to check back into the country."

"If I can fix the problem out there, then great. If not then we will go back into Puerto Vallarta for any parts and supplies needed."

I was mulling over the idea of sticking together for safety. Maybe they wanted us to turn around and wait for them to repair the problem. It could take a week if it was serious. I opted to continue our journey.

"Well, I wish you two the best of luck," I said. "I hope you can sort out the leak and get back on your way."

Darren said, "Ok guys, be careful out there. We'll see you in the Marquises."

"Yes we will my friends. Bye bye."

That was one less boat out there for possible help in case of an emergency. I got a bit worried, and began checking for any leaks in my rudderpost. Sure enough, there was a very slight leak. I didn't think it would be a concern. Nearly every boat leaks a little from somewhere. It's inevitable.

The day dwindled to evening, and we set up a watch schedule for the night. We decided on three-hour segments starting at 9pm.

On my first shift, I sat in the cockpit staring into the heavens with my mouth wide open. I was transfixed on billions of stars as the boat sailed onward leaving a magical wake of glowing phosphorescence. The bioluminescence leaves a green glowing trail near the surface, behind the boat. It's brightest on a moonless night.

On my second shift, I watched the sunrise. The winds were steady on a pristine clear morning. Land was nowhere in sight. There's something about looking in all directions and seeing nothing but water. Some people shutter at the idea. I find it angelic, flying across the surface of the ocean under sail with nothing more insight than puffy white clouds marching through the sky.

Figman woke up to his first sunrise on the deep sea. He wasn't feeling so good. He claimed he was a bit seasick and he might skip breakfast.

"Don't worry," I said. "You'll get over it soon buddy. It takes a couple of days to get used to the rocking and rolling."

"Yeah, I hope you're right," he said.

I ate breakfast as he watched me with a cringe on his face. My eating was making him worse. "Why don't you do something to get your mind off it?" I said. "Get out the fishing gear and try catching us some lunch."

Maybe that wasn't such a good idea. It entailed eating. Figman wasn't so concerned about eating the fish. He just liked catching them. I was more into eating them. We had a perfect relationship. He'd reel 'em and I'd eat 'em.

He pulled out the two fishing rods and ran them off the transom with a couple of bright plastic squid. We sat there and waited. Once you're cruising and the boat is steering itself, there's not a lot to do but sit and wait for fish to bite. This becomes the most exciting part of your day. You hear the drag start buzzing on one of the reels and one guy scrambles for the rod as the other guy grabs the helm to pull into the wind to stall the boat. This sparse activity keeps you from going insane from the monotony.

Staring off into the blue sky, I dropped into deep contemplation. It's hard to imagine what kind of thought processes the mind dwells on during the second day of a month-long quest into the unknown. All these wild ideas were swimming around in my head like piranhas in a fishbowl ready to devour each other. What kind of elements would we encounter—peaceful serenity, massive seas and storms, doldrums, pirates, whale attacks, or alien abduction?

I had read the book "Kon-Tiki", the account of the Norwegians who sailed across the Pacific on a balsa-wood raft. They mentioned in the crossing, seeing giant glowing eyes one night underneath the raft. Who knows what it really was, but it sure made me fabricate visions of fairy-tale monsters of the deep. This is somewhat entertaining because I knew there wasn't such a thing, but there's always the "what if".

When I wasn't busy concocting monsters of the deep in my head, I started envisioning giant pepperoni pizzas and juicy hamburgers. To this day, people continuously ask me what kind of stark realizations or profound thoughts I have when I'm at sea for such long periods.

"Pizza, beer, and sex," I dumbly reply. After this remark, I usually receive laughter, confusion, or disgust especially if it's a female asking the question. I do get plenty of profound thoughts, but they're usually outweighed by these subjects, especially the closer I get to my destination.

The second night the Figman said he was ready to eat something if I could cook, of course.

He said, "Being stuck in the hot galley bouncing back in forth trying to cook is what makes me seasick."

"Ok, I'll cook if you do the dishes."

"No problem,"

There are three kinds of people in this world: those who cook, those who clean, and those who say screw it and eat out. We couldn't exactly eat out.

By the third day, Figman was still seasick and getting a bit claustrophobic. He finally snapped. He said in a quivering voice, "Man, what if I'm seasick the whole way? I don't know if I can take this much longer."

"You'll get better,"

"It's been THREE DAYS and I haven't gotten better YET. This could be a serious problem. We might have to turn around."

"We're NOT turning around. We're four hundred miles from land. It would take us a week to sail back, straight into the wind." He looked away, knowing he would have to face the situation.

The trade winds were strengthening the further we sailed away from the continent. They were blowing a steady 25 knots and the seas were increasing in size to ten feet. An occasional wave would break and roll into the stern, spinning the boat to one side. It was nothing too dangerous, just uncomfortable.

Relaxing on a small boat in the deep sea is not possible. When lying down, braced up against the hull on the lee side, the boat is still bouncing off waves and rolling from side to side. I'm hanging-on even while sleeping.

I constantly have a voracious appetite when sailing. I eat a ton of food, but always lose weight. It's a continual workout at sea, even trying to sit on the toilet. If you don't have the ever-popular video "Nine Minute Abs", this is one way to build up your abdominal muscles.

We wore our harnesses when out on deck. The harness goes around your torso with a carabiner attached to the end. The carabiner clips into a "jack-line". Jack-lines are strap-like, nylon lines used for running across the deck of a boat. They are flat instead of round to eliminate rolling onto your ass when stepping on them. They run forward and aft on the starboard and port side of the boat. Securely fastened to the bow and the stern, they act as a safety line in case you fall overboard.

The days slipped by and the nightshifts seemed shorter, because we were both asleep during our nightshifts. The only difference between being on, or off, our night shift was the difference between sleeping down below in the cozy coffin or sleeping outside in the cold cockpit when you were supposed to be watching the horizon. We hadn't seen one ship or any traffic since our second day out of Mexico.

We were approaching two weeks at sea and our midway mark to our destination, the mystifying Marquises.

The water was so unusually blue it almost looked deep purple (maybe this is where the band got their name). You can't imagine how clean, clear and beautiful this water is until you witness it. This was true blue-water sailing and we were headed to the most coveted sailing grounds in the world, the South Pacific. I was still shaking my head from the dream I had made a reality in such a short time. Two months ago, I was frantically trying to get out of San Diego. Now here I was, nearly halfway to the Marquises and 1500 miles away from any point of land and safety.

Attack of the Flying Boobies

We finally reached the halfway point between Mexico and the Marquises. I thought to myself, what if something went wrong. It would take two weeks to sail to safety, if we could sail. We might be drifting in the inflatable donkey if something really went sour.

The intense pressure of our dangerous position was so unfathomable that it became dauntless. To be dead smack in the middle was the most unbelievable feeling. I became very passive of death. Mother Nature could snap me up in a heartbeat.

The fishing was average. We had only caught five fish in two weeks. Half of which were skippies (skipjack tuna, edible if you're tired of eating canned spam). I'll eat anything, but Figman was boycotting them. We had a break from the skippies and caught a small Mahi Mahi, which I sautéed up with onions and garlic.

Next, we caught a yellow-fin tuna. Instead of beating the thing over the head with the winch handle and splattering blood everywhere, we shoved this bottle of horrible tequila in its gills. It died in seconds with no mess. This is an old fisherman's trick.

Figman's dad gave us the tequila for the trip. It was so awful we couldn't touch it, so we used it to kill fish. If it was killing fish that easy, I wondered what it would've done to us.

I kept checking the leak in the rudderpost. It was getting worse. I didn't have the heart to tell the Fig. It would've given him one more reason to think I was crazy for taking him on such a hair-brained mission on a boat that was now sinking.

The sun sank into the sea and the stars multiplied by the billions. We had zero pollution, no city lights, and we were two thousand miles from land. The sky at night was a lighted pegboard minus the pegs.

That night I was reaching the end of my midnight-to-three-am shift when I heard this air-gasping scream from the cabin. It sounded like the uncontrollable scream of a restrained lunatic. I quickly jumped to my feet and stared down into the cabin to see Figman flat on his back, wide-eyed, and grasping the sides of his bunk. He just awoke from the attack of a nasty nightmare.

"Where am I?" he said with wondering eyes.

"You're on the boat."

"Oh God, I was just having a nightmare that I was stuck on a boat thousands of miles away from land."

I looked at him snickering. "And your point is?"

He shook his head and rolled over with a sickening scowl. He buried his head in the salty, sweat-drenched pillow to hopefully drift back to sleep. He was trying to muster up some happier thoughts.

The next day we were both trying to read our books sitting in the cockpit. Reading on a sailboat is challenging enough, throw in some rough seas and you might as well be reading Chinese on a pogo stick.

People give you all these sailing novels when they know you're a sailor. I was given books like "The Perfect Storm", "White Squall", and "A Voyage for Madmen". Just the quaint material I want to be reading on a rough passage to calm my nerves. Sadly enough, I ended up reading books like "Into Thin Air", or "The Tragedy of Flight 762". At least these are land or air-based tragedies instead of sea-based. It helps me get my mind off my present situation and think of someone else's misfortune for a change.

I was staring off into the fabled blue sky in a daze when I spotted a flying booby* circling the mast.

"Hey Fig," I said. "Look at this goofy thing. It seems to be looking for a place to land on the top of the mast."

The sea bird saw an opportunity to have a rest and a free ride. It continued to circle and attempted to land on one of the spreaders halfway up the mast. The booby sped in with its landing gear out and clipped its wing on the rigging. It spun 360 degrees in the air, spiraling downward. It had difficulty recovering, but it never hit the water.

After circling for half-an-hour, the frazzled fowl made a successful landing on the starboard spreader. We began clapping for the bird's success.

"Arggg," I said. "We've got ourselves a pet booby. I'd rather have a pet booby than a parrot any day. Although, we need a pair."

A second booby ironically materialized and began circling the mast. It was jealous of the other one perched up there, looking so cool in the shade of the sails. It circled around and around and finally went for it. It tangled itself up in the rigging and barely escaped.

After several attempts, it finally came swooping in and put its feet down on the spreader. It tucked its wings away and the

---

* booby = 1 : large, streamlined sea birds 2 : these birds have heavy bodies; long, pointed wings; long, wedge-shaped tails; and short, stout legs 3 : they fish by diving on their prey from great heights and pursuing it underwater; air sacs under their skin cushion impact with the water and provide buoyancy, as with pelicans 4 : the masked, red-footed (Sula sula), and brown (S. leucogaster) boobies are found the world over; the Peruvian and blue-footed (S. nebouxii) boobies, on the west coasts of the Americas 5 : the name booby is descriptive not only of the rather stupid facial expression of these birds, but also of their unwary, gullible behavior when hunted by man—a factor that accounts for their diminishing numbers

other booby disapprovingly moved over a bit to give the furry fellow some room.

They sat there for a few minutes looking around, when the first booby turned and started munching on the others head. The poor thing didn't fight back. It hunkered down and took the abuse. The attacker stopped and looked around. Then it proceeded to chew on the newcomer's head so ferociously it fell backwards off the spreader and dropped thirty-feet down into the ocean. It bounced off the surface and took off flying highly irregular at first, then corrected its flight and was gone.

I turned to Figman and said with a slow John Wayne drawl, "Son, what we have witnessed here was an aerial attack of the flying boobies."

"That sounds like a sci-fi porn flick," he said.

He was right.

The next day we were to cross the I.T.C.Z. (Inter Tropical Convergence Zone). This is an area where the trade winds from the Northern and Southern Hemisphere converge. Everyone warned us about this temperamental zone on the equator. Weather specialists were studying its behavioral movements and giving sailors the best longitudinal area to shoot through with the least amount of danger.

This zone lies on the equator, more predominantly in the eastern half of the Pacific. The area generally spans 150 miles north and south of the equator. It's known for having inconsistent wind and dangerous squalls. You'll be bobbing like a whoopee cushion for days without a puff of wind, then a squall comes and knocks the shit out of you. It's also one of the hottest places on the planet. We crossed at an area that was the shortest distance through the doldrums.

As we entered this area, lightning storms began brewing with electrical spiders hitting the horizon on all sides of the boat. I grabbed a set of jumper cables and clamped one end to the wire rigging where it meets the deck. The other end I dangled into the water. If lightening struck the top of the mast, the current would theoretically shoot down the rigging through the jumper cables into the water as a ground. If not, then it could explode the mast and fry all the electrical components on the boat.

The hair on my arms was standing to attention from the electricity like toy soldiers marching into a microwave. We managed to squeak through the storm without being toasted.

The next three days sailing across the equator was the most pleasant weather we had the entire trip. It was blowing 15 knots with calm seas. We sat in the cockpit under the bimini and made up silly songs playing the guitar. The song subjects were always hamburgers, hotdogs, or something we couldn't have.

We never did crack that bottle of champagne on the equator. I decided to save it for when we reached land. Besides, hot champagne in one-hundred degree weather would have made me sick.

We were clearly out of the I.T.C.Z. and well south of the equator clipping along with a change in the trade winds. We had entered the Southern Hemisphere and the trade winds were blowing from a southeasterly direction. This was the first time we had dramatically changed the sail pattern in three weeks. Before this, it was just small fine-tuning of the sails. We had three days to go and the excitement was rising.

Figman was on watch that night and I was down below asleep. Abruptly awakened by a nervous yell, I stared upward towards the cockpit. I saw Figman's face lit-up, peering down at me. Again, he yelled, "FLARE . . . FLARE!"

I jumped out of the bunk as he continued mumbling something. "You really saw a flare?" I said.

"Well uhhh . . . ahhh, I don't know." He continued to peer into the sky.

"WHAT?"

"I DON'T KNOW. IT LOOKED . . . like a flare." Slowly retracting from his hallucinatory statement, he said, "Well, maybe it was a shooting star."

"YOU GOT ME OUT OF BED FOR A FRICKEN' SHOOTING STAR?"

"Ahhh . . . well . . . sorry?"

I just shook my head, half-angered and half-laughing. I couldn't ever truly get mad at him. He was one of the funniest fellows I'd ever met. I retired back to the coffin and drifted off to slumber-land, still angrily snickering over the whole calamity.

The next day I decided to bring up the flare issue to make him feel a little better about himself. He was just trying to do his best.

"Listen, I didn't appreciate you waking me up last night for a shooting star. However, I have witnessed some in the South Pacific that are bizarrely big and bright, lasting for ages. One could easily mistake them for a flare *if* they had never seen a flare before." We laughed it off and broke the tension.

"ONLY TWO DAYS TO GO," I yelled. We proceeded with the fifth-grade sucker punching. We were both getting over-zealous with the intensity of arrival.

On the last night, I decided to do a double watch. I wanted to be sure that my GPS was correct, to avoid arriving into the side of a cliff. Engorged with energy, I couldn't sleep anyway.

Around 4 a.m., I spotted a large dark object on the horizon. It was in the direction of the island. It could have been a cloud on the horizon, so I didn't want to get too excited.

Over the next hour, it became prevalent that it wasn't a cloud. It was in fact an island and the first piece of land seen for 24 painful days. Engulfed with drunken divinity, my body swelled with elation. A feeling of safety and accomplishment fell upon me like a newly crowned king. Somehow, we had pulled it off. I figured I'd let Figman sleep. He'd find out soon enough.

Aliens of Stone

The sun rose and the island of Nuku Hiva revealed its rugged beauty. Lush green mountains shot straight up out of the ocean with 300-foot cliffs. Pine forests lined the top of the island. The lower regions were palm laden with a rocky shoreline.

Figman finally woke up and came up top-deck. He had a look on his face as if he had just come out of a month-long sentence of solitary confinement in a kennel. He looked sort of mangy.

He stared at land with wandering eyes. He began laughing with a strangely disrupted tone in his voice. You could tell his brain was spinning like a centrifuge and his body was fidgeting about.

"Why the HELL didn't you wake me UP?" he said.

"I figured I'd let you sleep."

He seemed angry that I didn't inform him the second I saw land, as if he was chewing on every minute that went by. It must have been the nightmares. He glared at the island, then at me, and shouted, "YOU'RE NOT INSANE AFTER ALL."

He was convinced I had arbitrarily sailed him out to the middle of nowhere with absolutely no clue.

He said, "I was getting a bit worried after nearly a month at sea. I wasn't sure we'd ever see land again." He was trying to hold back an unbearable need to grin. "You didn't trick me this time."

We began high-fiving and dancing around the cockpit.

We sailed closer to the edge of the cliffs and the smell of land hit me with intensity. I've never experienced this. It was something I didn't know existed. It's not as if I forgot the smell, it's just that I never noticed the absence of it. It was strange, though unique, much like the smell of your lover after they've been away for a month. This was the smell of prolific life, rotting jungle, seaweed, tree bark, pollen, and smoke.

A plume of mist mysteriously billowed into the air near the bow of the boat. A pod of dolphins arrived as our greeting party. They were riding the bow waves and leading us into the bay.

I stood on the bow, marveling at their simple and happy behavior. I had a flashback of home. It seemed so far away. I thought about the excessive pursuit of money back in the States. I pondered my existence in the U.S. and about how the first world has become far too complicated for my own mental and physical health.

After my daydream, we reeled in the fishing rods and prepared to anchor. As we pulled into Tahohe Bay, the beauty grabbed my being and rendered me a feeling comparable to the first time I fell in love. This was the most beautiful bay I'd ever seen. Detroit would have been beautiful after a month-long trip across the blue.

The symmetry of the bay was like the walls of a castle. Two large rock pillars marked the gateway into the bay. The back of the bay rose to a peak with a forest of pine trees. The water was changing colors to a lighter turquoise as we sailed in from the deep.

We dropped the sails and started the engine. We only used the engine *eight* hours total for the entire trip across the Pacific.

We anchored among the various sailboats that had arrived from across the Pacific. I pulled out the camera and a bottle of champagne in the bilge. I gave the camera to the Fig, ran to the stern of the boat, shook the bottle up and spewed it into the air. The bubbles landed on my head and I yelled, "WE MADE IT ALIVE . . . LET'S PARTY."

We both dove in the clear water and swam in the shallows. After the short swim, we got the donkey in the water and motored to shore. We landed on the beach and I walked up to the closest tree, wrapped my arms around it and gave it a big kiss. Tree bark isn't so forgiving on your lips.

"What the heck are you doing?" Figman asked.

"It's a tree; it's land,"

"Oh, right." He jokingly went over and hugged a tree too.

I skipped down the beach similar to Gene Kelly in the movie "Singing in the Rain".

The first person we ran into was a French sailor. With a huge grin on my face, though trying to appear normal, I said, "Do you speak English?"

"But of course. Can I help you?" he said with a French accent.

"Where's the closest bar?"

He laughed. "Did you just arrive?"

"Yes."

"You can find a bar right down the beach there," he said. "And they also have good food."

I wanted to hug the guy before we walked off, but I refrained. As we were walking down the beach, we came upon a garden of stone statues on the beach. All the statues resembled small extraterrestrials with giant round eyes. Stone aliens surrounded us. All the colors were too vibrant and the scenery was too surreal for reality. I felt as if I was on some peculiar drug. We meandered through a maze of ancient ruins and walked onward through the green jungle close to the beach.

We found the bar and walked in as if we were coming in from Earth for a weekend on Mars. We met a table of Scandinavian sailors. They had the same enlightened gleam in their eyes. Everyone was on a similar plane of thought. You could just look into their eyes without uttering a word. Everyone was ecstatic from the accomplishment of such a challenge.

Two beers later and I had a buzz. We ordered a couple plates of steak-frites (French for steak and fries). We chatted with the other sailors about each other's crossing. The food arrived and they politely let us eat. We turned and inhaled our meals like prisoners. We *were* in a small cell for a month.

After the meal, we staggered back to the boat and dove into our bunks for the first proper sleep in a month.

After recovering from the post-hibernation lethargy the next day, I went into town with our passports to check us into the country. I was walking into the small town of Tahohe and ran into a captain I had briefly met in Mexico. His name was Ralph and he invited me over to his boat for a beer a little later. I accepted his offer and went on my way to finish my chores on land.

I checked in with the customs office of French Polynesia and finished my errands. I was motoring back to the *Bula* when I spotted Ralph's boat up ahead. It was a 65-foot sloop with a strange Celtic name *Cershia*. I could never pronounce it correctly. I decided to spin over and take him up on the beer.

Pulling up to the boat, I could vaguely see some people sitting in the cockpit and Ralph swimming off the back of the boat. Ralph spotted me and started up the steps.

He yelled from the top deck, "Hey Carson hand up your line and I'll tie off your dingy."

Reaching for the tangled line in the bottom of the dingy, I could hear Ralph right above me waiting. I was passing part of the line upward with one hand and trying to free the rest of the line with the other hand. I happened to glance up and saw Ralph standing there in his birthday suit. I nearly had my hand on his hog and I retracted my arm. I said, "Whoaaa, hey, why don't you just pass that thing down and I'll tie my dingy off with it."

Ralph chuckled and tied off the line. He said, "Come aboard mate."

I climbed up the transom steps. When I reached the cockpit, there were three girls. Two of them were totally nude and a third one was topless. I had briefly met them before they left Mexico when they were clothed.

I said, "Hey Ralph, you got a harem here or what?"

Ralph laughed and two of the three girls got a bit embarrassed. They decided to go put on some clothes. The third one just sat there naked with one leg hiked up, displaying this unruly tarantula. Didn't they have razors on this boat? This was the one girl I *didn't* want to see naked. She proceeded to have a conversation with me, unwilling to cage that quilted quim.

"Sooo Carson," she lavishly said. "How was your trip across?" She looked at me with salacious eyes.

I couldn't look at her without developing a smirk. I tried to be polite, answering her questions. I finally faded out of the conversation with her, and onto one with a girl who had put on some clothes.

Ralph said, "There are some people throwing a small birthday party on the beach for a friend off another yacht. Why don't you go grab your buddy and your guitar and meet us there tonight?"

It was a full moon that night. I said, "Full moon party huh? I'm sure Figman will be excited to meet some girls, or anyone besides me."

I went back and told Figman about the birthday party and he seemed ready to rally. I think he was just happy to be alive and not seasick for two whole days.

I told him the story of my interesting rendezvous on *Cershia*. He coined their boat "The Nudes". They became the talk of the anchorage. We had everyone calling them "The Nudes".

Sailors are definitely an odd lot, and they're not afraid to lose their clothes. However, these people were taking it to extremes. Ralph was advertising online for crew positions on his boat with a strong emphasis on being part of the W.N.S. (World Nude Society). Ralph's girlfriend Tanya told me about how he went up the mast, during a rough squall, to repair the rigging wearing nothing but topsiders. Ralph had found his esoteric niche in society—extreme nudity. Of course, they had a German guy on board who refused to wear anything, ever.

We spotted the German one day standing in the dingy waxing the side of the boat with an electric buffer in his hands, wearing nothing but safety goggles. He had a female assistant who was leaning over the topside of the boat with her boobs hanging upside-down. She was hand waxing what he couldn't buff.

Boread pulled into Nuku Hiva safe that day. We hadn't heard anything about them since we left Mexico. They had repaired their rudderpost leak and sailed out of Mexico two days later.

We bought two bottles of rum at the local store. The prices were outrageous in French Polynesia. It was such an arcane outpost that everything arrived by ship from France or Australia. We paid the woman a fortune for the cheapest booze she had, and headed over to the party.

When we got there, we met everyone including Darren and Amber off *Boread*. After everyone got on the sauce and loosened up, the painful idiosyncrasies of the trip came out like bad gas. Everyone voiced how much the other person on the boat drove him or her insane. We all blew off some steam.

A new crew of people motored up on a 15-foot inflatable. They swamped their boat in the surf pulling up to the beach. We ran out to help them and they nearly fell off the dingy into the water. They clamored ashore giving us full responsibility to pull the massive inflatable up on the beach.

This young Canadian couple off the big inflatable introduced themselves. Then a short, balding fellow walked up and introduced himself. He was an American and the type of guy who gives you the Kung Fu grip handshake, stares you right in the eyes and proudly states his first and last name.

"Hi, my name is David Poltz." he stated. He immediately slipped me his secret bottle of Metaxa mixed with lemonade. Metaxa is a Greek brandy that doesn't mix well with anything.

He stealthily looked around and said, "It's my last bottle. Don't let the Canadians know about it, but please indulge in this fine Greek brandy."

This guy was hording it as if it was liquid gold. I took a painful swig. The taste was a cross between tree bark and toilet-bowl cleaner. I faked a nodding approval.

"Great stuff huh?" he said with a beaming grin. He glared at his prize and continued, "Yep, last bottle."

Making a secret ploy to avoid drinking anymore of that poison, I quickly stated, "Well, you'll just have to save the rest then, huh?"

"No way. It's me and you man, till we kill this sucker."

I couldn't lose him after I falsely confided with him over his stash. David spoke in a peculiar manner as though he was concealing information and involved in the tragically popular conspiracy theory. Another poor child raised in the era of the information crisis. Every sentence contained at least one of the key subjects: the Russians, technological infiltration, the CIA, neurological military spies, Hollywood, extraterrestrials, and internet espionage.

I pulled out my guitar, a conga drum, some shakers and random noisemakers I had brought from the boat. I passed them out to everyone who had an available limb. I juiced up a funky rhythm, or so I thought, and everyone joined in with dysfunctional order. We were creating some kind of wild ruckus. It sounded similar to a chimpanzee with a whiffle bat making music out of a set of hubcaps and a side of beef. When people are charged up and having fun you can't just pull the noisemakers away from the bad ones. It's the same as pulling a pacifier out of a baby's mouth.

The poor islanders were getting their first taste of white man's disease. We still had a good time beating up instruments, howling at the moon and mangling music together. We had defied nature and sailed three-thousand miles of open-ocean to a tiny rock in the South Pacific.

The Underworld of the Black Pearl

After spending a couple of weeks in the Marquises recuperating, we sailed out of Nuku Hiva heading for the Tuamotus. They are a chain of islands between the Marquises and Tahiti. My brother was flying in to meet us on the island Apataki.

Everyone had warned us about the dangerous passes in the Tuamotu atolls. An atoll is a ring-shaped island with a center lagoon. It acts like a fish bowl with each tide rising and falling through small passes. You might have 10 knots of current rushing through a pass during large tides. The *Bula* only motored at 6 knots. That meant we would be going either 16 knots inward or 4 knots backwards, depending on the tide. We were informed we needed accurate tide charts and a little luck.

We didn't exactly have a tide chart. We didn't even have a chart for that matter. The only fragment of information we had was a hand-drawn map on a cocktail napkin of the southern pass. A French sailor gave it to me the day before we left the Marquises. A little luck? We needed Neptune, Noah, or any bigwig with a finger on the game.

The sun was rising on the morning of our arrival. We were only 15 miles out, though we couldn't see the island. That worried me. After another hour, we were only eight miles out and still no island. You can spot a small island on a clear day 20 nautical miles out if it has some elevation.

I started questioning that French guy and his stupid cocktail napkin. The napkin had gotten water on it and now just resembled a "black spot" (a death threat among pirates made of a black spot or mark on a scrap of paper).

Figman was desperately scanning the horizon with the binoculars. He was scanning in every direction.

"Bingo. We've got an island captain," he said.

I tried to grab the binoculars and we began battling over them. He finally let me win since he had already spotted it. I located it, handed the binoculars back to him and grabbed the VHF. I wanted to hail someone on the island to obtain the times of the tides. I had an idea that high tide could be around 11 am by extrapolating a capricious oceanographic model through the art of bathymetry. I calculated the times of the tides in the Marquises and transferred them to our destination, roughly 800 miles west. I used enough formulas to baffle a professor of calculus, because I made them up.

I didn't know what to say on the VHF. "Apataki, Apataki, this is sailing vessel *Bula*. Do you copy?" It sounded ridiculous hailing an entire island. I was thinking about some ignorant foreigner pulling into any given port in America and saying on the VHF, "America, America, do you copy?"

Someone answered back in broken English with a French accent. I explained that we were about to enter the southern pass and wondered if the high tide was around 11am.

"OK . . . high tide . . . 11am," he said.

I looked at Figman and said, "That didn't sound like an answer to me." I said to the man on the VHF, "I am asking, *is* the high tide at 11am?"

"OK . . . no problem . . . high tide . . . 11am," he said. I just looked at Figman puzzled. He put his hands up and shrugged.

"Damn it, we're going in." I said.

We rounded the bend and that cocktail-napkin chart was spot-on, actually closer than some real charts I've used. We got to the correct coordinate, studied the pass and began motoring towards it. The pass was narrow. It'd be crazy to turn the boat around in the middle.

As we started into the narrow portion of the pass, I noticed we were sailing along rather fast. The tide must've been on the rise and flowing inward.

I backed down on the throttle in order to spot the small anchorage inside the pass that was scribbled on the cocktail napkin. I saw one sailboat in the tiny area to anchor. After studying the anchorage, I realized it also had a small entrance in the reef to squeeze through. We sped past it and the swift current pushed us into the lagoon. I turned the boat around and headed back into the pass towards the anchorage, making slow progress against the incoming tide.

I told Figman we were going to go past the anchorage entrance, turn the boat in the direction of the entrance, and then throttle it through the small gap at the right moment. It was very critical and the tide was gaining velocity.

Just as we passed the entrance, I turned the bow of the boat in line with the gap—waited for the current to push us into position, and then floored the throttle. We shot through the gap with maybe four feet to spare on either side of the boat.

Ok, I thought, we made it through that part, now let's anchor fast before we get pushed into the reef with the dangerous flowing tide. I motored over to a good spot to drop the anchor and yelled out to Figman on the bow, "DROP THE ANCHOR."

"Don't you think we should . . .?" he said.

Before he had a chance to finish his statement, I shouted, "DROP, THE ANCHOR." We were now drifting straight towards the reef sideways.

"Well, wouldn't it be better if we . . .?"

"DROP THE FUCKING ANCHOR!"

He dropped the anchor and entirely too much chain with it. I yelled, "STOP, STOP."

We were only in eight feet of water and the reef was about 20 feet away on every side. The chain was still flying out of the chain locker and the boat was drifting towards the reef. He finally stopped the chain and I desperately said, "Start pulling the chain back in and tie it off, I'll move the anchor by hand."

I quickly grabbed a mask and dove in the water. I picked up the anchor under my arm as if it was a football and tried to run along the bottom like an underwater cartoon character. I was carrying the anchor in the opposite direction of where the boat was drifting into the reef. I made it to an underwater rock on the other side of the anchorage and just got the anchor over the top of the rock when the chain went tight. The tail of the boat swung around and just grazed the reef.

I was so angry with Figman I could've killed him. When I surfaced, I took one look at him and mumbled to myself, "Idiot." Shaking my head, I swam back to the boat and climbed aboard.

He was pacing around on the bow with steam coming out of his ears. He then came back to the cockpit and said, "Don't call me an idiot."

That was the closest I ever came to punching him right in the schnozzle. I was engineering a plan to extract him off the boat somehow.

He walked up to the bow of the boat with his arms crossed, and I went to the very back of the boat with my arms crossed. We were fuming, staring in opposite directions—trying to get as far away from each other as possible. He was still only 36 feet away and I wanted him to be 36 countries away.

Maybe he had a good point to make about anchoring, but there was no time to query. Who is to say who was right or wrong? After spending too much time on a boat with someone else, that person is always wrong, in your mind.

Then I heard a familiar voice from shore. "*BULA*." It was my brother Greg, a.k.a. "Corn". He could not have shown up at a better time to save us from each other.

Corn is a bit taller than I am at six foot, barrel-chested, short sun-bleached hair, dark tan from years on the dive boats, and three years older. We used to look nearly identical back in college and pulled off some gags between our dates, who didn't know the difference half the time. He eventually put on more weight. It doesn't matter how much I eat; it just doesn't stick. We also sound a lot alike. I figure the only difference between us is our personalities. He was always convinced that he was Elvis and I thought I was Jim Morrison, but we were doing a bad job of both.

When we were kids, we used to beat each other up, but we have resolved our differences. Now we just have a good time. Every time we get together, somewhere in the world, things seem to fall right into place.

He got the nickname Corn from a friend of his in Puerto Rico who named the whole family with similar nicknames because we are from Texas and therefore we must be "hillbillies" and live on a farm. He was ordained Corn. I was given the moniker the "Kernel", because I was the youngest. And our Dad was named "Pop-corn". Their names stuck but mine didn't, probably because Corn didn't want his younger brother to have the upper hand with an authoritarian name like the Kernel.

Figman and I both looked over to shore, a mere 50 feet away, and there he was, arms in the air, doing an Elvis jig. A big grin came over my face. "THERE HE IS," I yelled.

"WHAT ARE YOU GUYS DOING?" he yelled back.

I didn't want to tell him that we wanted to kill each other. "HANG ON. WE'LL COME PICK YOU UP."

We forgot about the tense situation, for the moment, and dropped the donkey in the water to paddle over to see him. He gave us both a bear hug. He told us that he had nearly given up hope on our arrival. Without giving him any details of our trip, I said, "Why don't you two go grab a bite to eat while I clean up the boat." I needed a couple hours of space and there couldn't have been a better time.

Figman and I got back on good terms after our dissonance. However, if my brother had not arrived when he did, one of us would've hung the other. It's not easy living with someone else in the small cabin of a boat the size of a toaster. Even if it's your best friend, you'll still want to tar-and-feather them after enough time.

My brother Corn had a few friends on the island from a previous visit. One lived on the waterfront next to the anchored *Bula*. His name was Toa and he had a fishing boat. Toa was a young, schoolteacher from Tahiti. He was a large fellow with

Polynesian features and a constant smile. He was genuinely kind and warm. I was beginning to realize, the warmer the climate, the warmer the people. I didn't ever want to go back to the cold USA. He wanted to take us out fishing, spearfishing, and surfing. We couldn't have found a better friend.

Around four o'clock, we all hopped in his skiff and motored outside of the pass. Flocks of birds were feeding on schools of small fish on the surface. We sped over to the swarms of birds and tossed a couple of fishing lines out the back. We immediately caught two 5-lb Aku tuna. We got the lines back out for more.

We caught three more Aku and reeled in the lines. We motored back to the pass with our spearfishing gear before we ran out of sunlight. We anchored, geared up and dove over with a few other local guys who were also spearfishing. Tuamotans are the masters of spearfishing. They are legendary and have made it an art form. Some of the spearfishing champions of the world came from the Tuamotus.

We hovered on the surface, studying their adept techniques. They descended down to one hundred feet and hid in the reef for more than a minute waiting for the right fish. Once a good fish was in range, *click*, they pulled the trigger, spearing a tuna, all on one breath.

I took a deep breath and descended down to around sixty feet. I waited patiently without moving. A grouper came into range and I pulled the trigger. I speared my first fish of the day and began slowly ascending to the surface. On my ascent, I was working the spear out of the fish on my way up. Toa came over to me on the surface and said, "Friend, don't ever do that."

"What?" I said.

"The moment you spear a fish, bring it to the surface immediately and get it out of the water into the skiff."

"Why is that?"

"The sharks here are aggressive."

I nodded with bulging eyes and calmly said, "Right, ok, aggressive sharks, get 'em in the boat quick, got it."

My first day spearfishing in the Tuamotus I was three-for-three; three descents and three fish. Toa and my brother also speared a good amount of grouper.

Back on shore at Toa's place, we made sashimi with the Aku tuna and cooked up the grouper on the barbeque. We all sat around drinking beers, feasting on our catch from the sea and telling stories of our adventures across the Pacific.

After a few days of spearfishing and dodging sharks, we headed over to a friend's pearl farm on the other side of the lagoon. Toa gave us a ride over in his skiff. He dropped us off and claimed he would return in two days to pick us up.

We stayed with the Mau family from the main island of Tahiti. Part of the year, they lived on the atoll to raise black pearls in the lagoon.

They taught us the procedures of raising the Tahitian black pearl. It's a delicate process involving grafters flown in from Japan and clamshell nutrients extracted from the banks of the Mississippi river. The grafters insert arthroscopic tools into the live oysters, performing an operation to perfect the shape of the pearl by removing growths. They also insert the clamshell nutrients into the oysters to help facilitate rapid growth.

Mr. Mau told us a tale of his existence on a pearl farm in a tiny South Pacific atoll. He said, "A few days ago, I was out snorkeling in the lagoon, checking the pearl nets, when I spotted a pesky shark lingering around. I tried to *shooo* it away as I tended to the oysters. After a few minutes, the shark returned and continued to sniff me out. I felt a bit threatened, so I went up to the boat to grab the "bang stick" (a spear gun with a high caliber bullet in the end that fires on contact when it's jammed into an object). I was carrying it for safety and sure enough the shark decided to come in too close and I jammed the gun into the sharks head and the bullet fired. It was a direct shot to the brain and the shark died after thrashing about for a minute."

He paused and continued, "I tied the tail of the shark to the back of the boat and towed it to shore. Then I walked up and told my sons to go and pull the shark ashore. They went down and couldn't believe the size of it. It took five of them to haul it ashore. They measured it at four meters."

I thought Mr. Mau was lying until he showed us the pictures. One of the photos was of his son with his entire head in the sharks opened jaws. Mr. Mau had referred to the shark as being "pesky".

Cherry Pop

We set sail for Tahiti. It was only a day and a half journey. We squeezed through the tight pass unharmed. Luckily, the tide was going out, sweeping us past the turquoise shallows out into the depths.

We threaded our way past two more atolls near Apataki, sailing off into the deep blue. Within a half-an-hour, we were out of sight of land. Sea birds followed us for miles and the water was thick with fish.

I set the wind-vane on a compass course of 250 degrees and pulled out the fishing rods. The birds were hitting the surface for baitfish all around the horizon. My brother and Figman set the rods out trolling two Rapala lures. We then kicked back in the shade of the bimini and told stories.

Now with my brother onboard the boat, it was more crowded. He isn't a small fellow like Figman. *Bula* was maxed out for cruising capacity, but it didn't really matter. We were only island hopping on short trips. At least we had an extra hand for night watches. That meant we could sleep more, not that we ever stayed awake during our watches.

The next day, we averaged a much better speed than anticipated. We arrived early at the Teahupoo pass, unfortunately at night. My brother had been there before and claimed it was a large enough pass to enter at night. Thirty meters isn't exactly a wide pass. I've never been one to heave-to all night and wait until morning. I tend to go in blind. However, I was questioning my obstinate nature after the tight pass in Apataki.

I pulled out the spotlight as we approached the pass. Corn shined the big spotlight across the surface of the water to find any channel markers. "There aren't any damn markers?" I said. "Are you kidding me?"

"Nope, nothing," Corn said.

"Ooo kay, this is going to be interesting."

We could faintly see the surf breaking on both sides of the pass. There was an area where there were no breakers. I decided to head in through the area with no whitewater in hope that it was the pass.

Halfway into the pass, the spotlight battery died. We were already committed. I used my ears to judge how far away the surf was breaking on either side of the boat, shooting for the gap. We squeezed through unharmed and I shook my head at the risk.

We anchored on the inside of the pass near the shore in fifty feet of water. It was unusually deep so close to land. We couldn't see in the dark and hoped we weren't next to any reef that we could swing into in the middle of the night.

We drank a few beers and retired to our bunks.

We woke up to the sun shining behind lush peaks jetting out of the ocean. Luxuriant palms lined the shoreline with scattered beaches. There were dilapidated huts and rudimentary wooden houses painted in faded pastels.

The water varied in colors of aquamarine across the shallow barrier reef. The surf in the pass was overhead and breaking in a divine manner with the ocean spray whisking high into the air.

The three of us launched the donkey and motored out to the pass with our surfboards. Once we got out there, the surf was a lot bigger than it looked from the boat. We tied the donkey off to a mooring ball and paddled over to some heavy waves. It was about ten feet up the face and heaving thick barrels onto this shallow shelf a few feet below the surface.

I watched for ten or fifteen minutes to get a barring on where the larger sets were breaking and where the take-off spots were located.

There were only a handful of guys out surfing, which lessened the pressure. There's nothing worse than contending with a crowd when you're dealing with the power of Mother Nature.

My brother surfs goofy-foot* and I'm a regular-foot. The wave is a left giving him the advantage of ease and comfort facing the wave. This is a big advantage when dealing with dangerous waves.

He dropped into his first wave and disappeared as the wave passed me. I could tell by the back of the wave that he caught a long barrel pulling out at the end and giggling with excitement.

I looked up at the horizon and saw my opportunity coming with the next set of waves. I paddled into position and airdropped into a mini-bomb. I straightened up and got more comfortable on my surfboard. The wave began welling up and I managed to get into the barrel for a few seconds that seemed like eternity. Riding in the barrel of a wave is like being in a glass bubble in the eye of a tornado. The world is spinning around you while you're standing there on your board in a timeless state. One second seems like a lifetime.

We surfed for a couple of hours catching some good waves. Figman was charging the big stuff, impressing us. The sets were picking up to fifteen-foot and it was getting heavy. We decided to stop for lunch before someone got chowed by one of those meat hooks.

We motored back to the boat and I located my camera to get a few of the waves we just surfed on film. Teahupoo,

------

* goofy-foot = 1 : whether you're riding a surfboard, skateboard, snowboard or a two-by-four; if you stand with your left foot back, you're goofy-foot 2 : if your right foot is back, you're regular or natural-foot 3 : most people tend to be regular, therefore, anything that's different is goofy

pronounced "Chi-how-po", is one of the heaviest waves in the world. We pronounced it, Chow-*poo*.

We met this character named Cameron who sailed in that afternoon. He just arrived from Hawaii on his small thirty-foot Columbia named *Duet*. Cameron and I were around the same age. He was about six-foot tall, blonde hair, mysterious blue eyes and medium build. He wore a puka-shell necklace. We wore those when we were in middle school. He seemed as if he was still living out his days like a kid with a lot of wild energy for exploration and other sorts of odd behavior. He was anchored inside the reef in a well-protected area and told us there was plenty of room to anchor beside him if we wanted.

We decided to move over next to him that afternoon. We pulled the anchor and began motoring over to his boat. We were slowly working our way through this inner-channel towards his boat. I had Corn and Figman both on the bow to watch for the dangerous reef.

Cameron's boat was up ahead another hundred meters. I was plotting out a good spot to drop the anchor when I saw my brother with a surprised look on his face. He was standing there speechless and pointing into the water. He yelled, "REEF, HARD TO PORT."

I threw the wheel hard to port. We swung right into the reef. The keel and rudder screamed as we charged in sideways and came to an abrupt halt.

"MOTHER FUCKER!" I screamed.

I continued cussing and running around in circles. I was grabbing random objects and throwing things about, trying to organize a way to save the boat. Figman came back to help, only to stare at me in confusion. I was handing him ropes and devices that didn't quite fit in with the situation at hand. Turmoil was spinning in my brain. I was about to ignite with flames billowing off my head; I had to calm down. I was thinking to myself, here we made it all the way across the Pacific to Tahiti safe and I sink the boat the day after arrival.

My brother grabbed a snorkel and mask to survey the damage. He dove over the side and resurfaced after a short inspection. He said, "It's not that bad. We're not sinking."

Trying to remain calm, I spotted a large powerboat parked at a small dock next to shore. "I'm going for help," I said.

I jumped in the donkey and blazed over to shore. I quickly found the owner of the powerboat. He didn't speak any English, so I just pointed out to my boat. He got the hint and grabbed his keys.

I jumped back in the inflatable and he cranked up his engines. He pulled his boat over to the *Bula*. We threw him two lines, one securely tied to the bow, and one tied amid-ship. He tied off the line to his bow and put his engines in reverse. It took a bit of rocking to get her off, but she finally dislodged from the reef.

I thanked the local with all the Tahitian and French words I knew. I tried to pay him for the favor. He didn't want to accept anything. I forced him to take a six-pack of local Hinano beers. He gave in and accepted with a big grin. Beer is usually a more polite and acceptable means of trade.

I returned to the boat and anchored. I put on the mask and checked the damage. It wasn't as bad as it sounded when we hit. I guessed the ole girl was bulletproof after all. The bottom and back of the keel were scrapped up a bit and the tail of the rudder looked like a hedgehog had been chewing on it. I would repair it the next time I pulled the boat out of the water. She was floating and I needed an acceptable means of trade myself, cold Hinano.

We went to shore, loaded up on a case of Hinano and headed back to the boat. We all saluted the *Bula* for popping her cherry*.

---

* popping her cherry = when a virgin vessel goes aground for the first time

Just Tell Them You're with the French Film Crew

After a couple of weeks surfing Teahupoo, we decided to sail over to the beautiful island of Moorea. We pulled the anchor, said goodbye to Cameron and sailed northeast. It was about a six-hour sail. I had a funny feeling we would see Cameron again someday.

We sailed to the southwest corner of Moorea and entered a pass called Vaimiti. My brother had surfed there once before, claiming it was a good reef break.

We anchored on the inside of the pass, on a small pinnacle in ten feet of water. Surrounding us was a large green mountain ridge jutting out of the ocean towards the clouds. The water was so clear it appeared as though we were suspended in air above a multi-colored reef system. Tropical fish were darting in and out of caves and combing the reef for nutrients.

We took the donkey out to the surf break and paddled out. We met an Austrian out surfing named Flo, short for Florian. What kind of a guy has a name like Flo? He'd be working as a waitress in a dinner if he lived in the States.

He was tall and skinny with blue eyes and dirty-blonde hair, a typical Aryan European. He was a pro snowboarder and flew to Tahiti with a French film crew that was filming extreme sports. They were all staying at the Club Med.

I said to Flo, "So, how do you like the Club Med?"

In broken English, he said. "Great, I have nice room, great food, and I no pay nothing."

"Free?"

"The French film crew make movie of me snowboarding in Austria, and for payment, invite me down for two week party."

"Not bad there Flo."

"If you, your brother and your friend want to come over to eat at Club Med buffet tonight, tell front desk you're with French film crew. There are many peoples, they not know the difference."

Of course we hitchhiked down to the Club Med that evening. My brother said, "Let's go the beach route. I've done it before and it's as easy as just walking down the beach and right into the resort. Once you're inside, nobody asks any questions."

I said, "You sure about that?"

"No problem."

"Well alright then, we'll follow your lead."

We found our way down to the beach and began walking to the resort from the south side. As we neared the resort, it seemed to be an easy shot in. Just as we stepped onto the grounds, thinking we were in the clear, this big Tahitian sitting on a stool behind a tree shinned his flashlight on us. We froze. He said in a deep tribal voice, "You stay here?"

We responded unanimously shaking our heads in affirmation.

"Must go around to front entrance."

We haggled with him for a minute, claiming it was too far around and that our room was right there, pointing at some random room.

"Must go around."

Defeated, we turned and decided to try our luck at the front.

When we arrived at the entrance, we hadn't come up with a game plan. We just walked up and tried to wing it. As we approached the gate, there were two huge Tahitian guards sitting on stools next to the guard booth. Various guests were walking in and out of the gate. We confidently walked up with a few other people and followed them in. One of the Tahitian guards looked at us with uncertainty and said, "You stay here?"

"Yep, we're part of the French film crew," Corn said.

"You got a key?"

That stumped us. Corn looked back at us, as if it was our turn to come up with a subterfuge. My brain was trying to lock onto anything that could break the code. We just stood there for a moment too long. I mumbled the first thing that popped into my head. Nothing but verbal diarrhea fumbled out of my jaw. The authorities in the booth began to peer out at us. It would've been best if we had just walked off, but I tried to make a nice cover-up, continuing to get myself deeper. We finally turned and got out of there before things got uglier.

We walked on down the road, formulating our next attempt. We needed a human catapulting device to launch us over that tall fence.

Corn said, "Hey, I know of a drainage ditch up ahead. We used to sneak through it the last time we were here." Figman and I skeptically nodded in approval.

We found the drainage ditch, but the grounds men had patched it up with chain-link fence. They probably caught a few too many hoodlums like us sneaking through. We looked at each other in disgust.

"Foiled again," I said.

We continued down the road defeated. We eventually came upon a part of the fence that was close enough to a tree branch, conveniently leaning over it. We looked at the tree and at each other. I peered down the street one way and then the other for any cars and I saw nothing. I took off at a sprint straight at the fence. I hit the thing with enough speed to knock over a gorilla. The rebound of the chain-link fence nearly shot me backwards, but I held on and scampered up it. I made it to the tree branch, pulled myself over the fence, free fell ten feet and hit the ground. I saw a row of bathrooms and quickly ducked into one for cover.

I hid in the stall for a couple of minutes, listening to Corn and Figman outside the fence in an argument of loud whispering. I overheard Corn say, "Come on Fig. Help me up that fence."

"How the heck am I supposed to get your ass up there?" Figman said.

"Let me stand on your back." Corn chuckled.

"Are you kidding? You're gonna break my back."

"No I won't."

They were causing a ruckus. Security would spot them soon. I had been in the bathroom stall long enough. They would eventually find me at the buffet, if they got over that fence.

I slowly opened the bathroom door, checking for security. I saw the two of them fumbling around, one trying to climb on top of the other. It looked as if Corn was actually halfway up the fence standing on the back of poor Figman. The only problem, Corn was too heavy and he was bending the fence so far backwards that his back was nearly touching the ground. I quietly snuck off into the dark.

I got to Flo's room and knocked on the door. Flo opened the door and said, "Carson buddy, you made it. Come in, we were just about to make big hunger by smoking joint and then buffet. Where are your brother and Figman?"

I thought about the state of those two at that particular moment. "They're a little tied up right now, but they might meet us at the buffet." Flo looked at me confused as he was inhaling the smoke.

We finished the joint and headed over to the buffet. I grabbed a plate as we entered the restaurant. Flo joined his friends with the French film crew before getting food.

I was busy piling it high when I ran into Corn and his powder monkey* Figman. They were walking through the front entrance, covered in grass stains and dirt. They looked like they had gone *under* the fence. I just smirked. We had to stay incognito. They got the hint—grabbed a couple of plates and headed off in different directions.

---

* powder monkey = 1 : a gunner's assistant on a ship 2 : a small cannon is referred to as the monkey and the assistant is usually covered in gunpowder

We all met at Flo's table. He had a few seats for us. He introduced us to the crew and we tried to blend in with them.

I made multiple trips back to the buffet and managed to get six plates of food down. We talked with the crew for awhile about their different jobs on the set.

Resembling a bloated camel, I turned to my two accomplices and whispered, "Mission accomplished."

We figured it would be best to get on our way before anyone questioned us. The crew was sitting around jabbering in French. We politely said our goodbyes to the crew and told Flo we would see him out in the surf. Then we casually slipped out the backdoor.

As we walked away from the restaurant, the three of us tried to contain the grins on our faces. I was paranoid and felt mysterious eyes falling on my back as we continued out of the Club Med. It must have been the pot.

Shakhty and the Dreadlocked Gypsy

Corn flew back to Puerto Rico and Figman flew back to San Diego. Figman and I had been on the boat together for three months. At least we didn't kill each other.

I spent two weeks all by myself, just hanging out on the poop deck, living the life of a clandestine monk and surfing Vaimiti. There was no one around in sight, so I went naked most of the day on the boat. It was too hot even to wear shorts, but I found one functional problem. Don't ever work on the engine without shorts. I nearly got my jimmy caught in a moving part. Imagine a grown man naked and sweating in the hot tropics working on the engine—life isn't always daisies.

A single-hander sailed in through the pass on a small thirty-foot sloop named *Shakhty*. He anchored next to me on the same pinnacle and came over in his dingy to say hello. I heard a knock on the hull. I put on some shorts and came up top-deck to see this dread-locked feral in army fatigues sitting in his dingy.

"Hi, names Mick," he said.

"Carson, nice to meet ya," I said. "How's it going?"

"Good, good. Say, how's the anchorage here?"

"It's fine. I've been here for about two weeks all by myself. When the tide changes, it will spin your boat around, so it's a good idea to have your anchor chain free from any coral heads. Aside from that, it's safe. Where'd you sail in from?"

"I've been sailing through the Society Islands for awhile now, looking for some good surf. I've heard about this spot. How's it been?"

"It's been small. Last week was bigger. You can surf either side of the pass. The left is more consistent. Some mornings, I've had it all to myself. Where are you from?"

"South Africa. I left Cape Town on my boat a few years ago. I've been single-handing most of the way. I spent a couple of years in the Caribbean, and I came through the Panama Canal a few months ago."

Mick was a product of the rave generation. He also gave me the impression of a transcendental hippy. That or he was part of a commie, conspiracy cult. We connected immediately.

We kicked back in Vaimiti over the next week until the surf went flat. I was perfectly complacent until Mick came over to *Bula* one day and said, "Carson, aren't you getting bored?"

"No, actually I was enjoying just hanging out here, playing guitar in the day, and contemplating existence under the stars at night." I personally didn't care if I was sitting in the cockpit counting clouds, I was happy to be anchored in paradise.

He started telling me about a couple of girls he knew on a sixty-five-foot sloop anchored in Papeete. They were running around half-naked all day, taunting every perverted captain in binocular distance.

I was slightly interested at first, and then his story rang a bell. "*Cershia?*" I said.

He grinned—pointing at me. "You know Tanya and Lisa?"

"The nudes?"

"You call them the nudes?"

"It's a long story."

I told him my story and he told me his. He shyly relayed to me, how the big one, Lisa, was chasing him around and he was *running* from her. He had that look in his eyes as if he was running in quicksand.

I said, "You know, I haven't seen them since the Marquises."

"The captain has gone back to America for a couple of months and he left the girls in charge to watch over the boat. You want to go visit them and find a bit of a party in Papeete?"

I looked around and thought about it. "What the heck."

We looked at each other with wicked grins. "Pull your anchor pirate," he said.

Mick jumped in his dingy and motored back to his boat. We both started the process of stowing all the breakables and getting our boats ready for the sail to Tahiti. It was about a three-hour sail. I told Mick if he talked to the girls on the VHF to keep me a secret. I wanted to surprise them.

We both sailed out of the pass at Vaimiti and set our course for Tahiti. I put two fishing lines out the back for any possible lunch. The trade winds were blowing from the southeast at 10 knots and we sailed along close-hauled. The skies were clear with the sun overhead, illuminating the barrier reef off the southwestern tip of Moorea. The surf exploded onto the reef, sending spray into the air. The bottom was clearly visible at 150 feet deep.

About an hour out, Mick got on his VHF and hailed the girls, "*Cershia, Cershia*, this is *Shakhty*."

I turned up the volume on my radio when Tanya came on the radio.

"You wanna go up to channel 72?" she said.

"72," Mick said.

"Hey Mickey baby, where you at?" Tanya said in a lascivious voice.

"I'm coming over to see you two."

"Sounds like you missed us."

Lisa said, "Yeah Mickey, we can't waaait to see you."

"Girls, I'm bringing you a little surprise."

Tanya said, "Oooo Mickey-boy what have you got for us?"

"You'll find out."

The Stranger

We had a dreamy sail over to Tahiti and pulled into the Tapuna passage. The waves were breaking on both sides of the small pass and a few locals were out surfing. We weaved our way through the reef into the lagoon. Small houses and boat docks with outrigger canoes lined the waterfront. Small fishing boats sped past us, heading out to sea with dark-skinned locals onboard setting up the fishing lines.

We anchored our boats next to Marina Taina, among the other yachts from overseas. Many of the yachts were plush, multimillion-dollar outfits from all over the world. I felt as though we'd see Robin Leach pop in for an episode of Lifestyles of the Rich and Famous. I envisioned him with his film crew on one of the mega-yachts, boogying down with some false-breasted models, saying something suave like, "Oooo la la, look at those ta ta's— and at only ten thousand dollars a pop, they're not for the meek." Then there was Mick and I looking more like Lifestyles of the Poor and Stupid.

We jumped in Mick's dingy and motored over to *Cershia*. They were running around topless. We might have seemed poor, comparatively, but I wasn't feeling so stupid after all. We jumped aboard. They were happy to see their good friend Mick and really surprised to see me.

Tanya said, "Carson we hadn't heard anything about you and the *Bula* since Nuku Hiva. We've been wondering if you had gone missing."

It's a big ocean out there, but the cruising community is a tight-knit society who looks after each other on the high seas.

We sat around catching up. Tanya said, "We're heading into town for the summer games parade. Do you guys want to join us?"

We both said, "Sure."

I said, "Are we going in for the evening, or just for the day?"

Tanya said, "Bring clothes for both in case we decide to stay for the evening."

I said, "Sounds dangerous."

We grabbed what we needed from our boats and headed in to see the parade. We motored to the Maeva Beach Hotel with the girls in Mick's dingy. After tying up the dingy to the hotel dock, we walked up to the main street and hopped on the first bus for Papeete.

When we got into town, the girls said they were going to see the parade. Mick and I claimed we were on a mission to find a bottle of booze to save some money. Otherwise, we would've dropped a hundred bucks trying to get a buzz in a bar in Papeete. Tahiti makes Paris seem cheap.

They told us they'd be near the waterfront cafes and we could find them there. They went one way and we went the other.

Mick and I walked down the sidewalk on our search. All the stores were closed, so I asked a local policeman helping with the parade. "Parlez vous Anglais?" I said.

"Yez," he said.

"Do you know where we could find a liquor store that is open?"

He spoke English with a heavy, French accent. "Everyzing iz closed, it iz a national holiday."

I shook my head. "Wait a minute. There's no place we can buy any alcohol outside of a bar or restaurant?"

He then looked around and said in a soft voice, "Ok guyz listen. Zere is one guy down zee street zat you can get somezing at his house."

The cop was actually turning us on to some local bootlegger. It was Tahiti for that matter, and maybe it wasn't illegal. It was probably his cousin who sold the stuff out of his garage. He raised his eyebrows, cracked a bit of a smile and continued, "Well if you go all zee way down zis main street to the end and take a right, it tiz down on zee right."

I said, "Maruru." ("Thank you" in Tahitian)

We walked through the parade to the end of the main street, turned right and began looking for it. We couldn't find it, and ended up running into yet another Tahitian cop helping in the parade. I motioned to Mick, and we walked over to him.

I said, "Excuse me, do you happen to know of a particular store, or house here on this street somewhere, that might be selling liquor?" I left it ambiguously open.

"Sorry guys," he laughed and replied in good English, "that particular place you're referring to is also closed. Every store is closed on this day." With a big grin, he said, "Everyone is celebrating."

I thought to myself, yeah exactly, everyone is celebrating. Why are all the stores closed? They could be making some serious money on the sale of alcohol. It wasn't the States, and they wouldn't dare think about profit over tradition.

"Oh, of course, of course," I said. "Maruru." We sulked down the street, defeated.

Mick said, "Man this sucks. We sail all the way over here to party and we can't even get a bottle of liquor."

I said, "That isn't the best of luck."

We continued mopping down the street, dwelling on our lack of options. I spotted a pharmacy. "Mick, follow my lead," I said and pushed him in the direction of the drug store. He looked at me with one eyebrow raised.

We barged into this quaint pharmacy and walked up to the counter. An older French woman emerged from the back, wearing a revealing top, two buttons too low. She had articulate spectacles hung low on her nose as if she was just out of a ménage à trois in the back.

She asked us something in French with a lot of breath in her voice. For an older woman, she was still sexy. French women know how to put it on, whether they're 15 or 50.

There we were—two unshaven, dread-locked and nappy-headed villains, standing there in a contemporary pharmacy with nothing but bad intentions. Feeling uneasy from the pensive stare of the woman, I mumbled something undecipherable in her language. It sounded more like English with a French accent. She strangely stared at me.

With a wave of her body and an upward hand gesture, she said, "Would you prefer we speak English?"

Coming out of confusion, I said, "Yes, yes please." Mick and I continued to stare with mouths agape at her massive . . . wall of medication. I figured Tahiti would be somewhat like Mexico where you can buy prescription drugs without a prescription. "Do you have any aspirin?"

She walked away to the back room for a bottle of aspirin.

"Aspirin?" Mick said.

"Stall technique."

"Oh, right."

"What's the pharmaceutical name for yellow jackets?" I whispered.

"I don't know. How about butterflies?"

"Butterflies? What the heck are those?"

Not paying attention to my response, he continued staring at the wall of doom with wild eyes. We stood there squinting to read the labels.

"It's all in French." I said.

The woman returned with the aspirin. We tried to regain our lost composure. We were a couple of bungling morons under the scrutiny of a drill sergeant. I was desperately scanning the shelves for anything, even diet pills.

She was paying more attention to her hair than to us. With a bothersome stare, she said, "Would you gentlemen like anything else today?"

That question threw me off-guard. Time to abort. "No thank you ma'am," I said. I paid and we quickly exited without too much attention drawn to us.

We got outside and I said, "Man, I don't know what happened. I think that lady was a narc. She was using a sex tactic to lure us in."

Mick said, "I kept trying to convert street names to Latin."

"We were hoodwinked into nothing but aspirin. This aspirin is useless if we don't have anything to give us a headache."

We moped down the sidewalk with all the happy people parading past us in the streets of downtown Papeete. Just when we had given up hope, I glanced up to see this short fat fellow wearing a Panama Jack Caribbean hat, bee-lining straight for me through the crowd. He threw a shoulder right into my chest. I thought he was some drunken stranger until he peered up at me from under the retarded hat. He had eyes of a secret service agent.

"Pssst, quick follow me," he whispered.

"David Poltz?" I said. It was the engineer from the motor yacht in Nuku Hiva with the horrible Greek Brandy.

"Quick, let's go," He said, looking around as though I was blowing his cover.

Thinking fast, I said, "Is my friend ok?"

He covertly scanned Mick from head to toe. "He's fine, let's go."

We started following him into some dark back-alley. I was having questionable thoughts. "Where the heck are you taking us, to a peep show?"

"Not quite." I looked back at Mick and gave him a bit of a shrug in question. David finally stopped in a dark corner of the alley and produced an enormous joint. In a voice similar to Mike Hammer, he said, "Gotta light?"

I said, "No, I don't have a light. You've got a joint as big as a pregnant pickle and you don't have a light?" He was leering at us with beady eyes, just visible under the brim of his hat.

"I had to get out of there, fast," David said.

"I've got a light," Mick said. He brazenly unsheathed the lighter from his army fatigues. He stood there holding the torch in the air as if he was the Statue of Liberty.

David, unimpressed with his flamboyant behavior, quickly snatched the lighter from his hand and mechanically fired that mother up. Mick and I began hooting and hollering over our belated fortune.

"Shhh . . . keep it down." David said. "You're gonna get us busted."

"Sorry, sorry," we said in unison.

I said, "You have no idea what we've been going through to get our hands on anything." I introduced Mick to David. "So David, what's going on? Who are you running from and where did you escape from in such a hurry?"

After a few olympic drags off that Jamaican cigar, David passed it over to Mick and said, "It's the Canadians, and my girlfriend." Now David was sixty, looked forty and acted twenty.

I said, "Well, well, ole Dave's got himself a little honey bun."

"Yeah, yeah." David was still speaking in the Hammer voice. "She flew out from Kansas City to spend a couple of weeks on the boat while the owners are away."

"So why are you always hiding from the Canadians?"

Before I had a chance to get all the words out of my mouth, he said, "Insiders."

I giggled. "You mean like informants?"

"Yeah, yeah. I'm not really sure, but I try to keep them in the dark. They seem to know too much."

Now the Canadians were in their early twenties and seemed innocent on the surface. I thought he was having delusions, until I found out later that they did know a little more information than Dave would've liked. They were secretly conspiring against him to overthrow his reign. The human psychological interaction on a boat becomes quite intricate and sometimes mischievous due to the lack of physical and mental space.

David had a revered job as the soul engineer on a 120-foot, multi-million-dollar motor yacht. We eventually found out he didn't know Jack from Jill when it came to engineering. He was winging it with the little knowledge he had from working on his own twenty-six-foot sailboat.

We got extremely stoned and began walking back into the festival with a bent frame of mind.

"Listen guys," David said, "I've got to go find my . . . honey bun. I'll catch up with you all later." He disappeared into the crowd.

The last thing I saw was that blinding white Caribbean lid snaking through the parade, and he was gone. It was getting dark and Mick and I figured we would try to locate the girls.

The Piano Bar

We passed a few sidewalk restaurants and came upon a waterfront café called "Le Retro". By pure chance, we spotted the girls sitting at a table. They saw us and flagged us over. We weaved our way through the crowded café bumping into patrons and chairs due to our frazzled state.

We sat down and I grinned at Mick and said, "Well, ole Mick and I have had ourselves one heck of a time searching for booze, pills and just about anything that could get us sideways. Then we ran into the mystery man and he showed us the way to the back alley."

The girls looked at each other confused. They told us they wanted to take us to some place called "Mana Rock Café". They said we had to stop at the "Piano Bar" first. They both looked at each other when they said the Piano Bar.

After a few beers at the waterfront café, the girls were ready to take us to the Piano Bar. We walked through the downtown area along the harbor looking at all the sites.

When we arrived, we paid a small cover at the door and walked in with some unusual stares from the people outside the bar. The second I walked through the door a whole slew of transvestites attacked me. I turned to Tanya and said, "So this is the . . . Pianoooo Barrrr?" Three guys dressed in drag kidnapped me and hauled me onto the dance-floor. They sat me down in a chair in the middle, all by myself.

There were at least fifty people in the place, all circled around me, waiting for the show. The DJ cranked up some Egyptian belly-dancing music and three mahus* ripped my shirt off and proceeded to creep around me. They were ravenous vultures circling road-kill moving in for the thrill. They were shaking, gyrating, twisting and frolicking around. Then they pounced on me. I started peeling numerous paws off my goodies as they tried to tear my pants off.

I jumped out of the seat dodging a few mahus, grabbed my shirt on the side of the dance floor and ran out of there.

I was standing outside of the bar, putting my shirt back on, when my friends came pilling out of the front door. They were pointing and laughing at me. I turned to the girls and said, "Thanks a lot."

They couldn't stop snickering and snorting. Lisa finally said, "Ok, ok—we'll take you to a straight bar now."

They led Mick and me to this nightclub on the corner called Mana Rock Café. We walked up and stood in the back of the line to get inside.

After ten minutes, we were next in line to go inside when the bouncer said something to Mick about his shoes. We all looked at his shoes. They were a little tattered but they weren't exactly the worst pair. I think it was his nappy dreadlocks, but the bouncer couldn't keep a guy out of the bar for looking like Medusa, so he just made up something about the guys sneakers.

We didn't have time to wait. The line was pushing us through. We left Mick out there arguing with the bouncer, hoping he would sort something out soon.

Mick never got past the bouncer. Later, he told me that he met some people who talked him into going back to the Piano Bar.

---

* mahu = 1 : Tahitian word for a gay or a transvestite 2 : traditionally a family will raise one of the boys as a girl if there are no girls born in the family 3 : this is for the role of doing the household chores 4 : also known as a "Ray-Ray"

Poor guy, or maybe lucky? If you meet a "gorgeous" girl in the piano bar, don't forget to check the luggage.

I didn't remember much after that point, until I had my moment of clarity. That's when your whole world comes back into focus for a brief capsule of time. I was climbing a tall fence. I finally got over the top and landed on the other side. I remember walking onto a wide road. I looked at my watch. It read 4:01 am. I was just strutting down the middle of this road on the yellow line, feeling like Jim Morrison. I was humming my own version of the Doors, "Keep your eyes on the road, your feet upon the street", when I spotted the headlights of a truck heading for me. I decided to get to the side of the road.

As I moved to the shoulder, the truck began veering straight for me. I looked in disbelief, unsure what to do next. The truck came to a halt and two big Tahitian guys jumped out of the truck. They began yelling at me in French. I didn't understand them.

I drunkenly waved at them and said, "Yarana ("hello" in Tahitian)." I added, "Miti Roa ("very good"), maruru ("thank you")." I was throwing out the only Tahitian words I knew in no particular order. They frowned and shook their heads at the ground mumbling something. Then they both pointed at a commercial airplane parked a few hundred feet away.

"Oh shit," I said under my breath. That was no street. That was the airport runway.

They finally felt happy they had got through to me. They motioned me towards the bed of their truck. I hopped in the back and we sped off down the runway for safety.

They parked next to a small building off the runway. I jumped out of the back of the truck. The two guys grabbed me and walked me into their office. They motioned for me to sit there and wait. They probably thought I was a terrorist.

In walked the narcissistic French police, known as the Gendarme. They escorted me to their Range Rover and pushed me into the backseat. Two of them hopped in the front. The driver shifted the truck into gear and began driving without saying a word. Of the handful of times I had been thrown in a cop car, this was the first time I was actually enjoying it. The expensive leather shoes I was wearing were too small. Blisters covered my feet from a combination of dancing like a buffoon and stumbling for miles to find my boat. I will probably end up getting corns, bunions, and hammertoes from those shoes I owned for years. Damn impulse buy.

They had the A/C cranking and soft music on the radio. I was sitting in a comfortable seat with my arms stretched horizontal, grasping the full length of the back seat. I even had a smirk of contentment. All I needed was a cigar and some fine cognac. I didn't care where they took me. To jail or my boat, either way my feet would've been saved.

They were firing questions at me in an interrogating manner in French. I smiled and said, "Yarana—miti roa—maruru." For some reason, I decided to learn Tahitian instead of French. I thought it would help me out with the locals. The vernacular wasn't shining through. They were agitated and tried to speak to me in broken English.

One of them said, "What here doing? Where iz your passport?"

I said, "Boat. I'm on a boat."

"You, boat?"

"Yes, boat."

"What country?"

"America."

They continued with their barrage of cop questions, trying to stress that I was in "big trouble". I sat there comfortably reclined, answering questions in a broken manner similar to the way they were asking them. They realized they weren't getting to me. They pulled over on a side street.

The driver said, "OK, get out and walk to your boat."

That was the worst thing they could do, to make me walk in those torturous shoes. I think I would've rather gone to jail. I tried to reason with them. I said, "Do you think you could drop me off at my boat, so I don't get *lost* or into *trouble*."

"No, get out now." He said.

I sulked out of the air-conditioned Land Rover and back onto the dirty pavement. They sped off in the opposite direction.

After an hours-walk, I finally got to the dock. There was no dingy. It was gone. I sadly looked out at my boat anchored a quarter-of-a-mile away. I looked at the water and debated swimming. It was too far to swim in my condition.

I looked over at the hotel, near the dock. I spotted some lounge chairs next to the pool. I could crash there until morning. I pondered it and moved in that direction. When I got over to the lounge chairs, I saw a row of hotel kayaks. I skillfully surveyed the scene, looking for any stray security guards. I crept over to see if they had paddles.

"BINGO," I blurted aloud, cringing at my boisterous mistake. I looked around for any onlookers and whispered to myself, "No one." I covertly heisted a kayak and dragged it down to the lagoon. I hopped in and took off before anyone spotted me.

After a long squirrelly paddle, I got back to the *Bula*. I drunkenly scrambled onboard and thought to myself, if the police catch me stealing a kayak, they will definitely throw me in jail after the airport dilemma. I jumped in the donkey and fired up the outboard. I tied the kayak to the back and towed it back to the hotel.

I finally got back to the boat around five . . . thousand o'clock in the morning. I felt like I had:

1. Hiked the Himalayas in metal buckets for boots.
2. Drank Agent Orange.
3. Went six rounds in the ring with a kickboxing kangaroo.

It was a drunken triathlon.

A loud banging on the hull of my boat woke me up the next day. I sat up in a bit of fright with burning eyes and muttered to myself, "Cops." I was wondering if I had returned that kayak.

I staggered out to the cockpit, looked around and didn't see a kayak, or anyone for that matter. Was I imagining it? Then I heard the knock again. I didn't see anyone's dingy. I peered over the side and spotted Mick. He was swimming along side of the boat in his skivvies. It wasn't your normal pair of underwear either. It was a pair of speedo-type of underwear that all the men on the other side of the globe happily wear with pride.

I said, "What, are you doing?"

"Drop down the ladder, let me come aboard and I'll explain."

I placed the ladder over the side and he clamored aboard. He sat down in the cockpit with an exhausted look on his face and began telling me his story.

He stated in his South African accent, "I gave up on the Mana Rock Café and sadly went back to the Piano Bar with some straight people I met. I can't remember anything after that."

He took an arduous breath and continued, "I woke up this morning with my head spinning—looked around and saw nothing but these painted windows. I wasn't sure if I was still dreaming. I sat up and hit my head on a plastic ceiling. As I looked out of these painted windows, I realized I was on the top floor of the McDonald-land playhouse.

I began crawling to get out of there and took the slide down. When I shot out the bottom and landed on my feet, there were four or five of the morning employees setting up the outside tables. Frightened, they stopped and stared at me.

I said, "Morning." Then I walked past them slightly embarrassed with my head down and waving. I proceeded to the patio down by the waters edge, looked out to my boat anchored nearby, took my gear off, dove in and began swimming. Well, your boat is a lot closer than mine is and that's how I ended up here."

Once I finally stopped laughing, I told him my runway story. At the end of my long saga, I shook my head and said, "I've got to get out of here."

Tehani

It had been a solid week since my first night in Papeete. I hadn't remotely thought about having another drink until . . . now. I was getting the itch and it was Saturday night. What is it about this night that makes even the biggest homebodies feel as though they are missing out?

The sun sank behind the island of Moorea and I turned on the VHF radio, hailing every scabbard sailor in range. Everyone I contacted gave me excuses and some claimed fictitious ailments. I hung up the microphone and said to myself, "Bunch of old scallywags. I'm going in."

I threw together another disheveled get-up and pulled out the Dou Dou rum. I poured half of the bottle of rum into a container and filled the bottle back up with some opened fruit juice . . . 50/50. The juice had been open and sitting at room temperature for some days. Room temperature in Tahiti is oven temperature elsewhere. If anything were growing in it the Dou Dou would kill it.

I put those tortuous shoes back on and muttered, "I've got to burn these damn things." I grabbed the bottle and hopped in the donkey.

As I motored to shore, I glared at the distant lights of town with a feeling of wild excitement running through my veins. Going on a random adventure in a foreign port is what life's all about.

On land, I waited in the dark shadows at the bus stop swilling my bottle like a bum. The bus finally arrived. I jumped aboard the empty bus and headed to the back where I've always felt more comfortable. I sat down next to a couple of large speaker boxes pumping out a loud reggae beat. The black boxes stood about four feet with twin twelve-inch woofers in each. The night driver seemed a lot different from the day drivers I had seen.

I sat back there alone enjoying the thumping bass as I took long swigs from my bottle. I knew I only had half an hour to tank it. I looked out the window at the yellow streetlights passing by. Through the rear view mirror, the driver glanced back at me with an *irie* look on his face. The oncoming lights careened across his profile and created a merry-go-round of reflections on the ceiling inside the bus. The rum began warming my body and I grinned with the false happiness that it created. Mischief was churning in my head.

The loud bus bounced onward to the reggae beat like a basketball down the street. Nearing the center of town, I worked faster to kill the bottle. We entered the main street along the waterfront. All the people were walking on the boardwalk going home or going out. My stop was nearing. I drained the last bit of the rum down and tucked the empty bottle under the seat.

"Ici, s'il vous plait," (Here, please) I yelled to the driver over the music. He stopped for me. I slowly stood up and moved toward the door. "Merci," I said. He just nodded with a big grin and drove on as I stepped off the bus.

I looked at the bright yellow and white sign . . . Mana Rock Café. It brought back memories of the previous weekend. I grinned as I walked up to the entrance. There was a small line and I contemplated finding a girl outside to avoid paying the cover charge. I decided to play it cool instead and pay.

After waiting in line for ten minutes I paid the cover and stepped through the front door into the crowded club. My natural instinct was to go straight to the bar but I didn't need any more after half a bottle of booze. But I couldn't stand around without anything in my hand looking dumb. We always need something occupying our little claw in a social scene. I didn't smoke so I needed a drink to fill it.

I found the bar and studied the bottles on the wall. Looking for Crown Royal, I only spotted Wild Turkey. Close enough.

"Wild Turkey and 7up," I said, unable to say it in French. I hoped the bartender knew what I meant.

"No 7up. Sprite?" he asked in English with a thick accent.

"Oui," I replied. I paid and moved towards the dance floor.

Packed again with beautiful girls, I looked around the dimly lit dance floor. The DJ played some unusual French hip-hop. I was feeling good and the night was revolving like a new record. "Round two," I blurted aloud to myself.

I was sipping my cocktail surveying the scene when I spotted her smile from across the dance floor. It was dark and at first glance the only thing I could see were these bright teeth glowing in the dim light as she was laughing and dancing with her friends. Her long dark hair flowed around her like a silky dress. I could see her reflection in all the cheesy mirrors attached to the walls as she twirled in the refracting light of a miniature disco ball. Bent colors of light caressed her face. I stood there caught in a clammy trance of desire. Her laughter never seemed to end. The booze was catching up to me and everything was in slow motion. I felt as though I was a weird stranger watching in delight from the back seat of a movie theater.

I began to survey her entire body in a perverse manner. I couldn't find a single flaw. She was perfect and my heart began to pound in nervousness. She was wearing a tight maroon top that showed the shape of her small breasts. They pointed up to the sky like Hershey's kisses. The dark skin on her bare midriff shimmered with a moist glow. She wore a medium-length, light-colored shirt that fell down to her knees. Her legs were slightly thicker than the rest of her body, but not too thick, with the creamy radiance of healthy skin. She wore short black heels with straps that artistically crossed exposing her tan feet.

Everyone seemed to know her. They were dancing nearby smiling with her. She was a sunlit blossom beaming in a grey forest. It seemed as though people were fighting to get near her to feel her energy and capture some of her beauty.

I knew if I stood there too long I would never seize the opportunity. I had to go up to her and say the first thing that came out of my mouth, without thinking, which could be good or bad. I had to avoid one-liners or anything contrived, but I didn't want to sit there dwelling on the right thing to say while some other guy swept her away.

I haphazardly placed my unfinished cocktail on a random table as I walked on with determination to meet this ethereal beauty. I snaked through the crowd on the steamy dance floor and came upon her circle of friends.

I looked directly into her almond-colored eyes and pulled out a phrase that I had learned in a French dictionary, "Est-ce que vous aimeriez aller danser?" (Would you like to dance?) I put on my best French accent. I wasn't sure if I was even saying the right thing. I could have been telling her "I would like to massage your animal's buttocks.'

She turned—surveyed me in the dark and replied, "Avec plaisir." (With pleasure)

I guessed it worked. Her friends looked at me with disappointed stares. They didn't want me to steal her away from them. I put my hand out for hers and she gently placed her soft hand in my calloused hand. We moved away to a less crowded space on the dance floor.

"Comment vous appelez-vous?" (What is your name?) I asked.

She grinned with a look as if I didn't have a clue how to speak her language, but she appeased me because I was trying. "Je m'appelle Tehani. Et vous?" (My name is Tehani, and yours.)

That was a foreign name to me and I wanted to make sure I got it right, so I asked, "Pouvez-vous repeater ca?" (Could you repeat that?)

"Te . . . hani," she repeated.

"Tehani, oui," I affirmed. "Je m'appelle Bryan." (My name is Bryan.)

She then delivered too many words at once and I stood there like a jackass. She said, "Do you prefer we speak English?"

She saw through my hogwash and knew I was just another American who couldn't speak a second language. I was trying to play it off as if I was different. "Yea, I'm sure your English is a lot better than my French."

"No problem. I want to practice my English."

"Thank god, because I decided to learn Tahitian instead of French when I sailed into the islands. I've found out that the only people who still speak Tahitian are the old folks. It might've come in handy if I wanted to hit on your grandmother."

"Oh god, you would not want to do that. She might take you up on your offer." She laughed—looking away, probably with funny thoughts of me hitting on her grandmother. "So, where did you sail in from?"

"Well, I started in California, made it down the coast to Mexico and sailed across the Pacific to here."

"Wow, that was a long journey."

"It took a few months." She stood there entranced in a state of mental adventure. I felt like a mysterious pirate who sailed into her enchanted isle greeted with open arms.

She spoke good English with a velvety accent. I began to feel more comfortable around her as we danced staring into each other's eyes. Occasionally one of us would look away as if it was too much to gaze that deeply into the eyes of a stranger.

We got closer and I could smell her breath. It was warm and sensuous with a hint of booze. I quivered inside with yearning thoughts of kissing her voluptuous lips.

After a couple of songs, I put both arms around her and pulled her body into mine. She gave no resistance and fell into my arms. Engulfed in the immediate intimacy, we felt each other's heartbeat. She moved with the smooth gracefulness of a panther. I could feel my top lip tingling with adrenaline as we slowly revolved in a circular motion of rhythm. The internal drug took over my entire being.

I glanced at her profile out of the corner of my eye. She had striking features with high cheekbones that seemed European and eyes that seemed Asian. She appeared mostly Tahitian, but the combination gave her an international exotic appearance.

I whispered in her ear, "So Tehani, are you from this island?"

"Yes, I'm from Tahiti, though I went to school in France. I live here now and work on the inter-island cruise ship."

"What do you do on the cruise ship?"

"I'm a dancer." She smiled after that comment.

"What type of dancer?" I grinned at her, keeping my inquisition diplomatic.

She brushed her hair away from her face in the manner of a femme fatale. "I dance the indigenous Tahitian dance."

I thought to myself . . . thank god she wasn't a dirty pole-swinger at some seedy strip joint. "I would love to see you dance."

"You are," she jokingly replied.

I was becoming more intrigued. Not only was she good at English, she was even sarcastic. We continued dancing close to each other and I slipped my right leg between her thighs pulling her into my body. I began to get aroused and she sighed in submittal, pressing her habit into mine. It was getting a little scandalous for the public eye so we mutually signaled through body language to slow down.

"Puis-je vous offrir quelque chose a boire?"(Can I get you a drink?) I asked with questionable pronunciation.

"Oui, merci." She slid out of my arms and we squeezed through the sticky dance floor towards the bar. I was following her as she led me through, holding my hand. She glided gracefully through the club knowing the way as I stumbled over various hidden steps and random obstacles. I thought about the whereabouts of my last cocktail for a split second and figured it was probably gone by now. Cocktails were ten bucks a pop and that was the only reason why I entertained the thought. I wasn't in Mexico any more.

We found a spot at the bar and she knew the female bartender, naturally. She introduced me to her friend and said to me, "What would you like? It is my treat."

I was now in heaven, she was taking care of me. I whispered to Tehani, "Do they have any Crown Royal?"

She turned to her friend and rapidly spoke to her in French. Her friend looked at the assortment of bottles on the wall—turned to me and said in broken English, "No, zee only whiskey we have is zee Wild Turkey."

"That's fine," I blurted. "I'd like that with 7up, excuse me, Sprite on the rocks, s'il vous plait."

The bartender nodded—looked at Tehani and politely said, "Qu' est-ce que tu prends?"

Tehani looked into the air pressing her finger on her lips thinking for a few seconds, and then rambled off more than I could catch. Her friend went to work on our concoctions. Mine was rather simple and Tehani's took some more time and effort. The bartender neatly placed them before us after a few minutes.

Tehani happily paid and we moved to a small circular table in the middle of the club. I helped her with her chair.

"Merci," she said.

"Of course," I replied not knowing how to say that in French.

Nearly everyone that walked by said hello to Tehani. Some stopped to give her a kiss on both cheeks as is custom in Tahiti. She presented a genuine booming smile to everyone, which came straight from her heart. She lit up the room with her charisma. They all politely nodded at me or said a quaint, "Bonsoir." I nodded and responded back. She knew everyone. I didn't take her for a barfly; I just figured it was a small island.

We both finished our cocktails and I bought the second round. We sat and chatted for a long time at the table. Her world was very different from mine living on a small island in the South Pacific.

After what seemed like an hour getting to know each other, she motioned for the dance floor with an upward nod of her head. She was a professional after all. Without saying any words I put both hands out for her to lead the way. She took my hand again and I sank into a warm feeling of bliss as I followed her. I watched her sexy skirt bounce off the backs of her legs dreaming of the heavenly mystery underneath.

We entered the dance floor and found a more secluded spot in a dark corner, both knowing what could transpire. She spun around towards me moving her shapely body in an undulating fashion. The music was new to me. The DJ was switching from deep house to reggae-rap. Every now and then, he would throw in some French pop music. Everyone seemed to love the mix as I was trying to gain a bearing on his unusual eclecticism.

After dancing to the first two songs, the DJ threw on the Fugee's version of "Killing Me Softly". Tehani planted her sweaty body into mine. We slowed down to small steps back and forth with our arms draped around each other. I looked into her eyes and it seemed like the whole world was glaring at us including the mahus, though we didn't care. I moved my lips towards hers and she closed her eyes moving hers towards mine. Our lips pressed together and I could taste the sweat on her mouth. It was tender enough to know it wasn't just a drunk bar kiss. There was real passion.

She blushed and I looked over her shoulder pondering the possibilities. The crowded bar didn't seem to be so entertaining any more. It was getting too hot in there with only two fans blowing. I wanted to be somewhere else with her. The DJ launched into Whitney Houston's "I Will Always Love You". Everyone began singing along in horrible English. The flamboyant mahus in the bar were standing tall and belting it out as though it was their theme song.

"What do you say we go for a walk down to the waterfront?" I asked.

She looked up at me and nodded in approval. "Let me get my purse from behind the bar."

I thought to myself . . . my god I'm actually leaving the bar with the hottest woman here. She got her purse from the bartender and we exited. She only said goodbye to a few people on our way out the back door.

Once we reached the sidewalk out front, the smell and feeling of cool air coming off the ocean calmed our senses. We both stood there for a few seconds relaxing on the quiet boulevard. It was late and I turned to her and asked, "Hey, why don't we cruise out to my boat and sit on the top deck under the stars?"

She smiled and gave me a quick kiss. "Where's your boat?"

"You know Marina Taina?"

"Of course." She looked at me as if I was silly for asking her.

"Ok, well it's anchored off of the harbor there. Wanna go?"

"How did you get here?"

"The bus."

"Ok, I've got my car, I can take you there and I'll decide whether it's *safe* to come out to your boat once we get there."

She was either being safe or playing hard to get. One or the other, but I liked her little game. Who says you can't meet a nice girl in a bar?

We found her car on a side street. Any Midwest American would have balked at this tiny French car. We squeezed into the seats of her car slightly exhausted from the night. I was buzzing with the sense of misbehavior creating a bonfire in my brain. I was in the car with a beautiful woman in a foreign paradise with wild thoughts.

She pulled out a pack of Juicy Fruit and offered one to me. I slid one out of the pack and popped it in my mouth. She did the same. Maybe there were cops to bargain with and she was trying to mask the alcohol on her breath. Thank god she was driving because if the cops pulled *me* over it would probably be the same ones from the airport that found me on the runway.

She put it in gear and backed out of the parking spot. She sped out of the side street and I thought her speed was a bit excessive, especially if she was over the limit in cocktails.

"Are you ok to drive?" I cautiously asked.

"Do not worry, I am driver good."

Those are the last words you hear from a crash test dummy before you explode into a brick wall. My eyelids stretched as I stared out the window. I laughed to myself like a suicidal clown. I was hoping that it was simply a glitch in her English. Maybe she was just getting tired.

She sped onto the new highway and the noise from the automobile changed to a soft hum as it hovered onto the fresh asphalt. The heavy mist in the air created circular rainbows around the streetlights on the windshield as we passed them. Wet palm trees towered above the road glistening from the headlights of the car. There were only a few cars left on the highway at that hour. We glanced at each other from time to time and I put my hand on her exposed thigh. We raced onward towards the marina listening to a new Coldplay CD she told me she had bought on a recent trip to Paris.

After a ten-minute ride, that took me hours to walk the previous weekend, we pulled into the parking lot of the marina safe. She parked and turned off the car.

"I barely know you and it is wet," she said with a smirk.

I had amusing thoughts at that comment and replied, "I know, I know." Without a great comeback, I just leaned in and began kissing her. She put her hands around my head and arched her back to pull me into her sanctuary. I dove into her world crawling over the emergency brake. I think they made that car for monkeys because it wasn't big enough for one human per seat, much less two. She stopped me and said, "Ok, how on earth do we get to your boat?"

"I've got a small boat that brings us to the big boat." I used kindergarten terminology in case she didn't know what a dingy was.

"It seems safe enough; it is *you* I am worried about." She chuckled with a hint of sarcasm and a touch of seriousness.

We quickly got out of the car and began walking to the docks holding hands. I showed her the dingy tied to a small floating dock. She jumped in as if she was a little girl on an amusement ride. The perpetual grin on her face reassured me that she wasn't nervous in the least.

I fired up the outboard and we began motoring out to the anchorage. She looked out into the darkness as we pulled out of the marina and said, "Oh god, where are you taking me?" She squeezed my hand tight.

"Don't worry," I said. "It's not far."

We motored onward with patches of sky revealing bright stars that reflected off the calm surface of the lagoon. The moon was setting in the west behind a broken cloudbank. Tehani stared into the sky reveling in the adventure. She was letting go of her fears and trusting me, a total stranger.

We reached the *Bula* and I motored up alongside. I caught the side and helped her onboard. As she was climbing up the ladder her ass was sticking out and I was completely underneath her skirt. I thought about it for a split second but politely refrained.

I tied up the donkey and jumped aboard. I had somehow managed to capture the heart of this delectable woman and now she was standing onboard my boat. I was merely elated that she had enough trust in me to partake in a journey into the darkness. That or she was just plain horny.

I opened the hatch and showed her down the companionway into the cabin. I lit the paraffin lantern hanging from the ceiling, creating a soft glow.

"Wow," she exclaimed. "It's like a little house in here. It sure doesn't look that big from the outside." She continued to look around at all the interesting things. "Do you have a bathroom and a shower?"

"Sure, bathroom, shower, kitchen, oven. It's got pretty much everything but a garage."

She sat down on the couch and had a look as if she wanted me to join her.

"Care for anything to drink?" I asked.

"Just water, s'il vous plait."

Her accent was so sexy it made me melt every time she spoke in French. "I don't have anything cold. Is warm water alright?"

"Anything is fine, sexy."

I made two cups, handed one to her and chugged mine. I was hovering over the couch as she drank half of hers. She gently placed the cup on the table next to the couch and then grabbed my hand pulling me onto the couch. We began violently making out now that no eyes were upon us. Her hands freely moved about my body. She seemed to be initiating the action and I wasn't about to stop her. She licked my neck and I began looking over her shoulder trying to unfasten her bra. I had trouble at first but I finally managed to get the thing undone. Do the French have different clasps? I then stared at her perky little boobs. I began sucking on her nipples and she moaned deeply as if they hadn't been touched in ages.

She squeezed my bulge on the outside of my pants and I moved closer hoping she would put her hand down my pants. After a few seconds, her hand released and slid down inside grabbing a hold of my hard-on. Her hand was so soft and warm it got me even more aroused. I then put my hand on her exposed knee and slowly slid it up her warm thigh to the very top. She took a deep breath and I began rubbing her habit with two fingers on the top of her underwear. She shuttered and spread her legs for me to go ahead. I triumphantly eased my hand down inside her panties and rubbed her divinity. It was dripping wet and she gave an exalted sigh.

That was enough for me, I couldn't take it any more and began tearing her clothes off, careful not to rip anything, but going in like a kid at Christmas. She began undoing my pants. After throwing clothes about, we were both completely naked. I grabbed her hand and led her forward to the V-birth. She happily skipped forward and hopped into bed.

I lit a candle and placed it on a shelf. It flickered in a yellow brilliance on the ceiling of the cabin. I slowly crawled into bed and lay on top of her warm body. We were rolling around making out and I thought to myself . . . don't be an idiot, no matter how much you hate them you've got to wear a frog strangler. I hadn't needed one in months. I hope I have one, and if so, where the hell did I stash them?

"I've got to find a condom," I said rolling off her and searching through drawers and cabinets. "Found em," I said after a couple of long minutes. I threw the pile next to the bed wondering how many we might end up using.

I felt as though she was ready. I tried to slip on a condom gracefully but I had the thing backwards in the dim light. I flipped it around and tried the other way and that didn't seem to work either. Maybe it was so old it had seized together. At that point, I would've used plastic wrap if I had to. I finally managed to roll it on properly. I was shaky from the nervous pre-game build-up.

I slowly slid in a little bit at a time into her fertile wetness and her whole body shook. She looked deep into my eyes with her mouth open, gasping for air. I was on the verge of losing my Olympic-tadpole-swim-team but was trying to control the grenade with the pin pulled.

I managed to maintain and together we created a beautiful rhythm engulfed in felicity. The boat rocked to the slight ocean swell emitting a few creaking sounds. The smell of pheromones rose into the air intertwining with each other, forming a spiral staircase to the heavens.

Time seemed to erase itself though the intensity lasted for ages. I was rather proud of myself for lasting so long after my perennial celibacy. The sensitivity was remarkable even with the condom. I could've used a rubber glove and it wouldn't have mattered.

She seemed to be getting close to that special place and that just heightened my sense of nearness. I could feel she was on the verge and I wasn't sure if she was holding out for me. I gave her the reassuring gesture that I was right on her tail. We both hit the point of no return and she screamed in ecstasy. It lasted longer than usual as my body released everything it had. She squirmed and kicked, kissing my neck and tasting the sweetness there.

I finally slid off her hot body and stared at the ceiling in bliss as the candle flickered from the swirling breath in the air. I felt as though my entire core released as I lay there deflated.

The eastern sky was becoming light with the sun about to rise. The boat slowly bobbed and our wet skin slid against each other.

"Wow," she said entranced on the cabin top with her eyes wide open.

"Yeah," I replied, nodding my head.

She leaned over and gave me a lasting kiss, then flopped back onto her pillow exhausted. I pulled the sheets over us and blew out the candle.

The pre-dawn light was gaining intensity and I pulled the curtains shut. I crawled back into bed and Tehani was already breathing heavy as if she was on the verge of sleep. I laid my head on the damp pillow and pulled the sheets over me with a grin on my face.

"Bon nuit," she said, surprising me that she was still conscious.

"What does that mean?" I asked.

"Good night, silly."

"Oh, of course. Bon nuit."

Dou Dou Rhum

Tehani and I saw each other a few times after that night but we were both on two different paths. She was about to start a career as a flight stewardess and I was sailing across the Pacific. Part of me wanted to give it all up and settle down in Tahiti with Tehani. The other part was pulling me into the unknown across the Pacific.

Sadly enough we decided it was best we go our separate ways. I thought I could return someday to the island paradise and find Tehani after I had got the wanderlust out of my system, if that was ever possible.

It was reaching the end of October and I was ready to sail north to Hawaii. I needed a few days to provision the boat and prepare myself for the long journey. Secretly, I wanted to take-on the challenge for years, but not this soon. I continued reassuring myself of the legend Thor Heyerdahl, from the book "Kon-Tiki", who sailed across the Pacific on a raft. I had a modernized vessel, comparatively, with semi-state of the art equipment and 8,000 miles of offshore experience. I was confident enough to face the challenge.

I planned to sail up to Raiatea and then to Bora Bora. From there I would wait for a good weather window, and sail north to Hawaii. I planned to stop mid-way at Christmas Island to break up the 3,000-mile trip. There were a few other boats sailing to Hawaii around the same time and we began monitoring the weather. It was the end of October and the only weather window at this time of year, between Tahiti and Hawaii, was November. November marked the end of the hurricane season in the North Pacific, and December marked the beginning of cyclone season in the South Pacific. Mother Nature didn't leave much of a gap for sailors.

The rains finally cleared and my excitement rose. I had finished my repairs and provisions. The sun was blazing and it was a good day to set sail. I pulled the anchor and looked over to see two whales swimming 50-feet from the *Bula*. They came through the deep passage, circling next to the anchored boats. I headed through the pass and put out the fishing lines.

Two hours out, something enormous hit the fishing line and took off with the drag buzzing. I dropped the headsail—stopped the boat and grabbed the rod. I reeled for ten minutes when the line snapped and I lost yet another lure that set me back a blasted 15 hogs*.

I was near Raiatea, so I just reeled in the line and sadly put away the rod. I should have spent the money on fish sticks.

After entering the pass, I anchored next to a familiar sailboat named *Mondo*. They had passed me like a pleasure circus halfway between Mexico and the Marquises. I remembered Figman and I were desperately trying to change the headsail due to the escalated winds. We looked up to see this boat flying by us with people on the deck waving and snapping photos of us. It was blowing 30 knots and they were flying their damn spinnaker.

Hove to—head into the wind—the *Bula* was crashing into waves as we were scrambling to get a smaller sail on the head-stay. I peered over my shoulder for a split second and they were smoothly sailing downwind, having a posh cocktail party on deck.

Here they were to finally meet the myth and reminisce about that experience we had in the middle of the Pacific. They invited me over for dinner on their boat and we chatted about our sailing glories and tribulations.

---

* hogs = big fat stinking dollar bills, dead presidents, pesos, dinero, moola, cash

I spent a couple of days in Raiatea with them and then set sail for Bora Bora. This island definitely deserved its fame. Bora Bora was the epitome of a perfect South Pacific island.

The island is a small mountain that juts out of the ocean surrounded by a barrier reef. Inside the reef is an amazing lagoon with beautiful turquoise water.

I sailed around to the southeastern corner of the island weaving through the colorful reefs and brilliant white sand-flats. It was so shallow I slowed down for safety. I put the boat on autopilot, grabbed a mask and carefully climbed down the ladder into the water. I was hanging on to a line underwater to judge my clearance. Dragging under the surface, I watched the keel of the boat barely skimming over the bottom of the razor-sharp fire corral.

I found a great spot to anchor in ten feet of water with a white sand bottom. I grabbed my snorkel gear and swam over to the nearby reef. The intricate reef changed color and shape about every 50 feet. The ecosphere contained fire coral, soft coral, sea fans, brain coral, and odd types of crustacean life. There were hundreds of different fish and small sharks weaving through small holes and caves. The warmth of the water caressed my body as though I was wrapped in silk.

I spent over two hours in the underworld until my back began burning from the sun. I returned to the boat for some lunch.

After lunch, I began gearing up for the trip, doing all the necessary maintenance and routine checks. The weather window was looking favorable and I was ready to tie on the challenge and cast off for Hawaii. *Boread* was sailing out at the same time, along with two other boats.

The next morning, I motored around to the gas dock and filled up with diesel. I used the water hose to fill the 100-gallon water tank. I stepped back and took a good look at the boat studying the mast and rigging for one last check. She looked solid and I was ready. I started up the engine and untied the dock lines. I raised the sails and motor-sailed through the pass, trolling the fishing lines.

I was a bit nervous about the trip and depressed to have left Tehani. I felt as though I had made a big mistake by leaving her. I tried to relax in the cockpit under the mid-morning sun. Bora Bora slowly sank into the blue sea, disappearing into the *Bula*'s wake. 360 degrees of water surrounded me. I enjoy the feeling, as long as the seas aren't out to lynch me. I set the windvane to steer a course of 3-degrees true north.

The first night gracefully fell upon me and the weather was stable. I hailed *Boread*, who had sailed out an hour after me.

"*Boread, Boread*, this is *Bula*," I said.

"This is *Boread*, let's switch to six-nine," Darren said.

"Six-nine" We switched channels.

"How's everything up there *Bula*?"

"Everything's going smooth. How about you?"

"Everything's good back here. We just had a big bite on the lure, but it snapped the line. It was enormous."

"I've been losing more lures than I've been catching fish, lately. All I want is something small to eat."

"Yeah, us too."

"Anyway, I was going to take a nap and since I don't have a radar to alarm me of any ships in the area, I was wondering if you could yell loudly on the VHF if you spot anything. Hopefully you'll wake me up in case I'm in danger."

"Sure, no problem. Do the same for us if you see anything when you're awake."

"Roger that, good buddy. Alright, over and out. *Bula* back to one-six"

"*Boread*, back to one-six."

I didn't have a radar onboard, which makes it difficult to sleep as a single-hander. I decided to knock back a few shots of Dou Dou Rhum. It was the cheapest rum sold in Tahiti and I had stockpiled multiple bottles. It was dark brown and even looked like doo doo. It came in handy for various reasons. One, it was a kind way of killing fish. Two, for medicinal purposes in case I had an accident. And three, a sleeping aid in rough seas. Rum was my RADAR: <u>R</u>ight <u>A</u>bout <u>D</u>ark <u>A</u>dd <u>R</u>um.

I slept for a couple of hours that night and watched the sunrise. The weather was getting cloudy. I'd never been seasick before but I wasn't feeling so good. It could've just been nervousness about the clueless variables I might encounter out there.

The day got rougher with big squalls pounding me every hour. The squalls would hit with 35 to 40 knots of wind—back off, and then blow hard for about 15 minutes with rain and circling winds. The wind would die for about five minutes after a cumulonimbus cloud passed. Then the regular trades of 25 knots would fill back in.

This went on for a couple of days, making it tough without a crewmember. I couldn't sleep for fear that another squall might hammer the boat with too much sail up. I got sick and tired of changing the size of the sails, so I just left them reefed. I didn't care that my speed had dropped. I was about to drop.

I managed to get a few naps. After I was feeling a little better, I decided to do some routine boat checks. The first thing I checked was the bilge for any leaks. As I peered into the bilge, I saw enough water streaming into the boat from the aft compartment to frighten a beaver. I was already two days out and didn't want to turn back, but I debated it.

I used to care about things when I was younger, but I've changed. The answer to staying happy in life is; don't give a damn about anything. I hadn't been one to worry about things for a long time, until now.

The water was coming through the rudderpost packing, which I repaired in Tahiti. The packing I had used obviously didn't hold. The bilge was filling-up every 30 minutes, though the bilge pump was emptying the incoming seawater.

I got on the VHF and tried to hail any of the other boats that might be in range. One sailboat received my call and responded back. I informed them of my hazardous leak. They were concerned and told me they would pass-on the message to contacts in Hawaii via SSB (single-side-band radio). Two sailors in Hawaii were sending us weather reports over the SSB. They were staying in contact with those sailing north from the South Pacific. Sailors checked into a daily net. The handful of boats sailing north gave progress reports and any emergencies on the high seas.

It was comforting to know there were people out there who would help if they could. They were not going to be in VHF range for long. VHF range is 30 to 40 miles at best. No one is sailing down a highway in the ocean, so everyone spreads out due to weather and boat speed. I had a SSB receiver that could only receive and not transmit. The SSB transmitter was another one of the expensive items that I couldn't afford. I suspiciously thought the lack of it would accelerate my mortality if I got into serious trouble. I remained calm and continued north.

The Bermuda Triangle

After the fourth day out of Bora Bora, the weather cleared up a bit. The squalls had decreased and I was feeling more confident in the overall journey. The slight seasickness had subsided. I wondered how people managed with that horrible feeling. I had a very slight case, which was probably more nervousness than motion sickness. It finally caught up with me after giving Figman such a hard time about his sad condition. For the first time, I could relate with Figman and I was feeling bad for the guy. Getting seasick in stormy seas on a boat five-hundred miles out is similar to being strapped to the side of a rocket with a fear of heights.

That day I sailed past the tiny inhabited island of Vostok. It was just a speck of land in the middle of the ocean. One nasty cyclone could flush it to the bottom of the sea, forever. What sort of inbred aliens populated that place? I wondered what the locals did for entertainment. Bingo? Bridge? Or did they just sit around— eat rubber chickens and fart balloons? Their only entertainment was probably coconut football. You wouldn't want to get hit in the head by a 50-yard Hail Mary.

The mysterious palmed island disappeared after a few hours, leaving me in water world. The temperatures were rising the closer I got to the equator and the winds were slacking off. I hoped I didn't have to sit in the doldrums for days.

I began the daily routine of plotting my course on the chart and checking my progress. I turned on the GPS. It wasn't picking up a position. After some time, the unit began beeping alarms and malfunctioning.

I shouted, "GREAT. JUST FUCKING GREAT."

My main GPS unit was broke and I only had a small backup GPS. Frantically, I pushed every button on the main unit as a last resort. I finally gave up.

I was in an extremely remote part of the Pacific. Maybe there weren't enough satellites to lock-in a good position. My tiny hand-held GPS wouldn't pick up any satellites inside the cabin of the boat. I had to take the unit out into the cockpit to get an unobstructed reception.

I had a hold of that unit as if it was my last link to survival. If it went overboard, I might as well have gone with it, because I'd never find the tiny Christmas Island in the middle of nowhere. I could only imagine navigating by dead reckoning to a speck in the Pacific. I figured if I missed it, I could always turn and head directly west and run into China sooner or *probably* later.

The little unit was beginning to pick up satellites. I was relieved when it locked into a coordinate. I plotted my position on the chart. I had roughly a week left until I reached Christmas Island.

I lost all VHF contact with any other boats. I was completely on my own with nothing left but my decent knowledge of the sea and survival. I grew up around boats and the water and felt comfortable with that end, but what I lacked was knowledge of major mechanical or electrical failures. I figured they never had those things in the days of Columbus. I could get by without it, but it sure is nice.

I sat and stared out across the rough seas. Profound thoughts come to all of us at random times throughout our lives; while sitting in a coffee shop, waiting in traffic, or during a boring school lecture when our brains are redirected to some inspiring realization. However, the deepest thoughts come to us when we are isolated from the rest of the world.

I was lounging around on the "dungbie" (the rear end of a ship) in and out of consciousness, when something enormous hit the fishing line. The drag started buzzing so wildly that the reel began to smoke. I tightened down the drag, but it didn't help. The line was nearly at the end of the spool of 1000 feet. I immediately grabbed the helm to pull the boat into the wind. I dropped the headsail and tightened the mainsheet.

Once I stopped the boat, I shot back to grab the rod and started reeling. It was the biggest fish I'd ever kept on this long without snapping the 80lb-test line. I reeled for five minutes and it took off again with the drag screaming.

Exhausted, after about 15 minutes of cranking, I saw a huge explosion on the horizon. I looked up to see this blue marlin shoot out of the water and tail-walk across the surface. I'd been fishing for marlin for so long with no luck and here I was all by myself with no one to vouch for the biggest fish story yet.

I reeled for another 10 minutes and decided I had to document it with some live footage, so my story wasn't just a fish story. I tightened up the drag and ran to get the video camera. I rebounded out of the cabin and back to the reel. With the video in one hand, I reeled with the other. Just as I turned on the camera, the marlin came dancing out of the water. I yelled to the wind, "LOSEN YOUR SKIRT YOU PANSY MOTHER. LET'S SEE WHAT YOU GOT?"

After half-an-hour, I was winning the battle and the beautiful marlin was only 30 feet from the back of the boat. I continued to video with one hand, reeling with the other.

The marlin was almost alongside the boat. Its skin was changing colors from blue to purple and showing almost the whole color spectrum while swimming on its side looking me straight in the eye. If you have ever been close to taking an animal's life and it stares you in the eye with the look of mercy—forget it. You'll become a vegetarian and live on wheatgrass and sprouts for the rest of your days.

I knew I couldn't keep that bull anyway. It was probably 200 pounds, and all I had was a freezer big enough for a few TV dinners. It was not a large marlin by any means, but it was the biggest thing I'd ever caught. I just wanted my lure back and to set it free.

I got it alongside the boat and fetched some needle-nose

pliers to get the lure out of its mouth. I reached down in the water, grabbed its bill and pulled its head above the surface enough to pry out the lure. I was talking to the marlin, telling it how sorry I was. I gently pried the hook out of the side of its mouth and eased its head back in the water.

"There you go buddy," I said. "Be free."

It looked up at me confused still lying on its side. Then it turned and slowly swam off.

For lunch, I ate a cheap can of tuna fish. I felt suckered by the "sympathy stare". I was tired of catching giant fish. I just wanted one I could eat. I switched all my tackle to smaller lures.

The next day, I reeled in a six-foot oceanic white-tip shark. I had switched to small lures, but continued pulling in these things bigger than me. I was surprised the shark didn't chew right through the wire leader with its sharp teeth.

I got the shark alongside the boat, pulled its head out of the water with the fishing line and saw these long pectoral fins that resembled arms of a human. It could wrap those arms around me and give me a big smooch on the cheek. Maybe show me the Waltz or the Tango.

I just wanted my lure back. I pulled its head further out of the water with one hand on the fishing line, and reached down with the needle nose pliers in the other hand. It's jaw dropped open with double rows of razor teeth. There I was with a miniature pair of needle-nose pliers in my hand about to mingle with the jaws of a shark.

Just when I was sizing up my pliers and its mouth, it started shaking wildly back-and-forth and out popped the lure. The shark dropped back into the water, still thrashing about, and took off. That was easy. I sent the line back out and laid down on the lazarrete for a bit of a snooze in the shade of the bimini.

I woke up to a giant splash—bolted upright to see a tail fin kick out of the surface and dive back into the deep. I was running a lure ten feet behind the boat. Something massive took it, headed out with the drag winding out and the reel getting hot. It must've been another marlin. This time the spool was smoking even more than the last time and I thought I was about to get "spooled". (When a huge fish runs all your line out to the end and snaps it off the reel.)

As the fish had nearly run all the line out, it jumped out of the water and did a tail-walk across the surface. It was a huge Blue Marlin. It kicked completely out of the water, shook its head and the lure in its mouth went flying off. I said, "Thank god." I was happy the fish got off and I didn't lose another good lure.

As I reeled in the line, I found out the lure was gone. It must have snapped the line when it shot out of the water. My friends had talked me into spending five hundred bucks on lures in San Diego and my stock was dwindling down to nothing. They were eating everything.

I sat down in the cockpit to contemplate my next move when a thought came to me. Three days ago, I lost all contact with other boats, my GPS mysteriously lost coverage, and I started catching monstrous fish. I was fabricating illusions that I must've been in some sort of Bermuda Triangle of the Pacific. The phenomenon produced reports of navigational failures and the disappearance of ships and planes.

I looked around the horizon. Was I still heading north? I looked up at the sun. It was dead overhead. That didn't help. I looked at my compass. It read north. I just stopped and began laughing at myself. I'd been on the open ocean for too many days.

I woke up the next day after a 10-hour sleep. I had given up all efforts of night watches and adopted the Hindu belief that it doesn't matter what you do in life, when it's your time to go, that's it. I learned this from a fellow traveler while riding in the back of a bus in India. We nearly went off a cliff due to the frivolous driver's skills. It's your basic daredevil mentality. It helps to detach oneself from the present situation.

I was sleeping eight to ten hours a night, waking up feeling great. I put my faith in the spirits of the sea and let the details figure themselves out.

I went up top-deck to a beautiful morning with a blazing

hot sun at seven am. I did the usual routine of clearing the deck of flying fish and squid that had landed on the boat during the night. I couldn't understand how these squid ended up on deck. Did they wash onboard by waves? There had been no breaking waves in the past couple of days. Later, I learned that they actually propel themselves out of the water into the air to flee from predators. Flying squid? Yes.

I decided to check the leak in the bilge. It was getting worse. I had a few more days until I reached Christmas Island. I hoped nothing catastrophic would happen.

The sky was beginning to cloud over and the wind and seas increased that afternoon. It bothered me when nice weather changed to crap. It's not so bad once I'm used to the rough seas. I had finally gotten some descent weather to enjoy and the romance got rained out.

For the next three days, I battled my way through squalls and big seas. It's not fair when I couldn't fight back. Nature would have to be a mother, and I can't punch a lady.

I became so belligerent at one point; I had to put on some hard rocking Black Sabbath. I blasted it on full volume to calm my nerves. I figured I'd fight the evil spirits of the sea with someone scarier . . . Ozzy. It coincidentally worked. They backed off.

At last, I came in VHF contact with another sailboat as we were nearing Christmas Island. They were also having an interesting time getting beat up at sea.

That morning I spotted the island. I couldn't wait to pull into a calm anchorage and sleep for a solid year. As I rounded the corner of the island, the seas dropped and the water was clear enough to see 200 feet to the bottom.

"LAND HO."

Kirabati

There is nothing more enthralling than living through a death-defying passage and safely pulling into a mysterious paradise. I'm normally salivating for the taste of adventure with a myriad of convoluted thoughts break-dancing through my head. Will the locals invite a stray sailor into their hut to eat? Or will I end up in the black pot? Will the women be beautiful, or sumo wrestlers? Do they have cold beer?

I dropped the sails and anchored amongst two other sailboats in the lee of the island. The lagoon was too shallow to enter. The only anchorage was on the outside, which could get bad if the wind changed direction.

I dove over the side into the water that was clear as vodka. I swam for a bit with a mask and fins finding plenty of fish under the boat to spear for lunch later.

After the cathartic swim, I threw my mountain bike in the donkey and headed to shore to check into customs.

I found the small white building, with the help of some locals in the village. A big lady with dark skin wearing white official clothing checked me into the country of Kirabati and I paid a small fee for a visa. I got another stamp in my passport from some country I'd never even heard of before. I stepped out of the office and hit the road on my mountain bike to explore the island. One paved road circled the island, four kilometers long.

I pedaled out of the small village and cruised down the badly paved road. There were palm trees and thick foliage densely lining the sides. The jungle was trying to reclaim the road.

I rounded a corner and spotted a bicycle lying in the road. I thought that it was on odd place to leave a bicycle. I figured the owner of the bike had stopped to pick some coconuts or something. I had passed one truck speeding down the road and considered moving the bike to the side for everyone's safety. At that moment, I saw another large round object in the road not too far from the bike. It almost looked human.

As I got closer, I realized it was a body. I thought back to the one vehicle that perilously sped past me and postulated a hit and run. I apprehensively approached the body on the pavement. It was a huge man with arms and legs haphazardly strewn about. The body lay there in the road.

I rapidly dismounted my bike and forensically surveyed the scene for blood and damage. As I hovered over the massive islander, he made a huge gasping noise that nearly sent me backwards into a coronary. After his long gasp of air, that made me leave the pavement, he started snoring. The guy wasn't dead. He was *asleep,* in the *road.*

I'd seen some bizarre things in backwards countries, but this seemed like suicide. I surveyed the situation, trying to figure out why he chose that particular spot. Dense jungle and land crab mounds covered the side of the road, and he did have the only shade from a palm tree in the short stretch of pavement. I guessed it wasn't so strange after all. I left the guy in peace.

I got back on my bike and pedaled away. I could still hear him snoring ferociously. I got a chuckle out of being so concerned.

As I pedaled down the road, there were swarms of tiny white birds circling me. They were getting aggressive. It must have been mating season. They had a certain biological and impatient meanness about them.

They continued to swarm me. Occasionally, a bird would dive-bomb from up high and swerve just before it planted my forehead with its beak. I had to escape.

I spotted a trail to the left and decided to head off-road into the thick bush. I got about 100 meters down the trail into the jungle and ran into a thorny briar patch. I flattened both of my tires. "Son of a biscuit," I said. I was about four kilometers from town.

Defeated, I walked out to the road pushing the bike. I decided to wait for a passing truck to hitchhike. I hoped to see at least one truck on the road that day.

Devoured by the diabolical sun for an unpleasant hour, I finally spotted something in the distance like a mirage in the desert. It resembled a vehicle, but it was hard to tell from the heat waves rising off the hot asphalt.

I squinted from the tiny bush I was hovering underneath for any possible shade. It was a truck. I leapt out from under the stupid bush like a sweating bandit of the highway and stuck my thumb out. It slowed to a halt.

The gentleman driving the truck was not a local. He appeared to be Anglo Saxon. I said, "Do you speak English?"

"Yes, of course. Need a ride?" he said with a British accent.

"Yeah, I flattened both of my tires on that dirt road over there and I sure could use a lift back to town."

"No problem at-toll. Just hop in the back there, lad."

I threw my bike in the bed of the truck. I jumped in the back as well because his cab was full of local islanders. He looked back—I gave him the thumbs up and he drove onward.

After a short drive back to town, he dropped me off near my boat anchored offshore. I said, "Thanks a lot friend."

He just waved, looking at me in the rear view mirror and slowly pulled away. The big boys in the cab gave me a long silent stare and then looked out at my boat. Sometimes people of Oceania have a way of looking at me as though they want to eat me, but the second I gave them some form of greeting, their whole demeanor changed to that of a gentle giant.

When I got back to the boat, I added my bike to the endless repair list. I then grabbed my spear gun and jumped over the side with my mask and fins. There were plenty of reef fish hovering under the boat.

I held my breath and descended to the bottom. I hid among an outcropping of reef. A few fish were circling in search of food, but they weren't big enough to eat. Then a large blue parrotfish came into range and I squeezed the trigger. The spear went directly through its head and it died instantly. I brought it the surface and threw it into the cockpit.

Back on the boat, I cleaned the fish and fried it up with some onion and lime. I relaxed for the rest of the day, happily at anchor. Anything would be better than getting beat up on that tortuous sea.

Around sunset, I spotted *Boread* off in the distance. I hailed them on channel 16, *"Boread, Boread* this is the *Bula,* do you copy?"

Darren came back, *"Bula.* This is *Boread."*

"You wanna switch to our channel?"

"Meet ya there."

Channel 69 was our channel of choice between our young cruiser friends. The coast guard reserves channel 16 for emergencies and quick hailing of other vessels. Everyone monitors 16 on the high seas. However, some inconsiderate people get on channel 16 and chat for five minutes about nonsense until someone finally tells them to switch channels. Once you're off 16, and you've found a free channel, then you can talk for as long as you want.

We covertly chose to use one channel that we all knew, so we wouldn't have to voice that particular number over 16 where everyone could hear which channel we were switching to. Back in Papeete, it was a soap opera with bored sailing wives listening in on our conversations. We'd be blabbing about who got drunk here, who screwed whom there. Many rumors were spread by the VHF.

We switched to 69. Some anonymous sailor was probably searching the dial for our conversation.

"Darren, you there?" I said.

"Whoa, that was a rough one, huh?" he said.

"Yeah, I couldn't wait to get in the lee of the island and out of that madness."

"Thank god it's over and we made it safely. Amber is a little shook up."

"Call me the human martini."

"Shaken not stirred." Darren painfully laughed.

"So I'm anchored in about 20 feet of water. The bottom has

patches of sand and coral. You can find a decent spot to anchor on my left or right, equidistant from shore."

"Sounds good brother. Thanks. I guess it's too late to check into customs, huh."

"Yeah, worry about that tomorrow. It's easy if you can catch them open. They only seem to be open when they're not eating at the one restaurant, or drinking beer at the one watering hole in town."

Amber's voice came over the receiver, "Hey Bula, it's good to hear your voice. I can't wait to hang out with ya but we're too tired today. We'll see ya tomorrow, ok?"

Over the past year that I had known Darren and Amber, they had just resolved to calling me "Bula".

"It's good to hear your voice too. Alright, get some rest and I'll see you tomorrow. Over and out."

Life on Pluto

I spent the next few days recovering from the trip and hanging out with Darren and Amber. Our only entertainment was drinking the Kiribati beer at the local bar and playing fuze-ball on this beat-up table. Half of the men on the table were missing and the other half were duck-taped together. Some were just wooden pegs constructed by the kids who loved the game. It was their daily battle between buddies.

Everyday we had our one meal at the restaurant that was only open for three hours. I guessed that was a full day's work for these people who had next to nothing. Nevertheless, most of them had smiles on their faces and were genuinely happy. After traveling the world, I've realized that the happiest people seemed to have very little.

I was getting ready to head north to the Island of Fanning and then onward to Hawaii with *Boread*. Fanning Island is another small atoll, part of the Line Islands of the nation Kiribati. Very few people visit these remote specs in the Pacific, except for a few bone fishermen, salty sailors and an occasional pirate.

The next day, I sailed up to Fanning with *Boread*. We decided to have ourselves a race to Fanning, roughly 150 miles. We had perfect winds on the beam. We hoisted our sails and headed out.

I was in the lead for the entire day. They were barking at

me on channel 69 because I was taking them down as a single-hander. I responded on the VHF, "And there's *Bula* in the lead with *Boread* still dragging their anchor. Pull in those sails you scallywags. Ha haaa." I reveled in the victorious moment. Who knew how long it would last.

That night I decreased sails in order to sleep. *Boread* snuck by me in the middle of the night while I was asleep.

We both sailed around the bottom of Fanning Island as the sun was rising over the tropical atoll. The island had a shallow lagoon with a small pass. The pass was barely big enough for a sailboat to squeeze through.

Boread had already entered through the tiny pass into the lagoon. I was the second one to enter. The tide was dropping fast and water was rushing out of the pass as I approached.

I hailed *Boread* on the VHF and Darren said, "Hey Bula, we barely made it through the pass thirty minutes ago. The tide is even worse now. Maybe you should wait outside the pass until the tide turns."

"Oh really," I said with concern. "Ahhh . . . I think I'm gonna try first, and if it doesn't work, I'll just one-eighty the boat in the pass and try again later."

"Ok buddy, good luck."

I pulled out all my sails, trimmed them, started up the engine and floored the throttle. As I entered, I was making progress until I reached the halfway point where the water was rushing out the fastest. I gave the throttle one last push into the danger zone and asked the tiki god of Fanning Island for a rite of passage. The knot meter was claiming seven knots, but the boat was going backwards.

It was time to abort and turn around in the tight pass. I had to hug one side of the pass and turn towards the other in order to get around without running into the other shore.

To make my quick turn, I hugged the left side of the pass. A set of standing waves started breaking in the pass. One wave broke just behind the boat and the whitewater crashed into the stern. The wave pushed the boat deeper into the pass. A second wave broke nearly on the stern and jump-started the boat forward. I surfed down the small wave and realized I was getting past the threshold. A third wave broke behind me and pushed me into the lagoon.

"OH YEA" I yelled.

I pulled into the safety of the lagoon and got on the VHF. I said, "Did you see that? The *Bula* just surfed through the pass."

Darren said, "Yeah, I had a little help from some waves as well."

"I'm in. When's lunch?"

I sailed around to the north side of the palm-laden lagoon through opaque green waters. I motored up to a half-sunken barge. The rusty barge looked as if it had been there since WWII. I tied up alongside with plenty of fenders out and set up shop right on the deck of the barge that was at the same level as the deck of the *Bula*. I entertained the idea of throwing a barge party.

I launched the donkey and motored over to *Boread*, who had invited me to lunch. En route, I spotted another vessel in the lagoon named *Laughter*. I recognized them from Tahiti. I wanted to go over and say hello to the nice couple from California after lunch.

Amber made up another one of her unusual concoctions with lentils, green beans and some strange veggie meat in a box. I never understood that veggie meat, and no one has ever given me a solid answer to its contents. Like spam, nobody has a convincing explanation. I'm not sure the FDA does either. The military created spam during the war as food rations. But nobody questions the military for some reason. Soldiers took a liking to it, probably because they were stuck out in the middle of some war zone with nothing to eat but dirt or this mutant meat. Therefore, some marketing imbecile, or genius, sold it to the *masses*.

Amber is actually a good cook. But when you're dealing with a lack of resources, you get creative with canned goods.

After lunch, the three of us decided to go explore the island. I hailed Patrick off the boat *Laughter* to see if he wanted to check out the surf at a place called Whalers Bay on the north side of the island.

Patrick was an older surfer from Monterey, California. He

was still living in the '60s with long sun bleached hair, around five-ten, medium build and in his late forties or early fifties.

He was excited to go and said he would meet us on the beach with his surfboard for the walk. Darren and Amber didn't have a surfboard, so it would just be Patrick and me looking for waves.

Fanning Island has less development than Christmas Island. There was no concrete, only dirt roads and traditional wooden huts with palm-thatched roofs.

We walked through a tiny village with poorly maintained bamboo huts. The locals were hanging out in their front yards made of coral and shells. They were thoughtlessly doing nothing at all when the four of us walked by, totting surfboards. I wondered what they really thought about us. We weren't the first surfers or sailors walking through their village. However, we were definitely not passé.

We confidently waved to them and they waved back smiling. Some were in a dream-state of uncertainty, moving their hands back and forth mimicking our actions.

These islanders are of Micronesian descent. They have darker skin and are slightly shorter than Polynesians. The women have long straight or slightly wavy black hair. Some of the men and women had tattoos of matching design. Their demeanor was more innocent and inviting than Polynesians.

We emerged from the jungle to a white sand beach and looked out to see waves peeling over the shallow reef in a beautiful manner. We grinned at each other at our discovery. There was no one around.

Patrick and I waxed-up our surfboards and paddled out to the waves. We caught some long and hollow reef waves with an empty lineup. We were the only surfers around for thousands of miles.

We spent a couple of hours surfing while Darren and Amber explored the exotic coastline. After our surf, we walked back together through the village. The people were doing the same thing they were doing when we passed the first time. They all waved at us again with the same excitement as our initial greeting.

We motored back to our floating domiciles to escape the equatorial sun.

The next few days were spent surfing and spearing fish in the pass. I got a tiny reef nick on my toe from surfing. I didn't think much of it, until I got overly exhausted from hauling some heavy anchor-chain. Then a headache developed and I had to lie down. I looked at my toe and my whole foot was swollen.

I hailed Patrick on his boat. I knew his wife was a nurse. He said she was gone, but that I should come over and hopefully she would be back soon.

I got over to his boat and he was overly concerned with my situation. He had a friend off another boat that nearly died from a staphylococcus infection. It was obvious the infection was in the early stages of "staph". Patrick got on his SSB to hail any ship doctors that were listening on that frequency. The Hawaiian Coast Guard responded 1500 miles away in Honolulu. They transferred us to their ships surgeon onboard.

Patrick's wife Lindy returned to the boat while we were speaking to the surgeon in Hawaii. She took my temperature and other vitals and relayed them to the surgeon. I already had a fever of 104 within two hours and red streaks were creeping up my leg from the infection.

The ships surgeon treated the case as a full-blown emergency and began organizing a Coast Guard plane to fly into Christmas Island. They would pick me up and fly me to a hospital in Honolulu, immediately. That meant I would have to sail back to Christmas Island, 150 miles south, and leave my boat anchored off an unprotected shore of a foreign island.

I said, "Wait a minute here. I value my safety, but isn't there any penicillin or antibiotic I can take for staph infection?"

The surgeon said, "Ok, there are two types of staph infections reported from your area, both of which can be fatal. For Type-1 cellulitis staph infections, there are two types of antibiotics you can take, if you are lucky enough to find them there. For Type-2 cellulitis staph infections, which are indigenous to Kirabati, you would need to get to a hospital immediately and the closest one is in Honolulu. Now, Type-2 staph is only found in fifteen percent of the cases from the area. It's your choice."

Fifteen percent doesn't seem like a high percentage, unless you're gambling with your life. Dicloxacillin was one of the antibiotics he mentioned and common to carry on a boat. We hailed *Boread* and they thought they had some onboard. They were unsure of the expiration. They located the antibiotic and it was still in date. I was in luck.

I said to the surgeon over the SSB, "I have located some Dicloxacillin, and I'm going to give it a try first to see if my condition turns. If it doesn't, then I'll be interested in your plan of evacuation."

The surgeon said, "There was a similar case in Fanning Island where the US Coast Guard flew down and picked up a sailor who had staph infection just like you. He was taken to a hospital in Honolulu where he was treated with Type-2 staph. After his recovery, he was flown back to Christmas Island to his sailboat. He had to pay for the expenses, but at least he had his life."

I said, "Thanks for the story doc. That makes me feel really good about my decision to wait."

"Not to worry, it's a low percentage and you're lucky to have found the antibiotic. Please report to us tomorrow at O-nine-hundred and give us your vitals."

"Thanks," I said and we signed off the SSB.

I got my hands on those pills hoping for a miracle. After six hours, my fever dropped a degree. That was enough reassurance for me.

Some Days are like a Walk in the Park, Others are like a Walk on the Plank

The swelling had decreased in my foot from the staph infection and my fever had nearly subsided. The weather window for my solo mission to Hawaii was looking good. I didn't want to miss out on the opportunity.

I quickly stowed all breakables and lashed everything to the deck. I gave one last look around the boat to make sure everything was in order. I untied the lines from the old rusty barge and motored towards the pass.

The tide was going out, to my advantage. I motored through the pass at a swift rate. I spotted a school of brightly colored parrotfish swimming under the boat into the lagoon. The water was so clear I could see the details of the underwater reef outcroppings on the sides of the pass. The water turned into a deeper shade of blue as I moved further out to sea. I was going to miss the little island atoll and its simple people.

Darren and Amber on *Boread* sailed out of the pass just behind me. They were also sailing to Hawaii at the same time so we could stick together in case of any emergencies.

Safely out of the pass, I hoisted the sails. I pointed the boat to 20 degrees northeast on the compass and set the wind-vane to steer on that heading. I was close-hauled with the winds blowing out of the northeast at 15 knots. The weather looked favorable.

I planned on sailing 300 miles northeast to 157 degrees longitude, then turning and heading straight north. Once I reached the bottom of Hawaii, known for heavy trade winds, I could then turn to the northwest and sail at an easier angle to the wind.

Birds from the island continued circling the boat. They stayed with me until I got out of sight of land. They eventually flew back to their island home. The seas seemed a bit choppy, but I was optimistic about the trip and confident about the state of the boat.

Still a little worn down from the staph infection, my body was regaining energy. I knew I was on the rebound and that kept me positive. I continued northeast throughout the day, trolling two fishing lines, hoping to catch anything.

I sat in the cockpit under the shade of the bimini and read a sailing novel that wasn't too interesting. I just wanted to keep my mind off the dangers of sailing into the North Pacific in the middle of winter.

The day was long and hot, but I was making good progress. *Bula* sailed fast on the close-hauled tack, but it was uncomfortable from the seas breaking on the bow.

That evening, I cooked up the remaining fish I had speared at Fanning Island and listened to the weather on the SSB receiver. The forecast was changing for the worse. I tried to get some sleep that night.

The next day the winds picked up to 25 knots with the wind direction right on the nose. The seas increased in size with the escalated winds and I was already dreading the 10-day sail. I was looking forward to reaching that degree of eastern longitude to turn and sail at a more comfortable tack. I had 100 miles to go until I could turn at a better angle to the wind. I also had 1500 miles to go until I reached Hawaii. That seemed like a number I couldn't get my brain to grasp, so I focused on the 100 miles.

I was still trolling the fishing lines without a bite. It was strange that I had caught so many fish in between Bora Bora and Christmas Island and now that I was sailing away from the South Pacific, I was running out of luck.

The boat creaked along as the winds increased in power. I

was not feeling as confident as I was the day before. I began envisioning issues with the boat.

By the third day out, I was nearing my planned degree of longitude where I would turn at a better angle to the wind. A giant cumulonimbus cloud was rapidly approaching. The sky was clear on all sides, but this massive black cloud with a white crown towering thousands of feet above the surface was marching straight towards me. I couldn't turn and run away. There was nowhere to hide.

I spotted long lines of rain falling from the cloud, hitting the surface of the water from a distance. The lines of rain were falling vertically out of the bottom of the cloud and becoming horizontal before they touched the surface of the ocean due to the immense amount of wind and speed of the cloud.

I could see the strong winds moving across surface of the ocean towards the boat. I jumped down below to grab my raingear. I battened everything down and reefed the sails. Immediately, the brunt of the squall hit me with a 60-knot gust of wind. I heard the sheets screaming as they stretched and the rigging vibrating as it held up the mast.

It blew at a steady 60 knots for five minutes as I tried to ease the boat into the wind without getting pushed straight into the wind. The sails were fluttering so violently the entire boat vibrated and made sounds I had never heard. Then the rain hit me in the face with a stinging velocity. I was wearing my storm glasses; otherwise, I wouldn't have been able to keep my eyes open.

The winds began slacking, but continued blowing at a steady 50 knots. There was no way I could sail in that amount of wind, I had to heave-to and drop my sails. I heaved in the headsail with the furling line. I then clipped into my jack-line on the starboard side of the boat and crept forward into the torturous wind and rain. I worked at getting the mainsail down, but it wouldn't budge in that wind. I had to pull as hard as I could to bring it down.

I triple-reefed the mainsail to the boom. Exhausted but successful, I retired to the cockpit and hid behind the dodger.

I sat there for a couple of hours in the cockpit with the boat drifting backwards in the storm. Large waves were breaking and pushing the boat dangerously sideways. The rain fell on me and the wind whipped into my hooded raingear. I contemplated my position in the middle of the ocean, unable to sail, or do anything but wait for possible doom.

The huge squall passed, but the winds sustained 40 knots. I eased out a little bit of the headsail. I turned and continued north at a slow pace. I contacted *Boread* on the VHF. We were about 30 miles apart at that point and the connection was full of static. They also had to heave-to in that squall. The weather was generally deteriorating and the reports we were receiving from Hawaii were not good.

That day I got close enough to my preplanned longitude and turned directly on a northern path, hoping for a more comfortable sail. Soon after I turned north, the winds began to veer more from the north making it difficult to sail with the wind on the nose.

Day four was grim. I woke up after a long night of short naps that always ended with a crashing wave on the hull. The waves were so powerful, when they hit I thought the boat was coming apart. Quite often, I threw my arms over my head as if someone had dropped a hand grenade into the cabin. Water was working its way through the deck joint and various areas, soaking the interior, and saturating the seat cushions.

I heard a loud snap top-deck and a massive fluttering of sails. I quickly opened the companionway to see the headsail violently flapping in the strong winds. The furling line that holds the sail coiled up to a smaller size for the escalated winds had snapped and the huge sail had completely unrolled.

I put on my raingear, harness, and storm-glasses to head out into the bedlam. I clipped into the jack-line and crawled forward across the slippery deck to the bow. I found the break in the line. It snapped near the middle of the 40-foot line. I was able to tie the severed line back together as a quick fix and slowly reefed the sail back to its original small size.

After a few minutes, the wind filled the sail and I was

moving again. I retired below exhausted. The furling line was old and frayed and I hoped it wouldn't break again, but I had a bad feeling it would.

I spent another wet, sleepless night with the storm hammering me into a state of fatigue. I dreamed of dry clothes and hot showers. I envisioned myself sitting in a café, sipping tea and listening to jazz with a good friend. Upon reaching stable ground, I planned on crawling into a cave and never emerging.

I woke up the next morning to the same nagging problem with the rudderpost leak. I had repacked the gland in Christmas Island and now it was leaking worse than ever. The automatic bilge pump was turning on every 15 minutes. I was worried it might drain the batteries. The wind generator was taking care of most of the electrical load, but maybe not all of it. I could always start the engine to charge the batteries with the alternator, though the engine could fail with all the erratic movements of the boat. If my batteries died, I would have to pump the continual flooding by hand all day and night to stay afloat.

I received another bad weather report from Hawaii. I decided to check my position with the hand-held GPS. The hand-held rarely picked up a signal inside the cabin. I always opened up the companionway and held my arm out into the open air to get a clear shot of the sky to pick up a satellite signal. This time it wasn't responding.

I stood there with my normal death-grip on the hand-held GPS as I dubiously held it out into the cockpit. After ten minutes, the GPS finally spit out a response. It stated "poor coverage".

"SON OF A BITCH", I yelled, knowing I was in trouble. After my main GPS had malfunctioned, my hand-held was the last remaining contact with my position in the world, and now it was lost. Without it, I would never find Hawaii 1,000 miles away. I was angry for never learning celestial navigation. I tried to calm down. I'd try again later.

I tried the GPS again after half an hour and had no luck. Things were turning bad and I was in over my head. The news would say, "Single-handed sailor destined for Hawaii three months overdue." I would be sailing around in circles out there, going completely mad with no food or water like all the other survival stories I've read about. The best I could hope for was the idea that my survival story would be more than a mystery.

I continued to take the exploding waves on the starboard side of the boat as if I was sitting in a blood-red box in a bullring. Hour after hour, I took the beatings.

Day six, I finally picked up a GPS reading and gave thanks to every religious figure—Jesus, Buddha, Allah, Jah Rastafari, the Tiki God, and even the Black Christ. I saluted Satan as well, for he was probably the one who put me into this mess. The next time I go offshore, I'm going to carry no less than a dozen GPS units, and then a few backups.

I tried the VHF at random intervals for anyone to talk to out there. I finally contacted *Boread* and talked with them for about thirty minutes. Imagine feeling like the last human on earth, when you unexpectedly contact someone else. Darren was a man of few words, but he never wanted to end the conversation. Amber stole the radio transmitter and said she wanted to kill Darren and I was the only one who understood. She was speaking to me as though he couldn't hear what she was saying.

I was mid-sentence when a giant wave crashed on top of the boat. It submerged the deck and water gushed through the cracks in the companionway onto my head and the VHF. I was keeping the companionway completely sealed up due to the waves. However, there was so much water submerging the deck with each wave, the water would flood under the dodger and rush into the semi-sealed companionway.

After the continual flooding, I had to stuff the cracks of the companionway with plastic trash bags. Some of the bigger waves would blow apart my plastic jerry rig and seawater would shower down on my electrical components.

Each day that passed, the interior of the boat became more soaked with no chance of drying out. I longed for home, wherever that was.

Day seven, a loud noise woke me up from a lucky nap that I was able get from my normal state of insomnia. It sounded as if the headsail had unfurled and was whipping about. I shot out of the sealed companionway to see the furling line had snapped again, but this time from the unit itself. That was not going to be easy to repair with the intense winds.

I put on my raingear and unsealed the patched companionway. I went up on deck, clipping my harness into the jack-line and crept forward like a panther, avoiding all the booby traps lying await to trip me up. The deck of an offshore sailboat is an obstacle course. There are coiled ropes everywhere to hang me up, trip wires to send me over the side, and cables running in various directions. There's the boom to stay clear of, sails flapping to hit me in the head, whisker poles to knock me out, and a million metal toe-demons attached to the deck waiting in ambush to mangle my fragile feet. Then throw in a 25-degree angle of the boat heeling over and some heavy seas.

En route, another baseball hat was whipped off my head by the wind and into the sea, gone forever. This time I made it through the masochistic course only stubbing my pinky toe once.

I tightened the headsail sheet with the full 120% of sail out in 40 knots of wind. I was hoping the sail wouldn't shred or snap a shroud from too much pressure on the mast.

I went to the bow and tried to reinstall the furling line to the base of the furling unit. I spent twenty arduous minutes taking waves on the head and hanging on. Finally, I got it installed and realized I had done it backwards.

"Mother fu . . . ," I mumbled to the vicious wind. I had to do the whole process over again, eventually furling the headsail back to a small size.

I stopped, gazed across the metallic sea and realized there was no lonelier place. I thought about the gallant souls who single-handed around the world and felt for them. If the sea doesn't get me, the loneliness will.

I headed back to the safety of the cabin and dried off with one of my last dry towels. As I sat in my corner, I looked at random pictures of friends and family I had placed up on the walls.

I stared long at the few photos I had of Tehani. This was the only comfort I had in my diminutive world. I held some of the photos and tears came to my eyes thinking of all the things I wanted to say to them. I thought about how much of a selfish piece of shit I was for not spending more time with them or telling them how I really felt.

Davey's Grip

Day eight, I received a weather report that gave me a promise of clearing. That gave me hope. Immediately after the report, another squall hit me. I had to pull the sails in and heave-to for some hours.

It let up a bit, and I continued on sailing. I was down below trying to take a nap when I heard another rush of sails bashing about. I immediately thought that the damn furling line snapped again. I came out into the cockpit and looked forward in awe. My entire headsail had ripped in half down the middle.

I threw on my raingear and harness and quickly came out of the cabin. I stopped to stare at the dangerous flapping sail. I didn't want to go up there. Trembling and scared, I was thinking of any possible way to get out of that mess. I thought to myself, you're the stupid one who wanted to do this alone. I clenched my teeth with a mean sense of determination and crawled up to the bow. My harness line snagged on every entrapment that I passed, so I unlatched the carabiner to make it forward but forgot to reattach it to the safety jack-line.

I had to pull the headsail down completely. I released the halyard and began pulling the sail down. It whipped about, pounding me in the face. I couldn't do anything but take the lashings. A flailing sheet ripped another pair of storm glasses off my face and into the ocean. I saw them sinking into the abyss.

Once I got most of it down, the wind was pulling the sail and me over the side with the waves washing over the deck. The sail dangerously filled with seawater. I was hanging onto the sail for my life that was full of hundreds of pounds of seawater. I was having horrible thoughts that if I lost the headsail I could triple my time to Hawaii. I couldn't let go of it either because the folds of the sail had wrapped around me. I was slipping into Davey's Grip*.

I locked into survival mode. I wasn't prepared to go over the side forever. I managed to get the sail back on the boat and wrestled it to the cockpit in two pieces. I had to laugh at death—I couldn't let it laugh at me.

Luckily, I had a backup sail. It would be near suicide not to carry a backup in case I lost one. I located the storm jib and took it to the forestay to install it on the furling track. This was the most difficult thing I've done by myself in the high seas. I had to install a sail with a 3/16th inch luff-tape, carefully into a forestay track in 45 knots of wind. It's like trying to thread a needle in a hurricane.

I knew if I couldn't get the jib on the track, it was physically impossible to sail into the wind without a headsail. If I couldn't sail into the wind, I might as well turn and head downwind to an alternative destination, if that was even a choice. I had too many "ifs", but I wasn't giving in to pessimism. Even when the laws of physics were against Armstrong, he made it to the moon. I could make it to Hawaii.

I tried for over an hour, sitting down on the bow hanging on with my legs wrapped around the bow pulpit. Waves submerged the entire bow with me on it. While completely submerged, I continued to work. Upon surfacing, I gasped for air and let out a primal scream as if I was a Mohican warrior running into battle. I was feeling the intense energy of the present. I was scared to death but enjoying it.

---

* Davy's Grip = 1 : to be close to death, or frightened 2 : in reference to Davy Jones' Locker, the imaginary place at the bottom of the ocean that holds dead sailors and pirates 3 : Davy Jones was said to be an evil spirit lurking at sea, waiting to escort dead sailors or pirates to his place or locker at the bottom of the waters 4 : he went on to have a successful music career with the Monkeys many years later

I worked diligently with my hands and teeth to fit the storm-jib into the groove. I needed an extra person pulling the halyard up while I worked it into the track. I really needed five people. I figured out a system with bungee cords and my progress tripled.

After two intense hours, I got the storm-jib in the track and hoisted it up. I tightened the storm-jib sheet down and the boat began moving again. Covered in bruises, cuts, and lumps all over my hands, face and back; I retired to the cabin with bloody lips and knuckles.

The next few days gradually got worse starting with the weather. I spent two days sewing up the headsail. I broke various needles and punctured multiple fingers in the process. It's hard enough to stitch up an eight-ounce sail canvas by hand on land, much less at sea with waves exploding over the boat.

The cabin was entirely soaked and there was nothing dry to sit on anymore. My skin was constantly wet and chaffed. The sting of the salt in my wounds was the only reminder that I wasn't just having a bad dream.

The leak in the bilge had quadrupled and now the automatic bilge pump was running every five minutes. I calculated I was taking on 100 gallons of water a day. The water was coming from more areas than the rudderpost but I didn't know where.

Most of my cabinet drawers broke from dislodging during wave blasts. They all lay in the forward bunk in pieces. The starboard rub-rail had slid out of its track and was hanging over the side, dragging in the water. Various electrical lights and equipment shorted out. I was eating and sleeping less.

Whether it was the boat, or me, something smelled rotten. I hadn't showered in days because of the stormy seas. I could just imagine trying to shower on deck, dumping buckets of water on my head, slipping and going over the side. I didn't want to go over naked, not that it would make any difference. I'd just feel more comfortable drowning or being eaten by a shark with my shorts on. I don't know why, maybe it's some security thing in the face of death. Death doesn't care what you're wearing.

I was getting so little sleep that my brain felt hazy most of the time. Lack of sleep is one of the main reasons for human error.

I was talking to myself again, which is normal when I'm committed to solitude for long periods of time. I don't even think about it for a week or so, then something in my head just snaps and I begin blabbering to myself. It's sometimes comforting to hear my own voice when I'm deep in the dark abyss.

I cracked another can of tuna, which my diet had dwindled to for mere functionality and lack of desire to cook, or *eat* for that matter. I knew I had to generate some energy to make it through the last leg of the journey. I didn't aspire to put anything in a frying pan for fear I would have to eat it off the floor. My only desire was to lie on my back in the cabin sealed up tight. I stared at the ceiling as if I was waiting for a clown to pull my name out of a hat for a ride in the electric chair. Death was laughing at me, and I was laughing at my own silly demise.

There comes a strange time in a man's life when he feels as though the whole world has conspired against him, as though his own existence is just one big joke and everyone is out to get him. When you have been beat down for so long by the grand prankster, everything that transpires seems as though it is only another jolly poke of fun.

I was looking out the window when I heard a faint voice crackling over the VHF, "Hello . . . this is monkey looking for big banana." I shook my head, thinking I was imagining things again. I leaped over to the VHF and turned the volume up high. There was nothing but static. I must have been hearing things. This might be the first sign that my mind was slowly creeping into dementia. This little Asian voice came over the radio again, "This is monkey looking for big banana. . . . Where's my big banana?"

I stood there looking at the speaker in confusion when another strange distorted voice came over the receiver, "This is big banana. Is this monkey? Ha ha ha ha . . ." The first voice came back and began making funny animal noises and the second one chimed in with something that sounded like a cat with its asshole on fire. This baffling behavior continued for a brief moment until there was nothing but silence. I stood there waiting for something else, but heard only static. I sat down in my crazy corner and began laughing in derangement.

It had been more than ten days and I still had five hundred stinking miles to go. I just had to keep my mental fortitude for a few more days. I thought sailing was supposed to be fun. If so, then I've worked harder at having fun than any man alive.

Everyday that I heard the encouraging weather report from these two guys in Hawaii the more I wanted to dismember them. They gave me the same deluded information day after day—35 knots from the north, slacking the next day and moving more to the east. Never once did the winds slack or move to the east. I just wanted to hear the straight story. Don't tell me everything's going to be all right, because there are no rainbows in hell.

On the twelfth day, I reached the lee of the Big Island of Hawaii. Hawaii is the actual name of this particular island, though it is known as the Big Island because, well it's the biggest. The trade winds died, blocked by the 13,796-foot peak in the center of the island. The seas were about 15-feet, but smooth. I had to start up the engine and motor. There was no wind one-hundred miles off the coast. I didn't care if I had to motor all the way to Oahu; I was finally out of that diabolical wind. I clicked on the autopilot and fell into a deep sleep.

I woke up towards evening and checked my position. I was approaching the Alinuihaha Channel. This is the infamous channel between the Big Island and Maui. It rates in the top three most dangerous channels in the world for extreme winds. Trade winds from the Northeast funnel into this channel squeezed between two large mountains on both islands, creating the "Venturi effect." This is the effect of wind by the speedup of air through a constriction due to the pressure drop on the downwind side as the air diverges to leave the constriction. Often the wind velocity doubles from what the trade winds are blowing. I did the math. It was blowing 35 knots out there. I could expect double that.

Everyone told me to stay 100 miles out from the channel when approaching it from the south. I followed their suggestions and was confident the winds would defuse their intensity at that distance.

The sun was descending into the sea and I was beginning to pick up enough wind to raise the sails. I hoisted up full sails without too much fear of the Alinuihaha at 100 miles out.

I happened to see something on the horizon that resembled a current line. I thought it must've been the current from the channel. I didn't know it had a current that strong.

As I approached, I said to myself, "That's no current, that's a WIND LINE."

Before I had enough time to get the sails down, it slammed into me and sent the boat heeling over. I quickly pointed the bow into the wind and reefed the sails. This channel has broken the masts off many sailboats. I was lucky to have avoided that. I sailed along in 50 knots of wind for the next eight hours.

The sun had set and a few stars were twinkling through the patchy sky. I was sitting in the cockpit in the darkness when the boat descended deep down into a trough between waves. I looked over my shoulder at a 30-foot wave cascading down onto the boat. I quickly grabbed a hold of a cleat that was next to me. As the wave rushed over top of me, it sent me horizontal, hanging onto the cleat. I remember looking over my shoulder to avoid being hit in the face by the wave and seeing an avalanche of whitewater exploding over the top of the boat. It hit the boat so hard it spun the *Bula* 90-degrees.

I held onto the cleat until the wave had passed and drained off the deck. The cockpit was completely full of water and leaking into the cabin through the wooden slates.

I surveyed the boat to see if anything had been broken. The mast and sails were still intact and it seemed as though everything was still there.

I waited while the water drained out of the cockpit, staring at my feet underwater. The boat turned back on its course. The boat inexorably continued onward like a mean old man of the sea. I knew that one did some damage.

I sailed on through the night in the lee of Maui, Lanai and Molokai and into the Kaiwi Channel between Oahu and Molokai. I could see lights from Honolulu bouncing off a cloud layer in the distance. After the lights gradually intensified, I knew I was going to make it alive. I was so ecstatic I couldn't imagine sleeping. I also had to look out for the dangerous ship traffic in the area.

I spotted a large US Coast Guard vessel patrolling the waters off Waikiki. It was time to get on the VHF and state my arrival. I said, "US Coast Guard, US Coast Guard, this is sailing vessel *Bula*, do you copy?"

"This is the US Coast Guard, please repeat the name of your vessel," someone replied.

That was the first time I had spoken to a real human in nearly a week. It was comforting and gave me a warm feeling inside. Everything was going to be all right.

I said, "This is sailing vessel *Bula*," I phonetically spelled out the name of the boat, "Bravo, Uniform, Lima, Alpha. I'm flying an American flag, stating my future arrival into Honolulu from the southeast."

"Sailing vessel *Bula*, please state your position and number of passengers onboard."

"One-five miles southeast of Diamond Head lighthouse and single-handing." I almost wanted him to ask me where I had sailed from, so I could brag a little bit. But then again I didn't care to boast. The seas had drowned my ego.

There was a pause and the man whom I was speaking with said, "Yes, we have you on radar, please proceed and check into customs. Thank you sir have a nice day, this is the US Coast Guard, out."

They didn't have time to dally with me and were rather short. I couldn't wait to get to shore and talk to someone, anyone.

The sunrise created an effervescent red dawn. Oahu seemed like a dream. As I approached land, I was shocked by all the waterfront skyscrapers of Honolulu. It resembled New York City. In the past four months, I hadn't seen anything more than thatched huts and a few small buildings in Papeete. After a month of pure pain, I was sailing into something I wasn't sure I wanted. It was a concrete paradise. I had feelings of turning around and heading back south to solitude. Maybe I'd rest first.

Anchored in bliss. Morelle Bay, Tonga

Lands End. Cabo San Lucas, Mexico

Figman with the bottle of fish death

Brillant sunsets crossing the equator

Paddling the donkey in the shark infested waters of Palmyra

Shurd and I sailing in Hawaii in heavy winds

Palmyra lagoon

Tongan feast

Muzzy

Contagious smiles in Fiji

Bora Bora

Rope swings in Palmyra

Sailing into Pago Pago

Tahiti

Muzzy and I
looking for land

My only companion sailing alone in the Pacific

Giant coconut crabs

Anchored inside the pass at Teahupoo, Tahiti

Half sunken barge inside the lagoon of Fanning Island

Wahoo

Land

I pulled into Waikiki, dropped the sails and motored into the Ala Wai Harbor. I cruised up to the gas dock and got one fender out. I listlessly tied the *Bula* off to the dock. I stumbled off the boat, dizzy after no food or sleep. I left the boat there wide open with total unconcern for its safety.

Some old-timer came out of the gas dock shop and said to me in a raspy voice, "Aye buddy, you can't leave your boat there."

I looked at him apathetically and said, "Keep it."

I kept walking, oblivious to his next comment. The next person I ran into, I said, "Hey, where's the closest bar?"

He gave me a funny look, pointed and said, "Harbor Pub—right over there."

"How about pizza?"

He grinned, figuring I must've just sailed in from somewhere. "They've got good pizza too buddy."

"You've got to be kidding me?"

"Go see for yourself."

"That's the best thing I've heard in weeks." I was so happy I wanted to invite the old fellow, but thought better of it. I probably couldn't have a functional conversation with another human.

I staggered over to the Harbor Pub and walked into the below-street-level seedy place. It was dark inside and smelled like an ashtray. There were old sailing prints all over the walls, combined with photos of seventies surf legends. There were people hanging out in dim-lit corners, sipping pitchers of beer and cackling like pirates or wanna-bes. I sat down at the closest table and an old wrinkled waitress walked up to me.

She said, "Can I get ya anything honey?"

Coming out of my reverie, I blissfully looked up at her. I worked hard to form a smile. I could nearly hear my weathered, salt-encrusted face crackling as I forced a polite grin.

I said, "You sure can."

"Alright, what'll it be?"

"Cold beer."

"What kind?"

"Cold."

She glanced at me out of the corner of her eye with a puzzled look and walked to the bar. She brought me back a cold Killians Red in a pint glass.

"Here ya go honey," she said. "Would you like anything else?"

"Give me the largest pizza you've got with absolutely everything on it."

She began writing it down as if it was hard to remember. She then gave me another confused look. "You just come in from somewhere?"

"Yeah, I ahhh . . . just sailed in from Tahiti."

She stood back and put her arms on her hips. "By yourself?"

I had my head down like a dog who peed on the carpet and jokingly said, "Is that bad?"

"Well congratulations, glad you made it alive."

I humbly nodded. "Me too." She walked off, still shaking her head.

I realized that my speech was rather dysfunctional because I hadn't spoken more than a couple of words to another human in a long time. You lose dexterity of your tongue when you don't use it.

I ordered another beer while I waited for the pizza and started feeling the buzz. Drinking after no food or sleep is a bad combination. I began looking around for any cute girls, but most everyone at the bar were in their fifties. "Newlyweds and nearly-dead"—I guessed the saying for Hawaii was holding true. I figured

I was going to be there sooner than later at my pace and I contemplated getting old.

The pizza arrived and the waitress said, "Here ya go darling." She had a southern accent, and looked better with every beer.

I took down that large pizza and could've eaten another. I opted for another beer. She brought me a Killians and smiled at me with a set of teeth similar to keys on a piano—two whites, one black, etc. They didn't bother me a bit.

I had to escape before it was too late. I quickly paid my bill, left a huge tip and snuck out of there. I clamored back to the *Bula* and passed out. I forgot to check into customs, which might cost me a pencil whipping*.

My boat was still sitting at the gas dock the next day when I awoke to a loud knock on the hull. I emerged from a paralytic stint of narcolepsy and sloth-walked to the cockpit. I poked my pallid face out into the mid-day sun to see an official dressed in blue staring at me as though I was the missing link.

He said, "Is this your vessel?"

I tried to muster up a tender look of innocence and answered, "Ahhh . . . yes sir."

His demeanor lightened up. "You cleared in with the Coast Guard on the VHF, but not with customs."

"I'm sorry. It was getting late and I . . ."

Before I could finish, he said, "Not a worry, can I see your passport?"

I jumped to attention. "Sure, yep, ok. One minute please."

I scrambled down the stairs to find my passport. When I got down there, I didn't have a clue where to begin. The cabin was a junk yard. After a few stressful minutes, with the cop clock ticking, I managed to uncover it in the rubble and went back to the cockpit. I hoped that he didn't want to inspect the wreckage.

---

* pencil whipping = 1 : to get written up by the authorities 2 : another expensive ticket that goes to some politicians' pocket

He took one quick look at my passport and said, "Thank You."

"Is that it?" I said.

The nice gentleman extended his arm to shake my hand. He confidently stated, "Yes Mr. Carson, you are cleared into the country."

Trying to contain my elation, though confused over the ease of the process, I slowly put my hand out as though it was a trap and he was going to slap the cuffs on me. He gave me a stranglehold handshake.

"Yes . . . ok . . . thank you sir," I said.

I supposed if my name were Nayrb Nosrac, it would've been a little more complicated. I would've been greeted with a firearm instead of an extended arm. Especially since 9/11 occurred just a few months prior. Before I left Tahiti, I debated staying away from the States altogether and sailing to New Zealand to avoid the whole mess.

I turned and went back down below to face the carnage. I was happy to be alive and sitting still for once, but what lay before me was at least six months of work to get the boat back in shape.

I decided to go and use the public phone to talk to anyone I knew. I called every family member and friend I could contact, and told them I made it alive. I refrained from telling anyone about the extent of danger I had encountered and the volatile point of mentality I had reached, especially my mom.

I hung up the phone after the ecstatic conversations with everyone. I then debated my next move. Maybe I would find a church to pay tribute to my fortune.

I decided to deal with the boat first. After some legwork, I found a boat slip in the Ala Wai Harbor in Waikiki and began pulling the boat apart to dry her out. I laid everything out on the deck and went in with a hose. The deck looked like a yard sale. This arduous process went on for days.

In between the boat work, I meandered around the city in a dream-state. I was nothing more than a helpless fish out-of-water. I landed in a concrete jungle unable to breathe. I had a strange feeling as if I was roving around on a cloud after slipping through the fingers of tragedy. I was beginning to believe my thoughts had changed forever. If you think crazy once, you'll never think straight again.

I was walking back to my boat one day after eating lunch when I ran into a sailor I had met in Tahiti. He was a friend of the guys who were sending us the weather reports via single side-band radio while we were at sea. They wanted to throw a party in my honor for a successful, single-handed mission from Tahiti to Hawaii. I was flattered. I told him I would find a way over to the harbor somehow.

I got a ride over to the Ko Olina Marina the next evening. They invited me onto their large sailboat and offered me hors d'oeuvres and some expensive Scotch. I happily accepted. I was introduced to the two weather guys. My demeanor changed. Sarcastically angry, I said, "So *you* were the ones giving me those bad reports?"

One of them shrugged and said, "That's what you get for trying to sail to Hawaii in the winter time, Bub."

"I guess you're right," I said. "But why the hell did you claim day after day the weather was going to lighten up?"

"Hey, we were just relaying the weather, not predicting it."

"I have a hard time believing it was false day after day. I'd rather have been told it was going to be bad to prepare myself." We all shrugged and I concluded, "Well, I made it."

A few of the ladies shook their heads in disbelief. Some the men toasted to my arrival after such a tenacious odyssey.

I met an eccentric couple at the party that were close to my age and owned a sailboat in the Ko Olina Marina.

The guy said, "Name's Shurd." He looked at me as if we had met somewhere before.

"Excuse me," I said.

He used a fake country drawl, "Shurd, like bird, word, turd. And this here's the better half, Jane."

Shurd was around five-ten, one hundred and eighty pounds, thick-boned, light complexion, and a shaved head. His wife Jane was a beautiful redhead from South Africa who gave off the persona of a Southern Belle with a foreign accent. She was slender, graceful and moved about like an ethereal nymph weaving through a golden field of dandelions.

I introduced myself. We shook hands and began chatting about sailing, travel and music. We conversed for a bit, realizing we had similar interests. There was a familiar affinity about them.

Shurd was a Blackhawk helicopter pilot for the army, but the only thing army about Shurd was his silly hairdo. He gave off the persona of a quirky, globetrotting gypsy whose real interests were in music. Shurd enlisted in the army when he was down and out in Germany and in need of cash.

They were the only ones in the party close to my age and we continued chatting. Jane looked at Shurd, then back at me and said, "Say Carson, we're picking up a girlfriend and going downtown for the evening. Would you care to join us?"

I said, "Hmmm, I haven't hit the town yet, except for the harbor pub."

Shurd said, "Be prepared for most anything."

The Upside-Down Tequila Shot

The party was running out of steam and booze. I said thanks to the ones who threw the function in my honor. We left the boat and piled into Shurd's car, heading downtown in search of debauchery.

We picked up a bottle of vodka and spiked two big gulps from 7-11. By the time we got downtown to their friend Katrina's house, a 30 minute drive, Shurd and I had already tanked most of the bottle. We pulled up to her house and Jane went in to fetch Katrina.

They both came out after some time and jumped into the car. We sped off to this college bar named Magoos near the University of Hawaii.

Katrina was a cute and beaming girl from Alaska. She had moved to Hawaii to teach high school chemistry. She was in her late-twenties with long brown hair, brown eyes, a thin body and a nice smile. She had one crooked front tooth that didn't detract from her looks. It gave her a more realistic appearance. We were quickly acquainted before we reached the bar.

We parked and walked into the dive bar Magoos. Half the kids in there must have had fake I.D.'s. The entire place was set up with rows of long cafeteria tables and old classroom chairs. The bar owner must've made a deal with the campus to take all the rejects off their hands. Pitchers of beer and frosty mugs densely packed the tops of all the tables with hardly a spare seat. I felt as though we were entering a campus mess hall where the only thing on the menu was Pabst Blue Ribbon.

I surveyed the brutal mockery of our future intelligence and leaders of the world. I thought to myself, the only thing these people could lead was a beer-bong rally. There were people with beer labels stuck to their foreheads, pimply morons playing drinking games, and staggering meatheads with hungry eyes. I had an odd sense of comfort in this pagan crowd.

We shuffled over towards the bar. I said, "Anyone care to join me in an upside-down tequila shot?"

Jane said, "What's that?"

I said, "That's where you put a tequila shot on the ground next to the bar and do a handstand in front of the shot. You have to balance on one hand while taking the other hand and pouring the tequila down your throat upside-down."

I had no takers, except for this nerdy looking fellow in bifocals standing at the bar who over-heard the conversation. He gave me the thumbs up and said in an overzealous manner, "Yeah, sounds ahahahawesome. I'm in. But, ah, you do the first one."

I ordered the shot and placed it on the ground two feet away from the bar. I looked around and did a handstand up against the bar next to the shot. The impatient bartender was standing right there trying to give a large order of drinks to the cocktail waitress. This wasn't an ordinary bartender. She was a butch-haired beast. She probably got hired because the owner was too scared to say no.

As I was upside-down doing the one-armed shot, she started yelling for her two bouncers. I got back to my feet after a sloppy-but-successful mission and two rock heads were hovering over me ready to throw me out of the bar. One had slicked back hair resembling Rudolph Valentino from the 1920's and the other had a curly red bouffant.

They both grabbed me and Rudolph said, "Alright buddy, looks like you've had one too many."

"Wait a minute fellows," I said.

With no idea what I was going to say next, I wanted to reason with them. I knew I only had a five-second window of opportunity. My brain was furiously probing for the right words. I blurted, "You gentlemen have perceptibly misconstrued the situation at hand. Anyone who can perfunctorily execute a prodigious feat of this nature can *not* be that drunk."

I tried to confuse them with words. It stumped them. They looked at each other like two referees making a split-second call. They proceeded with their extracting-of-a-derelict exercise. They rushed me out the front door and pushed me out onto the sidewalk.

I was sitting on the sidewalk outside the bar, mocking the bouncers. Shurd came outside, pulled me off the ground, and put his arm around me. Only my true friends will pick me up off the street when I'm a stinking mess.

The girls were appalled at my behavior and opted to stay in the bar. Shurd carried me off to another bar. We staggered down the street to this bar called Anna Bananas.

We walked up with our arms around each, strictly for stability. Two drunks are more stable than one. Either of us could have fallen off the sidewalk walking alone, but together we just bounced off each other synergistically.

I was slurring my words and making random proclamations. I mumbled, "You know, Nietzsche once said, Insanity in individuals is something rare—but in groups, parties, nations, and epochs it is the rule."

Shurd just looked at me from three inches away as though I was making up that monkeyshine. We tried to regain our composure, undraping our arms from each other as we approached the bouncer at the door to the bar. He let us in. He must've been conditioned to drunk college kids.

We lumbered up the dim-lit stairs and headed for the crowded bar. I needed to pound some drinks to get some blood flowing to my brain and wake up. Why is it when you're already loaded, you convince yourself that more booze will pull you out of your drunken stupor?

We ordered a couple of Long Island Iced Teas and joined in the music of a live reggae band named "Ookla the Mok". I began dancing around like a baby in diapers with crud-in-the-bucket.

The girls showed up after awhile and got out on the dance floor. They seemed to be avoiding me. Occasionally they peered over at me with shocking stares.

Shurd walked up to me on the dance floor and tried to introduce me to this cute girl. I started mumbling something to her with a bad case of fat tongue*. She just smiled, snickered and walked away. I turned to Shurd with a wounded rabbit look on my face. He stared at me in befuddlement and walked off shaking his head.

We closed the place down and the bouncers politely extracted us. We all retired to the car. Then the question arose, who was going to drive? Jane volunteered to drive us to Katrina's house where we could crash for the night. We piled into the car and took off, happy that someone was going to drive. I was too tired to be concerned about our safety.

After about thirty minutes of driving in circles, which normally would've taken no more than five, we arrived alive. Everyone went inside to pass out. I lied down in the front lawn under the stars to get some fresh air. I was lying on my back in the cool grass with my head spinning. The entire sky revolved around me 360 degrees, and then it would stop and repeat the same 360-spin repeatedly. It's not a continuous spin like a merry-go-round. I sat up, puked a few times and passed out.

I woke up damp in the front lawn. It must've rained while I was asleep. It was still dark, so I crept inside Katrina's place and found a spare piece of ground to curl up on and slipped into a dizzy dream.

---

* fat tongue = unable to use normal speech due to a swollen tongue from an over-abundance of alcohol

Marooned on the Isle of Lava

I woke up the next day dehydrated. I vaguely remembered having the water dreams again, where I'm at a water fountain drinking for ten solid minutes. Then I find myself dreaming of guzzling cold pitchers of water and eventually large spectacles like Niagara Falls and I'm dog paddling around in the pools at the bottom of the waterfall lapping it all up.

I crept to the kitchen and began consuming multiple glasses of bad tap water. I stepped over my comatose friends and found the bathroom—stripped naked and hopped in the shower. I sat in there for twenty minutes, leaning up against the wall. I was convinced I could re-hydrate myself through osmosis. I began gulping more water from the showerhead. It wasn't working—my head still felt as though the LA Kings had used it as a hockey puck.

The others gradually woke up after I got out of the shower. I said, "So what the hell happened to me last night?"

They all smirked and stared in different directions. Shurd said, "Well, it all went downhill after that upside-down tequila shot." Nobody made any comments after that.

We all got ourselves together and went out for breakfast. There was a black cloud over the breakfast table. Conversation was undistinguishable and everyone resigned to just eating some food and trying to keep it down.

After breakfast, they returned me to my boat. I figured I'd punish myself and went to work on the boat with the hangover. I continued drying out the interior of the saturated boat. I took an inventory of everything broken and figured it would cost me about five grand in repairs. Numbers began rolling around in my head and I started talking to myself again.

I muttered, "Let's see Tahiti to Hawaii, Tahiti to Hawaii, one month of getting the shit kicked out of me and it cost me five grand. Ok five grand; I could have flown first class sipping cocktails, watching a movie in six hours time for five hundred."

All sailboats are *snail*boats that will cost you ten times as much to get your teeth kicked in. Although, I still had a voracious desire to sail the seas, but not for awhile.

I spent weeks repairing the boat and bought various expensive items including a new headsail, GPS, autopilot, and a laptop computer to install software with all the nautical charts of the South Pacific. Bills were stacking up and I needed a job.

I searched all the popular big bars and restaurants for a position but had no luck. After days of determination, I ended up with two jobs. Building houses and building boats, a couple of *easy* jobs.

After days of working out a system, I would get off work at the construction site at three and then head over to the docks, only to start work on the boats until dark and on the weekends. I was working seven days a week for months, trying to get enough money to get back to the South Pacific and true paradise. Some sailors make it to Hawaii after a frightening journey from the mainland and sell their boats. All I could think about was my time in Tahiti. I wanted to relive that experience.

I pulled the boat out of the water in a local boat yard. I needed to repair the rudderpost leak with fiberglass. I also needed to repair the rudder where I went aground in Tahiti.

Once I had her out of the water, I sanded down the bottom to apply the new anti-fouling paint. I came upon a mysterious crack in the hull on the port side, ten feet back from the bow. It started near the waterline and migrated down. I used a grinder to expose the crack. As I moved down the crack, I reached a length of two feet and started to worry. I kept moving down the crack finally reaching the end. It was a vertical crack over four feet long and fractured completely through the hull. This was definitely part of the leak. I had a serious structural issue and needed to assess the damage. I could not understand why the crack was on the port side of the boat. I took most of the waves on the starboard side.

I talked to some professional boat builders in the boatyard. They claimed it must've been a case of "oil-canning", where the lee side of the boat ends up with a fracture from the glass flexing in between structural bulkheads. They said I was lucky the whole bow didn't break off.

I purchased five hundred dollars in Nytex fiberglass and epoxy. I repaired the exterior crack with eight layers of glass and beefed up the entire bow past the vertical crack with a quarter-inch of glass on the interior.

After the repair, I felt as though the bow was bulletproof and could ram a floating telephone pole. I moved onto repairing the rudderpost and the reef crack on the bottom of the rudder. I finished all the repairs and put three layers of paint on the bottom. We lowered her back in the water and she didn't leak a drop.

Many months slipped by and I moved the boat to the Ko Olina Marina on the southwest side of Oahu. I needed to finish the boat repairs and get ready to head back out on the high seas after being on land for over a year. I was tired of living in the heart of hedonism in Waikiki.

I met a sailing girl named Misty in the marina. She owned a sailboat a few slips down from the *Bula*. We had gotten to know each other in passing and chatted about sailing and surfing. I had voiced to her that I might be interested in having a crewmember with me for the trip south. She seemed interested in cruising with me to the South Pacific. I vividly remembered the loneliness during my trip from Tahiti. I was tired of single-handing. I wasn't out to set any records or be a hero. So, I invited her along for the journey south. She gladly accepted.

She was tall with sandy blonde hair, mid-twenties, on the skinny side and crazy blue eyes. She always had a certain wide-eyed look of intensity. We were just friends and I wasn't planning on anything more than that.

The *Bula* was in better shape than when I left San Diego. My bank account was looking good and I was ready to get back to the South Pacific. The time for departure had arrived. Misty and I spent an entire day provisioning the boat. We loaded it down with two months of food supplies. We then went down to the customs office and checked out of the country.

Devolution

We cast off from the dock and began our mission on a beautiful sunny day. The wind was blowing hard through the marina. I nearly sideswiped a couple of boats as I reversed out of the slip. Backing up a sailboat is about as predictable as backing up a horse. You never know which way the ass is going to swing.

It was a rough exit but we made it out safe. We didn't need any setbacks. I was set free to the sea again after being a landlubber*.

We raised the sails and set off into the deep. The new headsail looked beautiful and the boat sped away as if it knew the way south. I was happy to leave Hawaii, but I was sad to leave the friends I had made. Now, I just wanted to get south of the equator in search of any place where they didn't speak more than ten words of English.

Everything down below, that wasn't stowed properly, was now finding a new location. I've soaked various National Geographic magazines in the toilet after forgetting to move them off the bathroom counter before sailing. Quite often, they soar off the counter and a direct shot into the toilet. It usually takes about

---

* landlubber = lubber was an old English word for a big, lumbering, clumsy person, and this term was aimed at those persons on ship who were not very skilled or at ease with ship life, as if to say, "You were no better on the land"

three days of drying before I can read them again. When I finish reading them, I trade them to other sailors for new material. They always say something like, "Oh, did you leave these out in the rain?"

I nod and reply, "Yep."

After the sorting-out process, then comes the devolution into a Cro-Magnon. This is the transition from walking and talking like a modern day Homo sapiens to staggering, crawling and banging your head on most everything. Speech becomes cave-like, dwindling down to a mumble or a grunt.

The nesting routine comes next. I had to wedge myself into a corner to avoid flying across the cabin. After I'd found my spot and locked in, next came the long lethargic stare off into the blue.

Palmyra was our first stop. I conservatively figured about eight days. Any cruiser knows—if you are going offshore, you have to factor in the forever theory. Anything could happen out there and it may take you forever to get there.

Sailing isn't like a plane flight with the time calculated down to the minute. I'd like to hear a stewardess on a small sailboat announce the ETA. Over the intercom, she would say, "We have a wind speed of 25 knots from the northeast and a boat speed of seven knots. Our ETA should be around seven days if we're doing good or twice that if we're doing badly."

The longer the passage, the more my interests turn strictly to catching fish and eating them. Yes, I love to eat on passages, but the trick is cooking. Cooking at sea is not easy. Some people wear a harness and clip into the stove with a carabiner similar to a rock climber. Sound crazy? I think it's crazy not to. My stove didn't have that capability. I have to do the three-point stance. When you are busy using your hands for cooking, you have to spread your feet as wide apart as possible and throw a hip into the counter. This goes back to my devolution theory.

I'm standing in the kitchen, juggling pots and pans and wondering if my half-cooked meal is going to end up on the ceiling or the floor. I dodged a flying pot that dislodged itself from the clamping device on the stove and hit the floor so hard that the top blew off and part of my spaghetti hit the ceiling. I still ate it, though I had to remove a few hairs.

BUZZZZZZ. "FISH ON," I yelled and ran to the cockpit.

I tried slowing down the reel by tightening the drag. Then I turned the boat into the wind to slow the boat down. I furled the headsail, tightened down the mainsheet, and grabbed the gaff. I jumped back there amongst all the equipment mounted to the stern. While I was reeling in the fish, I had to keep the end of the fishing pole out of the spinning wind generator. I also had to keep the fishing line clear of the wind-vane sticking into the water. Next, I carefully passed the rod around the backstay to the starboard side; all the while making sure the boat was pointed into the wind. I grabbed the gaff with one hand while holding the pole in the other and gaffed the fish. I heaved the fish into the cockpit over the lifelines. Then I located the winch handle and hammered it over the head.

I laughed at my good fortune. I filleted the fish and packed the freezer. I would have to eat the whole thing myself over the next few days. Misty was a vegetarian.

The days crept by with unbelievable sunsets and a full moon that lit up the night. I sat in the cockpit at night and played my guitar under the full moon. The songs got pretty weird at one point. It was such a strange place to be in the middle of the ocean at night, my mind was on its on journey.

The afternoon of the seventh day, I finally spotted land. I yelled, "MISTY . . . LAND HO."

She ran up top-deck and I pointed out the tops of some palm trees on the horizon. I could only see them on the crest of a large swell.

She yelled, "LAND." Then she turned and gave me a low five. She was playing it cool, trying to act a little less excited, but I knew.

It was getting late in the day and I wanted to get through the pass before dark. The winds had changed from northeast to southeast. We were at latitude seven-degrees north. The southeast trade winds were blowing up from the southern hemisphere. Trade winds occasionally cross over the equator by ten degrees or more.

The southeast winds were making progress toward the island tough. Bula was bucking straight into the wind and seas. I calculated I needed an extra two knots of speed in order to make it through the pass before sundown. I started the engine and began motor sailing. I normally run the engine at 1800-RPMs, though it wasn't giving Bula enough speed, so I bumped it up to 2200. That gave us what was needed. At a speed of six knots, I estimated two hours to the pass.

The familiar smell of land reached the boat and I turned to inhale that sweet sticky aroma that is only common in the South Pacific. It's a mixture of salty ocean air, lush humid jungle and a hint of fish. It strangely smells like sex.

The island rose out of the deep sea to greet us. It was hard to believe such a tiny island existed. Surprisingly, the mighty ocean had not extinguished it. Nonetheless, it was shelter from the wrath of the sea. I dreamed of anchoring in a jade green lagoon in placid waters, barbequing coconut crabs.

We motor-sailed closer to the island and the motor began sputtering. I scrambled to the cockpit to find out the problem. The engine slowly died. I looked at the temperature gauge. At first, I thought I was reading it wrong. It was up to 260 degrees Fahrenheit. "What happened?" I muttered to myself. I had no time to worry about that. I had to utilize my sails to get me through the tight pass before dark.

As I was surveying the situation down below, I heard Misty yell something from the cockpit.

"WHAT?" I yelled back.

She was hand steering the boat and said, "I just saw waves breaking on the reef 100 yards off the port bow."

"We are two miles north of the island and the charts show the reefs extend only a mile offshore. Are you sure it wasn't just a wind wave?"

"It looked like reef waves."

"Maybe head away from the island a bit."

I was still standing down below when I looked up and saw Misty's face. I saw the same stare on my brother's face before we ran aground in Tahiti. I didn't want to register the inescapable idea. Unable to speak, she stared into the water and pointed.

She finally found the words and yelled, "REEF." Before the words even left her lips, I was airborne, leaping into the cockpit. I grabbed the helm, whipped the boat to starboard away from the reef and into the wind to slow us down.

I spun the wheel and *SMASH*. We collided into the reef, sending both of us flying off our feet. The *Bula* bounced over it and continued at a much slower pace. We kept waiting for the next explosion as we moved slower through the shallow waters. The water was so clear it seemed as though the reef was just under the surface. I was surprised we were still moving.

The boat slowly crept along sailing away from the reef. After a few minutes, I felt confident we had escaped. I said to Misty, "Take the helm." She grabbed the wheel and I darted down below to check for any leaks in the bilge. I threw open the floorboards and stared into the bilge. I was talking to myself, "No apparent leaks, that's odd. We slammed that reef hard enough to knock over a dump truck." I heard enough reef crunching under the boat to dismantle the keel. I looked up at Misty and said, "Strange, no leaks."

The collision probably mangled the keel to the point of impeding smooth forward movement. We would have to find the closest island that had the means to repair it. The closest island to do any major repairs was Hawaii or Samoa, both a two-week sail. I'd worry about it after I got safely through the pass before dark.

I hailed the island on the VHF, "Palmyra . . . Palmyra this is sailing vessel *Bula*, do you copy?"

After a long pause, there was a crackling response, "This is Palmyra, please go ahead."

"Hello, this is sailing vessel *Bula*, flying an American flag. I'm approaching your island from the northwest and requesting permission to enter the pass."

"Permission granted," a kind female voice said. "There are three other boats in the lagoon. We will assist you in finding a place to anchor away from the fragile coral. The lagoon is a protected marine sanctuary."

"Thank you very much. I also have a bit of an issue. My engine has overheated and I'm wondering if it is possible to sail through the pass."

"Please stand by."

After a few minutes, a man came on the radio. In a laconic manner, he said, "Sailing vessel *Bula*. My name is Matt. I'm the caretaker of the island. Can I help you?"

I explained my predicament. He said, "It's getting dark so we have to work fast. I'll meet you at the entrance to the pass in my skiff and try to tow you into the lagoon."

"Thank you very much for the help," I said.

Ten minutes later, I saw his white skiff motoring through the pass and we sailed towards him. As we approached, I was able to get the engine started again because the temperature had dropped. I told him the engine was presently working. He turned the skiff and told me to follow him closely.

Five minutes later, the engine overheated again. I informed him on the VHF. He then came around the boat, tied off to the bow and towed us the rest of the way into the lagoon. He towed us over to a spot and told me to anchor there for the night. He'd move us in the morning. It was pitch black at that point and I would not have been able to do it without him.

Matt's wife was onboard the boat as well for help. After I dropped the hook, they said to us, "Welcome to Palmyra."

I said, "Thank you. It wasn't easy. We endured seven long days from Hawaii without too many problems. Then we get within two and a half miles from the island, the engine dies and we ran aground. That's some greeting."

Matt said, "You're one of the lucky ones. That reef has taken many boats. The charts for this area haven't been updated since the 1800's. They're about a mile off."

I painfully laughed. "Well that explains everything. We were a mile north of where the reef was located, according to the chart. I'll have to check out the damage tomorrow. At least we're not sinking."

"Well, you two should get some sleep and we'll help you find a new anchorage in the morning," Matt's wife said.

I said, "Wait a minute." I ran down below and grabbed a bag of frozen salmon, a six-pack of Hawaiian beer and a bottle of champagne. I came up top-deck. "You like salmon?"

Matt said, "Wow, we don't get salmon down in these parts."

I handed them the care package. "Thanks again for your help."

They took the gifts and Matt's wife said, "Hey, you don't have to give us your bottle of champagne. Don't you want to save that for when you cross the equator?"

"Nah, we've got plenty more," I said. They all said thanks and motored off in the skiff.

Misty and I sat on the deck of the boat staring at the millions of stars overhead. Seabirds were squawking their last salute to the day before retiring to their roosts. We were enjoying sitting still for the first time in a week. Palms enveloped us on all sides of the protected lagoon. The feeling of comfort returned to me. The humidity was thick inside the sanctuary and the air was heavy with the smell of fertility. An occasional fish jumped through the surface and splashed back into the calm waters. There were no lights visible except for one sailboat anchored nearby.

We cooked up a big feast, had a few cold Guinness stouts in celebration and retired to our bunks. I never sleep as hard as at the end of a long crossing.

The Forgotten Isle of the Purple People Eater

I crawled out of bed as stiff as cold oatmeal. Misty had already been up for hours. I didn't understand that girl. She never slept. She was the best crewmember anyone could have. She cooked, cleaned, never got seasick, and only slept a few hours a night. I thought of all the things I could get done if I only slept three hours a night. Nah, I liked to sleep.

Matt motored over in his skiff to help us find a better spot to anchor in the lagoon away from the protected areas. I was anxious, yet scared, to see the bottom of the boat.

After we anchored, I strapped-on a mask and snorkel and dove over the side to survey the damage. I swam down to the bottom of the boat and studied the keel. There was nothing more than a long, thin gouge out of the solid lead keel about five feet long and an inch deep. I couldn't believe it. I kept circling the boat looking for more damage, but there was none. The *Bula* was tougher than I thought. I came up and ecstatically told them of my findings.

After the fortunate results, we went ashore. Matt showed us the Palmyra Yacht Club. It consisted of four rusty chairs, an old tube TV, a sunken bar (sunken from dilapidation), and a new ping-pong table.

Admiralty flags covered the walls from many countries and yacht clubs. Graffiti peppered every corner with long quotes, poems, drawings, names, dates, and sea-lore. I found an untouched area on a wall to put my two bits of the good ship *Bula*.

We went exploring the island after visiting the yacht club. We found a 34-foot Beneteau shipwrecked on the beach close to the side of the island where we ran aground. That could've been us.

We wandered through the thick jungle and came upon the wreckage of an old WWII plane. Florid vines and green foliage had a grasp around the metal fuselage as if they were trying to pull it back into the ground.

We stumbled upon our first coconut crab. These rare crabs are found on tropical islands near the equator. It was purple and the size of a basketball. It had the movements of an android. It looked like something a cryptozoologist had created for Hollywood. I learned they are the best tasting crabs in the world. Their meat is sweet because they live on coconuts.

The mutant alien looked hostile. Maybe it was tired of the same old diet. It viciously stared at me with beady eyes, extending-out, surveying me in a forensic scrutiny. It had ferocious claws, the size of my own hands. I slowly backed away and cautiously crept through the jungle.

After motoring back to the boat for lunch, it was so hot I needed to go for a swim to cool down from the equatorial heat. I dove in the clear water of the lagoon. I had my eyes open underwater and spotted a couple of dark figures moving under the boat. I didn't linger around too long in the water and swam back to the swim ladder. After boarding the boat I looked over the side to see two sharks swimming just underneath me. I stared at them and a third and fourth joined them in their search for food. I started talking to myself, "I can't even go swimming. They have me boat-locked. First the jungle and now the sea."

We ate lunch and Matt hailed us on the radio. He was going to take a group of sailors on his skiff outside the pass to go snorkeling on the reef. He asked if we wanted to go. I looked at

Misty, she gave me a positive nod, and I said, "Sure, we'd love to go."

"OK then, get your gear together and meet us at the small dock in half-an-hour," Matt said.

"See ya there."

We motored over in the donkey, watching the sharks under the boat. I was wondering if they had ever attacked a rubber dingy before. I put my feet up on the top of the bench seat, just in case. The small outboard engine died. I pulled and pulled on the starting cord and finally gave up. This was the beginning of a Jaws movie. Luckily, we had oars.

As we paddled the rest of the way, we carefully scanned below. One shark tooth to that rubber inflatable and we'd be finished.

We pulled up alongside the small dock. There was an older man, waist deep in the lagoon with two manta rays frolicking about in the shallows. The mantas had about an eight-foot wingspan and were doing underwater loops and acrobatics around the guy's legs. He caressed the back of one with his hand as it flapped its wings on the surface in response. They were very friendly and seemed to love the attention.

We boarded the skiff with Matt and his wife, a marine biologist from Hawaii, a millionaire on vacation, an older couple off another sailboat, and Misty and me.

Palmyra, owned by the Nature Conservancy, is a unique island that receives very few visitors. There are only three possible ways to visit the island. A biologist sent to do research. Someone with a lot of money who gives the Nature Conservancy mega bucks as a tax write-off, or the lucky cruiser who sails there from distant lands. They allow cruisers to anchor their boats up to ten days in designated areas of the lagoon.

We motored out of the pass, watching flocks of blue-footed boobies flying in from the sea. They were trying to land in the trees that lined the shore. Boobies are terrible at landing. They spend most of their lives flying out at sea and never get the practice. It's a spectacle to watch these big birds soar into shore, pull out their landing gear and go slamming into a mess of tree branches. The wild-eyed bird goes tumbling upside-down into the foliage. Sometimes they try to land on the beach, usually misjudging their speed. The second their feet hit the ground they summersault beak-first into the sand.

We got outside the pass, motored around to the west side and tied the boat off to a mooring buoy. We put on our snorkel gear and entered the warm turquoise waters. The clarity and colors ignited my visual sensory. The tropical fish swarmed us. They were very interested in us. Palmyra has had very little contact with the outside world since WWII. There were schools of Moorish idols, multicolored parrotfish, stripped convicts, sea turtles, octopus, jellyfish and plenty of sharks. I followed some of the larger fish, knowing I could've easily speared them for lunch had it not been a protected marine reserve.

After a couple of hours, everyone got back onboard and we untied the bowline and motored towards the lagoon. As we re-entered the pass, every fifty feet or so, we would spot a massive manta ray then a sea turtle then a large shark. The ocean definitely owned this tiny outcropping on the equator.

Misty and I spent five days hanging out on Palmyra getting to know the other cruisers, biologists and caretakers. Everyone felt lucky to have the chance to spend time on this esoteric outpost.

Danger Island

The weather was looking favorable and we decided to head out that day for our first destination in the South Pacific . . . Samoa. It was 1300 nautical miles, roughly eight days if the winds were conducive.

We said our goodbyes, loaded the donkey onto the deck, pulled the anchor and sailed out of the pass. As we sailed past the last piece of land, there were flocks of seabirds flying in and out of the trees. I spotted one last booby mishap. It was high in a tree hanging-on upside-down with its wings spread wide. It was trying to right itself in a frenzy, twisting back and forth. It finally lost its grip, fell a few feet bouncing off a couple of limbs and latched onto a branch safely. I felt sorry for the fuzzy fellow.

We motored out of the pass, pulled all the sails up and I set out the fishing lines. It was a bright clear day with the winds blowing from the southeast at 15 knots. If only it could've been like that everyday. We settled into our normal lethargic routines, reading or snoozing in the cockpit under the shade of the bimini.

The day was long and hot as we sailed closer to the equator. As the sun was setting, it turned the entire sky a glorious pink. Clouds near the horizon turned fire red. Puffy purple clouds drifted overhead and gained intensity. The closer you get to the equator, the more spectacular the sunsets. It's caused by the humidity and light scattering through particles in the air. It makes for a natural phenomenon in the sky. Some evenings, I couldn't resist putting on Pink Floyd's album "Dark Side of the Moon".

The following day, we hit the doldrums. The wind dwindled down to nothing and the temperatures escalated. There was just enough wind to keep the boat moving. We had too much distance left to start up the engine. We continued to creep along in the stifling heat, sailing straight into Satan's barbeque. I was having visions that the water was on fire and we were sailing through the flames of hell.

The next day the wind completely died. We sat there with the sails flapping back and forth. The boat swayed erratically from the ocean swell. It was nerve racking, so we pulled the sails down and sat there bare-poled, rocking back and forth.

After 15 hours of no wind, I was hallucinating from the heat. I'm not sure what's worse, no wind or too much wind? I think they share a fine line of insanity. In one situation, I'd be shitting my pants, thinking I was going to die. And the other, I'd be pissing on my toes thinking I could fly.

I sat on the side-rail of the boat with my legs dangling over the side, staring long into the blue abyss. I got the spookiest feeling it was staring right back into me. I wanted to jump over the side and go for a cool swim. I looked over the side at the enticing water and finally dove in. I swam down ten feet and opened my eyes to a vast sight. We were out in the middle of the Pacific, thousands of miles from land and floating in ten thousand feet of water. I was looking into infinity. All I could think about was something enormous coming straight up from the bottom to engulf me. I got back on the boat.

I wondered how long we could be stuck in the doldrums. Days? Weeks? I couldn't take it any longer. Something had to happen, soon.

The setting sun produced a magnificence of colors that took our minds off the present. The temperatures thankfully dropped and Misty decided to cook up a vegetarian meal. She pulled out a box of veggie ribs.

I stared at the box and asked, "What the hell are veggie ribs? There's no such thing as veggie ribs. You can't have *ribs* if you don't have a *carcass*."

"Well it's not actually ribs," she said. "I think you have to form the ribs yourself."

"So, we're eating playdough? Why don't you just shape miniature cows and fry them up? If you're a vegetarian, then what's with the fetish of eating something that looks like meat?"

Misty shrugged and pulled out the contents of the mystery box. It was nothing but a bag of soybean mash and a packet of barbeque sauce.

I faded out of the conversation. "Ribs, yeah right. Who in the world . . . ?"

I hadn't caught a fish since Palmyra, which was adding to my madness. I was trolling two fishing lines with no luck. I changed lures every few hours. I staggered the trolling lures ten to twenty feet apart. I even tried rubbing food products on the lures for smell. I thought about bottom fishing. I would need about 10,000 feet of line. I could only imagine the sci-fi mongoloid I would pull-up from the bottom. It would implode from the pressure before I got it halfway to the surface. I would end up with nothing but blue fish lips.

We woke up the next day to an ocean so still God could've taken a crap from heaven and seen his own ass in the reflection. I tried to divert my thoughts to boat repairs. If you've ever owned a boat, you know there's never a lack of them.

I launched into various electrical issues until it got too hot to stay down below. I gave up and went out to the cockpit to lay my head down on a hot pillow. My head was no longer swelling; it was now shrinking from dehydration. We had no cool water onboard and I had no desire to drink warm water. I had myself a bona-fide, Peruvian shrunken head.

We had reached 24 hours without a puff of wind. I started the engine to motor for a couple of hours, if anything to create a slight breeze.

Three hours later, we picked up a small breeze. We killed the engine and pulled up both sails. We were only moving along at one knot, but it was a towrope out of hell. It lasted about two hours and then died. We pulled the sails down again and sat there with Satan snickering at us.

I stood on the stern, dumping multiple buckets of seawater on my head. The water was only slightly cooler than the air. I repeated the process hourly.

A slow trickle of wind would come and visit us about every fifth hour. It would only hang around for an hour or two and then disappear. This continued for the next day until we crossed the equator.

There is a tradition among sailors to drink champagne in celebration of crossing the equator. This was my third time to cross the equator on *Bula* and never once did I feel like drinking champagne. I'm not a fan of champagne, but I'll drink it on certain occasions like wedding receptions, birthday parties, anniversaries—you know, happy times. It's hard to be happy sitting still with no wind in a hundred degree heat.

It took us three splendid days to get through the doldrums. We picked up the southeast trades around two-degrees latitude south. At least we were moving again. They increased with strength and we clipped along towards Pago Pago, pronounced "Pango Pango".

I was trolling my best lures with no luck. Maybe the surface was too hot for fish. They were probably down deeper where it was cool. I wanted to be down deeper.

The days passed at a more enjoyable pace, as we sailed into the southern hemisphere. However, the winds never cooperated with us. They continued to blow straight out of the south. It was sending us too far west to make Pago Pago.

That night while plotting our route, I realized we were on a dead-set course with some place called Danger Island. It's the most western island in the Cook Island chain. The name didn't sound too comforting when negotiating a sailing route past it. I found some information about the island in an old book on the South Pacific. It gained its name from the powerful currents near the island.

I wasn't in the mood for playing any games of chicken or chance, so I opted to sail to the west of it. We would pass it sometime around two in the morning. Two a.m. was not a great time to be dodging an island. This was the time when I was on my watch in the cockpit, dead asleep.

I decided to stay conscious that night. I checked the GPS about every hour. Every time I checked it, we would be back on a collision course with the island. I adjusted the wind-vane to steer us away from the island, and again the winds would turn us back into the same direction. It was confusing. The winds must've been veering, or maybe it was that fierce current mentioned in the book. Either way, I couldn't seem to get away from that stinking island. According to the GPS, we were fairly close to it, but it was a cloudy, moonless night and I couldn't see a thing. We luckily passed it to the west, according to the chart. I never got a glimpse of that mysterious island. We continued charging south to Pago Pago.

Muzzy

Pago Pago stood before us like a green leviathan slowly rising out of the depths. The sun rose, igniting the rippled mountain peaks into a beautiful splendor. My plan of eight days had turned into eleven due to the doldrums.

I got the fishing lines out, hoping for anything. I would've been happy to catch some seaweed, anything to hear the buzz of the drag and get my adrenaline going. That sound became an addiction.

We were about 15 miles out when it hit. *BUZZZZZZ* . . . I shouted, "FISH ON."

Misty whipped the boat into the wind, and I pounced on the rod. She furled the headsail in and I continued reeling. The fish busted through the surface and did a tail-walk. It was a mahi-mahi. "Quick grab the gaff," I said.

She put the gaff in the cockpit and kept the boat moving at a slow pace into the wind. I got the fish alongside and handed the rod to Misty. I gaffed it in its side and hauled it into the cockpit. It danced around on the floor and I located the winch handle and hammered it over the head. "FINALLY." I yelled.

"Yeah, nice one," Misty said with a smile, only to appease me.

With crazy eyes, I said, "ELEVEN DAYS . . . and only ONE FISH. That's a pretty bad record."

The mahi-mahi was probably 15 pounds and was plenty for me. I wondered what poor Misty, the vegetarian, thought of the whole episode of dragging a healthy organism aboard, beating it over the head, filleting it up on deck and washing all the blood back into the sea.

I filleted it up, not bothering to turn-on the freezer. I was going to cook the whole thing and eat as much as possible. I was sick of eating that veggie meat she was feeding me. It was creating a gastric phenomenon. I could've melted a Mexican mule with that veggie gas.

We pulled into the steep-walled bay of Pago Pago. This bay inlet is the most protected in the South Pacific islands. It was a glorious paradise surrounded on all sides by lush green mountains cascading out of the heavens. However, it had a shipping wharf and a smelly tuna factory.

We pulled up to the quarantine dock, tied off and hailed the harbormaster. He sent for the customs agent to come down and check us into the country of Pago Pago, better known as American Samoa. It was easy checking in as an American. We were still charged a fat fee.

We untied the boat from the dock and motored away from shore. We anchored deep in the bay and began cleaning up the *Bula* after the long passage.

We took the inflatable to shore and met a young fellow at the dock named Muzzy from New Zealand. He was short and stocky with a buzzed haircut. Tattoos covered his upper body. He was wearing a pair of baggy surf trunks that nearly reached his ankles.

He introduced himself, "Hey there mate, name's Muzzy."

I wasn't sure I got his name right. I said, "Mozzie, short for mosquito?"

He said, "No mate—Muzzy," then he spelled it out. "M, u, zed, zed, y. It's a nickname for Murry where I come from."

"Oh, it must've been your accent that threw me off."

He was crewing on a 60-foot motor yacht from New Zealand with an old rich couple that was driving him insane. He said, "It's nice to meet some people my own age for a change."

"There's not too many of us out here," I said. "Most of the cruisers are retired couples. I just retired early. The only difference is, they've got a couple-hundred thousand in the bank and I've got a couple *thousand*."

Muzzy was a surfer and we decided to grab our boards and search for some waves that day. The three of us squeezed our boards onto a local bus and circled the south shore in search of any reef pass with an inviting wave.

It was interesting to see how people lived on a South Pacific island that was politically an American territory. Years ago, I spent a month on Western Samoa and recognized a major difference. In my opinion, the people on American Samoa lacked respect for their island. It was a beautiful paradise with trash lying about and a general sense of indifference.

We sat on the bus, staring out the window, intent on finding some secret surf break all to ourselves. The trade winds blew across the reefs, creating an onshore flow, making the surf conditions dismal.

Unsuccessful, we returned to town on the bus and found a local restaurant on the waterfront for some food and beers. We sat down at a weathered table on the porch near the water. Muzzy explained to us that he was sick of the captain's old lady.

He said, "Mate, the wench is working me into the ground. She's complaining about fingerprints on the dining room table. I'm just waiting on a job position at a surf camp in Fiji. It's coming available in the next month. I should be getting an email from the camp owner any day now. When I get that email, I'm off that slave ship and on a plane for Fiji."

Muzzy and I got a local platter of meat and rice. The meat was some unusual pork product that Misty was staring at with a suspicious eye. She got vegetables over rice.

Muzzy got up to use the toilet. I spoke to Misty while he was gone, "This Muzzy character seems like an alright fellow. What do you say we invite him along to sail with us to Tonga? You're flying back to Hawaii soon and I could use the company when I sail on to Fiji."

She said, "Yeah, sure, he seems like a nice guy."

Misty and I looked at each other and nodded in agreement over inviting him along on the *Bula*.

He returned from the bathroom and sat down. I said, "Hey Muzzy, if you want to get off that stink pot and jump on the *Bula*, we're heading to Tonga where Misty is jumping ship. You can have a free ride to Fiji."

He grinned and said, "Oh yeah?"

"Sure. You know how to sail?"

"I own a 26-foot sloop back home."

"Well alrighty then, what do you reckon mate?"

"I'll have to check with the owners of the boat to see if it's cool if I split. I don't want to leave 'em hanging if they need me help."

"Do whatcha gotta do and let us know. We're heading to Tonga in less than a week."

I briefed Muzzy on the particulars of the *Bula*. I clued him in on the fact that I was kind-of sailing on a budget and couldn't afford all the expensive safety items that most cruising vessels had onboard.

He didn't seem to care and happily said, "You got room for a big surfboard-bag?"

"Yeah, we can just put it front with mine."

"Alright, I'll let ya know as soon as I have a chat with the owners."

I spent the next day buying a new marine battery. One of my boat batteries was slowly dying. I was also searching for a new outboard engine. The sidewinder was pronounced dead. I had two outboards when I left San Diego. The first one was a classic, 1957 Johnson, seven-and-a-half horsepower. It seized on me in Hawaii. I'd gone through two outboards in two months and I couldn't find an outboard in Pago Pago for any less than a grand. I gave up. At least I found a new battery.

Muzzy hailed me on the VHF and said, "Alright mate, I'm in. When should I move my stuff over?"

"Bring it over now if you'd like," I said.

"I'll be over in half-an-hour."

"See ya then."

He brought his board-bag over and heaved it onto the deck. It was the size of a body bag and weighed as much as one. I said, "Did you take the old lady out? You want to dump her offshore?"

He started snickering, moving the limp missile towards the cabin. I said, "Leave it in the cockpit until I chainsaw down a few bulkheads to squeeze 'er in there." He also had a full size backpack stuffed to capacity. I looked at it and jokingly said, "Oh good, you brought a life raft as well." He dragged it onboard.

After he got onboard, he said, "So I began telling Jim, the owner of the boat, I wanted to sail to Fiji with you all."

Jim asked, "Which boat?"

Muzzy pointed and said, "That one over there."

"Are they experienced sailors?"

"I'm not sure?"

"What kind of offshore equipment do they have onboard?"

"I don't think they have much."

"Well, do they have a life raft?"

"No."

"Do they have an SSB?"

"I think it's just a receiver."

"So they cannot transmit in case of an emergency?"

"I guess that's right."

"How about a radar?"

"Nope, no radar."

"Well if nothing else, do they at least have an EPIRB*?"

"Yep. They've got one of those."

"So let me get this straight. You want to move onto a tiny sailboat with a couple of kids, who have no life raft, no SSB, no radar, and you want to sail to Fiji?"

Muzzy had two options, one of which he couldn't take another day of, and the other he figured he might not live too many

---

* EPIRB = 1 : Emergency Position Indicating Radio Beacon 2 : it's a distress signal and when activated this device notifies the U. S. Coast Guard via satellite of your present location anywhere in the world

more days. He didn't care at that point and said in a defeated tone, "Yep."

"Well, it's your life."

After Muzzy finished his story, we all laughed, but I stopped short and thought to myself, were we actually some kind of ship of fools?

I said, "Ah who needs all that crap. They never had it in the olden days. We're all just monkeys with material anyway. We don't need all that technology."

The conversation redirected into going snorkeling in a national park on the north side of the island. Everyone seemed interested and we gathered our gear and headed to shore. We spent the rest of the day exploring the untouched north side of the island.

Deeper into the Kingdom of Tonga

We spent nearly a week in Pago Pago provisioning and doing repairs. We decided to head-out for Tonga. We wanted to disembark before the weekend. According to ancient sea lore, it's taboo to leave on a Friday. If we left on Saturday, the corrupt port captain would charge us double. It was Thursday, so we packed-up, fueled-up, and checked out.

We weighed anchor and motored out of Pago Pago around noon. On our way out of the harbor, Muzzy came to me with a sheepish look on his face and said, "Mate, I've got to tell you something." He looked around for the words. "Every now and then I get a bit seasick."

"What? Now you tell me," I said, acting angry.

He tried to defend himself and said, "Yeah, I got a little ill on the last boat, but I was still able to do all the boat duties." He continued about some story of leaving New Zealand in a storm and he was puking over the side. However, he was on the top-deck securing everything and manning his post. From then on, I was on his case.

We raised the sails and cut the engine as the wind strengthened outside of the harbor. The weather was not looking so good. There were no reports of dangerous storms, but it was rough as we sailed out of the pass into the big swells. The wind was blowing 25 knots and increasing as we sailed further away from the harbor. The sky was black with ominous rainsqualls across the horizon.

The boat was heeling over burying the starboard toe-rail. We were taking waves over the bow. I was trying to steer to the left of this red floating beacon up ahead in the mist. As I approached it, I saw shallow reef underneath the boat. I got worried, gave the wheel to Misty and ran down below to check the local charts. I'd made a mistake. We were to sail to the right of the red beacon, marking a shallow reef. I erroneously thought it was the channel-marker.

I yelled to Misty, "FALL OFF. FALL OFF."

She quickly turned the wheel to starboard and sailed downwind before we ran aground on the shallow reef. We got away from the reef and back on course for Tonga.

We had gone from a calm anchorage to big seas, strong winds, and a narrow escape. Muzzy said he wasn't feeling so good. I began feeling a bit uneasy myself with the boat bouncing off the waves. I'd never been seasick in all my days at sea. I felt a bit queasy when I had left Bora Bora, but never threw-up. I sat in the cockpit feeling green. I was trying to hide it. The captain doesn't get seasick.

"Hey Carson you don't look so well," Muzzy said. "Are you ok buddy?" He chuckled.

We hit one wave too many and I dove to the side rail. I puked once, and that was it. I felt better and turned around to see Muzzy rolling in laughter. I just stood there with puke on my face and said, "You know you're in trouble when the captain pukes."

He couldn't stop laughing. I stood there looking dumb. I tried to defend my diminutive position and said, "Well, there's a first time for everything."

We sailed on through the night with calmer conditions and woke up the next morning to the sound of the drag buzzing. I stopped the boat and let Muzzy reel in the fish. He quickly got it onboard and we had ourselves a perfect 15 lb yellow fin tuna. I filleted the fish and we had sashimi for breakfast. Misty ate some weird veggie meat again.

Over lunch, Muzzy began telling us about his trip from New Zealand on the last boat. They stopped in Tonga on their way to Samoa and stayed in the northern Vavau group of Tonga, where we were heading.

"Man," he said, "I was hanging out with this lunatic kiwi named Poko. He was building hurricane houses for the people of Tonga. Poko had this speed boat we took out one day with a bunch of 16 year-old girls and a couple cases of beer."

"Sounds scandalous," I said.

"You would've loved this character. He'll probably be gone by the time we get there. He was finishing his job and heading back to New Zealand."

I had estimated arriving in three days, but we were sailing much faster than normal. I was worried we would get there too soon and arrive in the middle of the night. I tried to sail more conservatively to slow the boat down.

The next day we caught another yellow fin tuna. We made another huge pile of sashimi for dinner. We were still smoking-out the miles as we charged south. *Bula* usually averaged six knots with one or two people onboard. We were averaging seven and a half knots with the winds blowing at a perfect angle for speed.

The third day out, we spotted Tonga in the distance. It was around three o'clock in the afternoon. We were not going to make it before dark. I planned to get to the lee side of the island and heave-to until morning.

"Mate," Muzzy said, "I've been through that entrance many times. I know it like the back of me doe-joe." I gave him a homophobic stare.

He continued, "All we have to do is sail through these two tiny islands that are three hundred meters apart and we're home free."

"And what do we do when we pass through the tiny islands?" I said.

"We head straight into Morelle Bay. It's probably another three kilometers from there. No worries at all."

The northern Vavau group of islands has no outer lying reefs. All the islands jut straight out of the ocean with steep cliff-lined shores.

"It's a straight shot through the entrance to the anchorage at Morelle Bay," Muzzy said.

I said, "I'm not sure we'll be able to see when we get closer."

The sun was setting as we approached the island. In no time, it was pitch black with no moonlight to help us navigate. I spotted the lights of another sailboat going through the pass in front of us. I got on the VHF to talk to them. An old man came on the VHF and said, "We're motoring into Morelle Bay and I know it quite well. You can follow us through if you'd like."

I replied, "Sounds good. Thanks captain."

I stayed on his tail until we safely arrived at the anchorage. We found a spot to throw the hook among ten other sailboats.

I could hear the faint cries of tropical birds in the trees on the shore. The feeling of safety and warmth came over me. We quietly floated at anchor under the stars in a windless, protected bay. I did my last round on deck, securing sails, making sure everything was in order, and then retired down below.

"Alrighhht," I said. "Welcome to Tonga. We don't have any cold beer. How about some warm ones?"

They looked at me as if they had secretly cashed a few while I was securing everything. I found out later that Misty was secretly taking nips off some hidden booze she had kept in the closet the whole time she was on the boat. We cracked a round of warm beers in the dim lantern light of the cabin and sat around grinning at our successful mission to Tonga.

Poko

The red sun rose to blue skies and a palm-lined beach. I grabbed the snorkel gear and dove over the side into the clear water. The first thing I spotted was a school of neon colored squid. They had diaphanous skin and they changed colors in unison from fluorescent pink to blue, then various colors.

After the swim, we cooked up banana pancakes. The three of us sat out in the cockpit enjoying the meal and the scenery.

We heard this loud outboard whining in the distance at full throttle. It gradually got louder. An aluminum skiff flew around the bend steering into the anchorage. This bald-headed maniac in dark, menacing shades was at the wheel. He was straight out of the movie "Mad Max". He fired through the middle of the anchored boats at 50 miles an hour. Seconds later, he was gone around the other bend.

"What the hell was that?" I said.

Muzzy looked at me and said, "Poko."

"He's out of his mind. What if little kids were swimming in the anchorage?"

Muzzy got on the VHF, "Mermaid Bar . . . Mermaid Bar, this is sailing vessel *Bula*, do you copy?"

"This is the Mermaid Bar," Replied a young female's voice. "I didn't catch the name of your boat, but go ahead."

"Hey Angela, it's Muzzy," he said with a hint of interest.

"Muzzy what are you doing back here? I thought you were off to Samoa." She sounded excited.

"I was, then I met some crazy sailors on this boat named *Bula* and sailed back down here with them."

"Welcome back. Where are you located?"

"We're anchored in Morelle Bay and I wanted to get a hold of Poko. He just flew past us a minute ago and he's heading your way."

"I'll relay the message. When ya coming into town sailor?"

"We have to come in today to check into the country. I'll stop by for a beer."

"Ok. Good to hear you're back."

"I'll see you later."

I glanced at Muzzy and he said, "Oh yeah mate. Maybe I'll introduce you to that one."

Ten minutes later, we heard the same whining of an outboard coming towards us. Muzzy looked at me and we both stared at the corner of the bay. Poko exploded around the bend in an unbridled fury. He came powering up to the anchorage weaving through the boats creating pandemonium. He spotted Muzzy waving his arms. He shot over to the boat, did a hot-lap around us and pulled the throttle back to a stall. There were two poor souls sitting in the back. They were white-knuckled and teary-eyed.

Poko was of medium height, thick as a barrel, light skin covered in freckles, and a shiny bald head.

He said, "Muzzy, what are you doing back here mate?"

Muzzy said, "I couldn't leave ya here to pillage this poor place by yourself."

Poko shouted, "IT'S ON."

"I'd like you to meet Captain Carson, and Misty." We said hello.

Poko said, "When are you guys coming into town?"

Muzzy said, "We've got to check in today. We'll be heading in there soon."

Poko was in a hurry. "Well alright, I've got to get back to work. I'll see ya at the Mermaid Bar, eh?"

He stood up tall like a Russian Czar—cocked his head sideways staring at us, and floored the throttle. He yelled over the loud engine, "SEE YA WANKERS IN TOWN."

The people in the back nearly fell out of their seats as the boat stood up at a 45-degree angle. The boat rocketed out of the quiet anchorage. Every sailor in the vicinity shot him the stink eye, then turned and shot us a few.

We got organized, pulled the anchor and began sailing through the lush archipelago into the small town of Neiafu. We weaved through a labyrinth of cruising yachts that were flying flags from many different nations. We anchored 50 feet from the Mermaid Bar on the waterfront.

After we checked in with the Tongan customs, we paddled over to the Mermaid Bar. We tied up the donkey to the back porch of the bar that hung over the water. The bar resembled a western saloon on the waterfront and we were three outlaws coming in for a drink.

Swashbuckling sailors and salty vagabonds were spinning yarns about deep-sea tales. Muzzy ordered a round of local beers. When the beers arrived, I looked at the slew of bottles. I said, "Strange, they change consistency and color from bottle to bottle."

These beers were all from the same local brewery, but one might be cloudy and the next clear and stronger than the first. I liked the variety. I supposed it all depended upon who was brewing the beer on that particular day. The quality personnel were probably paid in product.

A cute girl walked up to the table and said, "Hey Muzzy, it's good to see ya."

Muzzy stood up and said, "Hey Angela, I just couldn't leave ya here all alone, so I got a ride back with these sailors. This is Carson and Misty."

We shook hands and she said she had to get back to work helping with the bar. Muzzy had his eye on her, but I think she was preoccupied, or running from poor Muzzy.

In walked Poko and everybody in the bar knew him well. He was bouncing from table to table, laughing and carrying-on in a booming voice. Everyone stopped to stare. He was the town celebrity, buying rounds of local beer for various circles of friends and strangers.

Muzzy said, "Poko is pulling in the dough. He's the foreman on a local job site."

Poko finally made his way over to us and began firing off jokes, offensive remarks and a barrage of verbal garbage. He was a walking Rodney Dangerfield.

"The locals from my work site named me Poko," he said. "Poko means *baldy* in Tonganese."

"That's what they told *you,*" I said. "It really means homo."

That stumped him and he just laughed. He sat down and had a beer with us. He introduced us to a sailor he knew sitting next to us at the bar. His name was Hugh from London. We introduced ourselves and shook hands with Hugh. He had blond hair, fair skin and a medium build. Take the lead singer Simon Le Bon from Duran Duran, add ten more years of booze and narcotics—throw in some novelty teeth, and there you have him.

Poko left us after a couple ludicrous comments, and continued his social campaign around the joint.

Hugh and I continued to chat for a while. He was on a 46-foot catamaran he bought in Australia. He had sailed it up to Tonga with his wife. His story was similar to mine. He had quit his job back home and sold everything. He was seeking out more in life than a secure job in the mundane middle class of a British bourgeoisie society. He was a quick-witted Londoner, but liked to drink a little more than your average pomie*.

I said, "Hey Hugh, tomorrow is the Fourth of July and us Yanks have been known to do a bit of celebrating on this day. What do you say we all get together and have a party on the *Bula*?"

He said, "How about on my yacht? I've got a load of deck space and I'm sure my wife Blair would be delighted."

---

* pomie = 1 : slang word for the English 2 : nobody knows the true origin of the word, but there is speculation it could have derived from the acronym Prisoner of Mother England: P. O. M. E.

Muzzy, Misty and I looked at each other in agreement and I said, "Well ok then. We'll bring the margaritas and some musical noise makers."

"See you tomorrow."

The Swingers

The Fourth of July started out hot, and only escalated from there. The three of us went down to the local market and bought a bottle of vodka and a watermelon. We planned to saturate the melon with the vodka.

We got back to the boat, loaded up our stuff and headed over to Hugh's boat named *Easy*. The three of us arrived with a guitar, conga drum, tequila, vodka, and a watermelon.

Hugh said, "Welcome aboard. What's the watermelon for?"

"You'll see," I said.

We ambled aboard their plush catamaran, impressed with the amount of deck space. They could have staged an episode of "Soul Train" on their boat.

Hugh's wife Blair introduced herself. She was a tall brunette with a body that was probably good in its prime. She was the quintessential Amazon cougar on the prowl.

"Let's get into it." I said. "Hugh, have you got a long thin knife?"

"What do you plan on doing with it mate?" he said.

"Well, I need to bore a round hole into this watermelon, big enough to fit the neck of that bottle of vodka."

He thought about it for a second. "I've got just the thing."

He went down below and reappeared with a cordless drill and a bag of large drill bits. He sized up the neck of the bottle, pulled out an inch-and-a-half drill bit and flamboyantly clipped it into the drill as though it was an AK-47. He said in his British accent, "Now where's that melon?"

I grabbed the melon like a football and Hugh motioned me towards the transom. He said, "Let's take it to the swim platform in case it gets messy."

As we moved to the rear of the boat, I said, "Maybe you should wear safety goggles."

He gave me a preposterous look as he stood the melon upright on the swim step. He lined-up the drill and pulled the trigger. Melon guts spackled both of us from the waist up. Covered in watermelon juice, he looked up with a glistening coated face like Lucifer.

"Goggles?" I said.

He just nodded in a forfeited approval. We peered into the melon. It was a perfect round hole about 10 inches deep.

"Nice work," I said. "Stage two." I walked over to my backpack and procured the bottle of vodka.

Hugh said, "What do you think about rum instead? I've got an old bottle of Caribbean rum I've been trying to get rid of for awhile."

I stopped and queried aloud with a peculiar system of nomenclature, "Vodka comes from potatoes—rum from sugarcane—watermelon is fruit, which equals sugar. The formula calls for rum. Lay it on me."

He went down below and reappeared with a bottle of dark rum. It had a picture of a fat black lady on the label. I twisted off the sugar-crusted lid and shoved it into the top of the juicy watermelon. I began rubbing my hands together and said, "Splendid, splendid—it's a perfect fit doctor. Now we have to wait for the rum to fill up the melon. Ha ha haaa."

Blair had given up on our little boy's project. She had taken the initiative to mix up some tasty margaritas. She passed them around to everyone. We held our glasses in the air, all saluting the 4th.

"How ironic," I said, "the English celebrating with Americans over our independence from them. Then there's Muzzy, the kiwi, who probably descended from an English convict, exiled to the land Down Under. What a sad lot where are."

Four margaritas later and I began wondering whether the watermelon was ready. The bottle of rum was empty. I pulled it out of the top and began carving away with a foot-long kitchen knife. I handed the slices out to everyone. We took our loaded melon slices to the swim steps to eat.

We stood around with sticky hands, spitting seeds into the water. Misty and I were the first to grab a second slice. We competitively looked at each other and devoured them.

People were dropping out of the race. Misty and I picked up speed with every slice. I was spitting the seeds out at first, but by my third slice, I couldn't be bothered and just swallowed them with the rest—it saved time.

Hugh bailed-out after three. Misty and I finally quit around five or six. I lost count and we didn't even figure out who won or why we were racing. I figured each slice contained roughly a shot of rum. I tried to do the math.

We were watching the sunset with a good buzz when Hugh approached me. He said, "So Carson, is that your girlfriend?"

I looked at him judging why he would ask. "No, Misty is just a friend," I said.

"I've got to admit, I quite fancy her. How come you two haven't shagged?"

I giggled at his choice of words, "Well, I knew her ex-boyfriend in Hawaii and he treated her pretty badly. Their relationship was on the brink, so I asked her to sail south to enjoy some freedom. I really didn't want to hook up with her, I just preferred having a girl as a crew member for a change." He went on to tell me that he and his wife had a bit of an . . . open marriage, and he had an eye for Misty. "Well Hugh, you can certainly try all you want. She's all yours. But I've got to warn ya. She's been with maybe two guys in her whole life. I'm not sure you're gonna be the third, there padre."

Hugh mixed a cocktail and moved in. I was sitting on the cockpit couch chatting with Blair when the two of them disappeared down below. I thought to myself, Hugh doesn't waste any time. Once Hugh and Misty were gone, Blair's demeanor changed. She began getting cozy with me. She said, "I'm going to fetch a blanket." She reappeared with a leopard-print comforter. She jumped up on the couch next to me and threw the comforter over us.

Muzzy gathered what was going down. He said, "I'm out of here mate," and quickly exited the cockpit. He dove over the side and began swimming back to the *Bula*, which was anchored fifty meters away.

Blair said, "What's up with Muzzy?"

"I can only guess."

She shrugged off my statement and boldly said to me in her London accent, "So Hughie has obviously gone down to shag your girlfriend, and I'm gonna shag you." She looked at me with her lips pursed and her eyebrows raised in a matter-of-factly pose of perversity.

"Weeell, I don't really. . ."

"Oh Carson, you're not a prude are you?"

"I'm just ahhh . . ."

Misty catapulted into the cockpit from below with a helpless bunny look on her face. "I've got to talk to you in private," she said.

Just before I got up from the couch, Hugh came sauntering into the cockpit with a cocktail in his hand. He had a cheesy look on his face, resembling Austin Powers. He even had the bad teeth.

Blair said, "Oh look there's Hughie, he's dropped the ball again." Blair put on a sympathetic voice and said, "Look Misty, I'm not much into girls, but after I've shagged Carson here, I'll come and shag you next."

Misty's fright doubled. I mixed up some more cocktails to feed to the theater. Misty tried to act normal and began conversing with Hugh again for some stupid reason. I sat down next to Blair, but not too close. Once she realized we weren't going to shag, I felt more comfortable.

Hugh and Misty disappeared down below again. How did he do it? Blair told me that she and Hugh had a bit of a competition of who could shag the most people. There were points involved. The highest points went to shagging a captain.

I said, "Poor Hughie doesn't have a chance. Number one, most captains are men. And two, a woman can practically get laid anytime she wants." I intentionally used the word *practically* in light of Blair's pursuit of me.

"He's losing badly." Blair said. "I took down a boatload of Italians last night, and to tell you the truth, I'm quite knackered." She looked into the air as if she was calculating her points. "The only time Hughie gets laid, is when I force women to believe he's irresistible."

Misty burst into the cockpit a second time and said, "Maybe we should go soon."

I nodded in approval and motioned for the dingy. Misty and I said our goodbyes in a polite manner, though exited quickly. Hugh and Blair just stood there in the cockpit looking defeated and lonely.

We drunkenly paddled off in the darkness in a lackadaisical manner. Misty lost an oar en route and nearly fell off the dingy trying to retrieve it. We crawled aboard the *Bula* on all fours. I passed out in my wet clothes.

What Kind of an Idiot Would Sacrifice a Virgin?

We escaped town and sailed back to the secluded Morelle Bay. We were attending a traditional Tongan feast that evening on a beach around the point from Morelle Bay.

After anchoring and showering in the ocean, the three of us paddled to shore in the donkey. We pulled the inflatable up on the beach above the high tide mark.

We had a short jaunt through the thick jungle and arrived at this palm-thatched hut. The locals invited us into their rustic home. They were outfitted with indigenous Polynesian regalia. The men and women donned tribal grass skirts and black fabric tops. The women wore white flowers behind their ears. Both men and women had Tongan armband tattoos. Genuine smiles lit-up their faces as we entered their hut.

A spread of foreign seafood dishes cluttered the long table. Spiral shells baked in breadfruit, octopus in coconut milk wrapped with banana leaves, and abalone cooked in miniature pumpkins. Baby pigs were fire-roasted bright red on the spit. There were piles of yams, taro, and sweet potatoes. A cornucopia of fresh fruit was ornately displayed with multi-colored flowers on large, green banana leaves. White candles flickered among the spread down the length of a long wooden table.

The locals pointed at the table for us to begin. I stacked my first plate with as much as I could. Everyone indulged in the Polynesian food.

I kept going back for more. I ended up eating five plates and dropped into a food paralysis. Laid out on the dirt floor, I tried to breathe, but my stomach was crowding my lungs. I continued taking short breaths.

After the dinner, we thanked the islanders, leaving them gifts of money and waddled back through the dark jungle with flashlights. I was barefoot and careful not to step on the army of land crabs or any dirt demons lurking in the dark shadows.

We made it back to the donkey and paddled back to the *Bula*. I retired to my bunk and laid there in pain. I finally drifted off as the boat quietly rocked me to sleep.

The following day, I woke up and felt as though I had to pass a petrified dinosaur. I skipped breakfast and went for a swim. I spotted Hugh and Blair on their catamaran *Easy* sailing into the bay. They anchored nearby in the protected bay.

I yelled out from the water, "Good morning."

"Morning Carson," they both said.

Blair said, "We were thinking about going for a sail around the islands today. Would you all care to join us on our little romp?" There was usually some sexual innuendo in her choice of words.

I said, "Sounds good to me. Can we bring the dive gear and find that spot that people have been talking about? Muzzy mentioned something about a hidden cave as well."

Blair looked at Hugh and he nodded in interest. "Bring those two, your gear, and come on over when you please."

"I'll tell the others. I'm sure they will be up for it."

I swam back to the boat and when I boarded I saw Misty staring at me. She said, "So you wanna go sailing with the Swingers huh?"

I laughed and said, "Oh come on, he's not gonna try anything. Don't worry I'll protect you as long as you protect me from Blair."

She laughed and said, "Alright, but I don't want to hang out on their boat too late."

I nodded. "Ok, ok."

We loaded our gear onto the donkey and paddled over to their boat. After transferring the gear, Muzzy helped pull their anchor and we motored out of the bay towards the neighboring islands. It was great sailing on someone else's boat for a change. It doesn't seem like work. We sailed around to this hidden spot called Mariners cave. Muzzy had been there before.

We got to the cliff-walled location, grabbed our masks and jumped in the water. Hugh stayed onboard. The bottom was 14 fathoms deep and too much trouble to anchor. The four of us swam over to the cliff-lined shore with no sign of an opening in the cliffs.

We reached the limestone, sheer wall. There were large fruit bats flying in and out of caves closer to the top. We listened to the eerie screeching of the bats. I had visions of those blood-sucking creatures latching onto my neck. I stayed lower in the water.

Muzzy said, "Ok, you have to swim about six meters down, then through the opening in the underwater cave and up to the surface. You can swim down and watch me do it once and then follow me the second time or just trust me and go for it."

I said, "I'll be the first. Let's go."

We were wearing masks, but no fins. We both took a deep breath and went under. I followed him down and through the underwater archway. As we entered this dark blue corridor I began thinking . . . if I were a man-eating sea creature, this is exactly where I would live. Large schools of fish were frantically swimming out as we were entering the cave. What was chasing them?

As we continued swimming underwater, I was hoping it wasn't much further. I spotted what looked like a silvery, circular air pocket about six meters above us. We finally surfaced and I gasped for air. I questioned Muzzy's sanity halfway though the corridor. Would I grab a large snake with fangs if my buddy said it was safe?

The distance was long enough that you had to commit. There was no chance of turning back once you were inside.

There was a lot of pressure in the cave. I had to equalize my ears continuously with the rising and falling of each swell. When the swell rose, the pressure increased, creating a thick fog in the air. I couldn't see a foot in front of me. When the swell dropped, the pressure decreased and the fog completely disappeared in one second.

Muzzy swam back through to usher Misty and Blair into the cave. I was worried about those two. I'm a good swimmer and I was questioning whether they were going to panic halfway. Misty was a surfer, she'd be fine. I was concerned about Blair who didn't appear to be in shape. However, she was the type who would do anything if dared.

The three of them finally surfaced. After gasping for air with slight terror in both of their eyes, Blair said, "My god Muzzy." She was trying to catch her breath. "If I would've known it was going to be that far I would've brought a dive tank."

I added, "Yeah, I was second guessing him halfway through that dark hole."

We were all treading water and glanced at Misty, who hadn't said a word. She was busy scanning the cave still trying to catch her breath.

The cave was large with a ceiling twenty feet from the surface. We climbed onto the rocks and sat on a flat bank above the water. The ceiling had limestone stalactites hanging down with water dripping off the ends. The water drops echoed as they hit the surface. The light from the underwater entrance refracted upon the ceiling. It resembled the lights from a swimming pool at night.

While we were inside the cave, Muzzy unleashed its unique history. He said, "Back when Tongans were still sacrificing virgins—bloody wankers, they were to throw another innocent female into the ocean. A young boy was in love with the virgin girl. Troubled, he created a plan to save her. He secretly knew about the cave and insisted if they threw her off the cliff to the ocean gods then they had to throw her off a sacred cliff of his designation. They granted his wish. The young boy in love explained to the virgin what to do when they tossed her over the side. When she was tossed to the sharks, she swam down and into the cave. The boy had left her enough food and fresh water for a month stashed in the rocks inside the underwater cavern. The girl remained there long enough to consume the supplies and resurfaced after a few weeks. She returned to the village astonishing everyone. The people thought she was a ghost and the chief thought she was a deity."

We had spent about ten minutes in the dank cave and I was ready to leave. I couldn't imagine a month. Misty was practicing her breathing exercises, hoping to get out alive. Blair had a look as if she might be staying.

Muzzy and I let the girls go first. Misty took a dozen deep breathes, shook her head in submittal and swam down like an erratic frog. Blair followed, after cussing and crossing herself. Muzzy and I nodded at each other and descended down. We resurfaced and the girls had already begun swimming to the catamaran.

After boarding the boat, we motored over to a tiny island nearby to scuba dive a spot called "The Wall".

We put on the cumbersome dive gear and duck-walked to the swim platform. I was contemplating a new Olympic race, "The Quarter-Mile Sprint in Full Dive Gear". It would entail one lap around the track wearing a thick dive suit, booties, gloves, mask, snorkel, fins, buoyancy compensator, and a tank. Just to make it more interesting, you had to breathe through your regulator. If you didn't self-combust or pass out from heat exhaustion, then you would probably trip over your flippers, face-plant the asphalt, crack your head open from the extra weight on your back, and explode if the tank got dislodged.

I made it into the water without too many snags. We gathered around for a quick debriefing. I said, "Ok everyone, it appears we are in 70 to 80 feet of water. Let's descend down to the bottom and work our way along the wall to the north against the current. Then we can circle and use the current to drift back to the boat. Let's stick together. Does everyone know all the hand signals?" Everyone nodded but Hugh.

"Can you run through them for me," he said.

"Sure,"

I spent a couple of minutes to refresh his memory with the signals. "Ok, are we ready?"

Everyone nodded in approval. Blair stayed on the boat this time while the four of us went down.

I began my decent into the underworld. The visibility was over 100 feet. I drifted deeper with the sound of the boat motor fading away to pure silence. I could only hear the sound of the air bubbles escaping my regulator. The water was cooler as I reached 50 feet. The reef was prolific with intricate outcroppings formed on the wall.

Once I got down to 60 feet, I looked up to see everyone had gone in four different directions. Where did we go wrong? I waited for awhile and Misty finally made it down. She let me know Hugh was having a little trouble and he was ascending back to the boat. I gathered the information through underwater sign language, charades, and a mumbling argot she shouted through her regulator.

I turned and kicked north next to the wall, looking for big fish. I had my spear gun. After a few minutes, I looked over my shoulder and Misty had disappeared. I scanned in every direction and she was gone. She was a competent diver; I figured she would be all right.

I continued through the multi-colored reef, spotting familiar tropical reef fish and a few new ones. I spotted a few grouper that I could've speared, but I was waiting on the grand daddy. I was just about to make my turn to drift back to the boat when I spotted a school of snapper.

I snuck over in a stealth manner through the reef. I propped my spear gun on the top of a rock and waited. I breathed slower, so the bubbles wouldn't scare the fish away. They swam closer to me and I searched for the largest one. They were maybe five pounds apiece. I'd have to spear two or three to make it worthwhile.

I was scanning the pack with my finger tight on the trigger waiting for one to swim into range. I happened to see something large move directly below me. I slowly glanced down to see a big grouper that looked maybe 30 pounds. You never can tell until you get them on the boat. I could have reached out and petted it. Here I was trying to pick out a puny snapper, when I was lying on top of the mother load. I felt like I was standing on the back of a whale and fishing for minnows.

I maneuvered upward a bit, got my spear gun pointed straight down and waited. It stuck its head out of the hole and . . . *click*. I nailed it in the back of the head. Furiously it tried to swim off with the spear in its head, but I pulled it in with the line connected to the spear. I wrestled it into my game bag, removing the spear. I ascended to the surface foregoing my safety decompression stop. I had only been to 80 feet for a short amount of time.

I waived for the boat. Blair spotted me and motored over to pick me up. I didn't want to linger around in the water longer than necessary. I had heard too many stories of huge tiger sharks in Tonga. I handed them the catch bag. They marveled over the catch as I clawed my way aboard the boat with that heavy tank on my back.

It was a good size grouper, but I still felt like a bad sport spearing it while using dive gear. The real sport is holding your breath and free diving to that depth. That's when it becomes a real challenge. But a man's gotta eat.

The others were already onboard and we began slowly motoring back to the anchorage. Hugh said, "My regulator was fouling up and I couldn't fix it underwater. I decided to can the operation and return to the boat."

I turned to Misty and said, "I looked around for you at one point and you completely disappeared. I didn't know if you had gotten inhaled by a giant piss-clam or what."

Misty said, "I went up to help Hugh a second time, then lost you, so I went on my own."

I said, "What the heck happened to that coordinated dive plan? I got to 60 feet and everyone was gone." Everyone stood there, up in arms.

We sailed back to Morelle Bay with a gentle breeze pushing us through the lush archipelago. We anchored and I filleted the grouper for dinner. Hugh and Blair naturally invited us over to eat on their boat that evening.

After showering on the *Bula*, we paddled back to their boat in the donkey. Hugh was getting the barbeque ready for the fish with a cocktail in hand. Blair was putting on a sexy dress, also with a cocktail.

I heard that familiar whining of an outboard maxed-out. I looked up to see Poko speeding around the corner in his aluminum battle-boat. He did a hot-lap around the *Bula*. He finally spotted us on Easy and raced over.

He tied up and jumped aboard with a 12 pack of beers. He began spouting off about his party we missed. All I heard was free beer, all night party, loud music, cops, and teen-aged girls.

We quickly exhausted the twelve-pack listening to more of his outlandish stories. Poko yelled, "BEER RUN. WHO WANTS TO GO?"

"Beer run?" I said. "Where can you get beer around here?" He said, "IN TOWN."

"It took us an hour-and-a-half to sail from town. How long is it in your skiff?"

"TEN MINUTES."

"Ten minutes—right."

"LET'S GO."

"Yeah?"

"BRING IT ON SEPO*."

Muzzy and I jumped in the skiff. The second I got my two feet on the floor, Poko punched it. I nearly fell over backwards. I happened to glance at my watch just as we took off.

He got the boat up on a plane going 50 miles an hour with the engine screaming. I ducked under a huge, flying water beetle. It zipped over my head. Had it hit me in the sunglasses, it would've cracked a lens at that speed.

---

* sepo = 1 : Australian slang for an American 2 : they think all Americans are polluters; septic tank rhymes with yank

It was man-against-machine as we sped onward. Pulling into Neiafu town, Poko weaved through a slew of sailboats pissing off most everyone. He slid the boat up next to the dock and I looked down at my watch.

"Ten minutes, exactly," I said.

Poko shook his head in reassurance. I couldn't believe that it was ten minutes exactly. That coincidence confounded me more than the short amount of time.

He leaped off the skiff and bought a case of the local beer from a store located steps away from the waters edge. He promptly returned, tossed the case in the skiff and blasted off through the slew of boats in the tight anchorage. We received a repeat of middle fingers and cursing as he powered onward in a delinquent manner.

We arrived back at *Easy* and hopped aboard with a fresh case. Poko kindly administered the beers and I began putting the fish on the grill. We cooked up the grouper, listening to his endless barrage of fanatical stories. He kept everyone entertained.

We sat down to a nice meal from the sea, enjoying the moment. A warm breeze blew through the anchorage as we ate. We told stories until we finished the beers. Poko motored back to town and we retired to the *Bula*.

Escape to Fiji

Tired of partying like a college kid, I craved a cleaner existence. I had to get out of that scene and get back into surfing. Misty was flying back to Hawaii in a few days. I asked Muzzy if he wanted to sail to Fiji soon. He was more than ready. It was a repeat in Tonga for him. The weather looked good with 15 to 20 knots of southeast trade winds. We decided on Monday to sail to Fiji and *Easy* wanted to sail with us.

We dropped Misty off at the airport and said our sad goodbyes. I was going to miss her, she wasn't the best sailor, but she was a dependable crewmember. Muzzy and I checked out of the country and spent our last night in Neiafu.

We woke up early in the morning to a partly cloudy sky and good winds. I listened to the weather on the SSB. The morning net called for benign weather for the next few days.

We weighed anchor in our pristine little bay and sailed out into the deep sea for Fiji. It was about a three-and-a-half day trip and we were looking forward to the sail. We both wanted to get to Fiji for the renowned surf. The boat was destined to get there with a name like *Bula*. Everything was pointing in that direction including the wind as we sailed dead downwind.

Easy pulled out of Tonga a few hours after we left. We wanted to be somewhat close in order to help each other in case of an emergency.

The first night slid by painlessly and the weather was holding up fine. The winds were picking up a bit, but we were at a downwind angle and sailing along comfortably. We didn't get in contact with *Easy* until the second day.

That day we caught a 40 lb mahi-mahi and hailed *Easy* to see if they wanted any fish. It was about two o'clock in the afternoon and they said they could see us up ahead on the horizon. We were about two or three miles in front of them. Hugh thought about it for a second and said, "Sure mate. I'll pull up some sail and try and catch you guys."

"Roger, we've got a huge bag for ya," I said.

They caught up to us three hours later, and we maneuvered the boats as close as we could to throw the bag of fish over into their cockpit. It was blowing 25 knots and the seas were a bit rough with 10 to 15-foot waves. We tried to get as close as possible, but it became too dangerous.

I hailed Hugh on the VHF and said, "Ok Plan B. We're going to run one hundred-feet of line out the back with the bag tied to it. You pull up behind us and use a gaff to pull it onboard."

"Yeah that sounds like a safer idea," Hugh said. "Every time I went up on the top of a wave, you were down in a trough making it impossible to catch a flying bag of fish."

"Right, just keep the line and give it back to us in Fiji."

Muzzy tied up the big bag of fish and ran it back behind the boat. *Easy* maneuvered behind us and pulled into position. Blair went up to the bow with a gaff in hand, wearing a harness clipped into a safety line in case she fell overboard. She went to gaff the line but missed. The bow was bouncing off the waves. The second try was successful. She pulled in the bag and Muzzy immediately untied the line. She pulled the long line aboard. She threw a victory arm in the air as she cautiously crept back to the cockpit.

Hugh got on the VHF and said, "Operation Fish Transfer successful."

"Roger, O.F.T. successful," I said.

"Mate, we didn't have a clue you were going to give us this much fish."

"We've got the same amount as you."

They said their thanks, and we all got back to our usual sailing routines.

Muzzy and I began chatting about the whereabouts of this secret surf camp. The owner was keeping Muzzy in the dark about the location for some odd reason. I was contemplating a surreptitious new surf break.

I said, "Well I'm going to go anchor at this little island called Yanuca. I was there about six years ago surfing a place called Frigates Pass. You're welcome to come along if your job doesn't work out, or if you have to wait until the position comes available."

He said, "I'll find out soon enough when we reach the capital Suva."

At sunrise, we sailed into the Lau Island group of Fiji. This group of islands is the eastern-most archipelago. You can only visit them with a special grant from the government. We sailed past the low-lying green islands onward to the capital Suva.

We caught a glimpse of a young islander boy who stepped out of his grass hut. He stood on the beach looking out to sea at us. He was the only form of existence visible. He was limply holding a stick in his hand and staring at the *Bula* sailing past. We were only a quarter of a mile offshore. I thought about how different our lives were. We sailed westward out of site of the little boy.

The Hungry Cougars

We reached Suva in 35 knots of wind and dangerous seas. We pulled into the calm waters of Suva harbor happy to have escaped the storm at sea. The harbor was a squalid shipping port. We were not impressed with our introduction to Fiji.

We motored past a defunct fleet of foreign fishing vessels packed with sweaty Asian men. They were languidly smoking cigarettes and boondoggling about in the many cracks and crevices of the vessel. Many of them had a look as if they were waiting for the end of the world to arrive.

We anchored off the Suva Yacht Club. Muzzy began cleaning the boat while I went ashore with our passports to check into the country.

At the insipid customs office, there was an Indian man who started processing me. He said, "Name of vessel?"

"*Bula*," I said. (Bula means "hello" in Fijian)

"Yes Bula," he said with an Indian accent, "but what is the name of your vessel sir?"

"Who's on first?" I said as a joke.

He shot me a confused glance and I explained, "*Bula* is actually the name of my vessel." He finally broke down and laughed at himself.

I was a hit with the customs agents. They were amused that a vessel from the U.S. had the name *Bula*. After visiting over 70 countries, this was the first time I got a customs agent to laugh.

They filed my paperwork swiftly and I was free to sail for four months in Fijian waters.

I hitchhiked back to the boat. Muzzy had morphed into a caged orangutan from cabin fever. He was dying to go ashore to have a brew and check his email.

We went to shore and found him an Internet café. He received some good news. The surf camp needed him in the next week and they were wondering when he could make it to Fiji. Excited, he sent a message back, stating he was presently at the Suva Yacht Club. The guy left a phone number and Muzzy went to call him.

Muzzy came back with news that the guy running the surf camp Chuck, was coming down to the yacht club in ten minutes to meet us. We sat around and had a beer.

When he arrived, we introduced ourselves. Chuck told us the camp was on the island of Yanuca.

"Hey," I said, "that's where I'm sailing."

"You own a sailboat?" Chuck said.

"Well, I guess that's how we got here."

"When are you sailing out there?"

"Maybe in a couple of days."

"What if I pay you to give us a ride out there?"

"No need, I'm heading that way anyway."

"Excellent, that would be really kind of you."

Things were falling into place. Chuck showed us some enticing video footage of the perfect wave at the island. Muzzy and I were desperate for some surf and getting excited over the video. We continued talking about the island and their plans with the camp.

Chuck had to meet someone in town. He left us at the bar sipping the local Fiji Bitters and mulling over our mission out to Yanuca. We didn't want to sail out into that cruel sea with the wicked storm brewing. We decided to stay in Suva until the storm subsided. The Fiji Bitters were sliding down easier than nickels in a slot machine.

It was time to celebrate the end of another successful passage. We paid our tab and took a cab into the dirty town of

Suva. The cabbie dropped us off in the center of town. Walking down the sidewalk, we haphazardly found some nightclub called Traps. We meandered through the front door.

It was dark and crowded inside. We weaved our way to the bar. Muzzy ordered two margaritas. We grabbed our cocktails and walked through a small door into another part of the bar.

I had sipped maybe a third of my cocktail when Muzzy turned to me and said, "Ready for another mate?"

I looked down at my drink and said, "Well, I'm only . . ."

"You're ready for another." He walked to the closest bar.

He kept buying these stiff margaritas the entire evening. He would walk up to me with a new one about every 15 minutes. I'd be standing there with half a cocktail and he would show up with another Mexican hand-grenade.

"Hey, you've got to slow down with those things," I said. "I've still got half-a-cocktail here."

He gave me that staunch kiwi stare and said, "Finish it mate, or you'll be keelhulled*."

"Yeah, I'm trying maaate." He was hammering me into oblivion.

I was standing there with two margaritas, slurping down the new one. Some girl, not looking or able to see, slammed into my elbow. That sappy green juice went down the front of my white shirt. The girl continued onward unapologetic at what she had done to my only clean shirt. I astonishingly stared at the back of her head, waiting for some response. A few onlookers scoffed at the negligence of the passerby and felt sorry for me. I bent forward to let the juice drain off my soaked shirt. My hands were full and I couldn't do anything but stand there with my shirt sticking to my abdomen like fly paper.

---

* keelhulled = instead of committing a villain to walk the plank, pirates would tie a long line to each of his ankles and toss him over the bow of the ship with each line pulled tight on either side of the vessel, then dragging him under the keel of the ship till he was severed in two

I regained my composure after the embarrassing mishap, though I resembled a wet college kid at a toga party. I began surveying the scene with a silly grin on my face. There were groups of local girls standing at the side of the dance floor waiting for someone to ask them to dance. Tourist girls had taken the initiative to get out on the floor by themselves.

Six margaritas later, Muzzy and I got cougared♥. Two ravenous tourists forced us onto the dance floor. They were backing their asses up. We just stood there confused.

"Awww . . . what the heck," I said. These two old birds were grinding their asses into us and we kept cackling and spilling our cocktails on them and ourselves.

After dancing with them for three songs straight, we had enough. At the same moment, we glared at each other through the fog and simultaneously started yelling. We turned and began scrambling out of the joint. However, we couldn't find the exit. We went from one room to the next, getting more lost in the dark labyrinth of debauchery. A Fijian guy, the size of a Yugo, finally helped us find our way out.

"No wonder they call it Traps," I said to the Fijian. "We could've been in there for the rest of our lives had it not been for you."

The guy turned to us with a shady grin and said, "You guys want to smoke some weed?"

We looked at each other and nodded at the guy in approval.

♥ cougar = derived from a hierarchy of women as follows:
<u>cub</u> – 1 : girl under the age of eighteen 2 : illegal, stay away you dummy
<u>bobcat</u> - young but legal and ready to pounce on seductive prey
<u>cougar</u> – middle-aged, married, divorced, or still single and looking for young meat
<u>silver fox</u> – 1 : anything with silver hair, paying for everything and promising to fly you to her condo in Maui for the weekend 2 : sugar mama

The rest of the night was a blur. I vaguely remember riding in the back seat of a cab for over an hour, driving back into the dark hills of Suva. I have cloudy memories of sitting in the cab, around four in the morning, out in front of this small Indian store. Muzzy was inside scoring the pot.

Muzzy jumped back in the cab and said, "Maaate that was caaa . . . lassic. After I landed the grass from the little Indian man behind the counter, I turned to walk out and he desperately said to me." Muzzy spoke with an Indian accent. "You must buy someting. You can't just walk out wit nuting. It look too suspicious." Muzzy bought a cheap loaf of bread that never made it back to the boat. It ended up soaking in seawater in the floorboard of the inflatable. We crashed out just before sunrise.

Dangerous Dale

The storm subsided after a few days. Muzzy, Chuck and I set sail for Yanuca. We made our way through the tricky reefs of the lagoon and caught a mahi-mahi and a tuna en route. We passed a tiny, white sand island with only one palm tree in the middle.

I said, "If you were stranded, that's where you'd end up." We stared at the island with different thoughts.

We pulled up to the island around sunset. I sailed past the surf camp on the south side to show Muzzy his new home. He stood on the deck in a trance over this hidden gem.

The mountainous island was only a half of a kilometer long with beautiful sea cliffs and a small village tucked in the middle. Outer reefs protected the island on all sides from the large ocean swells. A few makeshift fish-camps scattered the shoreline on the lee side. Blue tarps were tied to the palm trees for protection from the rain and blistering sun. Smoke rose into the air from the campfires. Commercial divers inhabited the small camps. They combed the reefs for sea cucumbers, which were sold to the Koreans at a high price. But the poor ethnic divers were paid pennies to risk their lives, doing multiple-dives, exceeding safety limits.

The reefs close to Yanuca contain some of the best soft corals in the world. A few dive boats operate around the area bringing tourists to the underwater sanctuary.

I anchored on the west side for protection from the trade winds. Muzzy and Chuck went to shore to meet the island chief and have Savusavu, pronounced "Sabu Sabu". This is a ceremonial drink of kava root among Fijians. It's a polite offering for an outsider to bring the chief a gift of kava and join in the ritual. I'm not so fond of the drink. It looks and tastes like dirt. The root is supposed to give you a feeling of euphoria. It just puts me to sleep.

They slept in the camp that night and I finally got the boat all to myself. I'm not an introverted hermit, but living with another mongrel in a fiberglass bobber could turn the kindest humanitarian into a misanthrope.

I went to the village to meet the chief the next day to offer my own greetings of Savusavu. The village had a small soccer field with young kids playing an unorganized game. The youngest kids where just milling around until they spotted me. They ran over to see the foreigner. A handful of boys and girls gathered around me. One little boy held my hand as I walked towards the center of the village. I stopped to take a few photos. Some got excited and others were bashful, jumping out of the way of the camera. The excited ones genuinely smiled and held up the peace symbol they had learned from some tourist. The others that avoided the photo were kicking around in the dirt. They were batting objects with sticks for entertainment.

They kept saying the only English word they knew, "Mister, Mister."

"Chief?" I said.

A couple of them knew the word and led me down various pathways past rudimentary huts. The young boy held my hand again as if he was my personal escort.

The little kids led me to the right spot. I saw some of the elders of the village congregated inside the largest of the huts. I peered into the open window and one of the Fijian men got a big smile on his face.

"Greetings my friend," he said. "Please come in."

"Bula," I said. Some said Bula and others smiled with an upward flick of the eyebrows, a common gesture in Fiji. "I have come to offer Savusavu to the chief."

I removed my flip-flops before entering, as is customary. They accepted the offer and asked me to join. I sat down in the thatched-roofed hut with ten other locals cross-legged on a reed mat. We sat around a large wooden bowl. The wise old chief slowly scanned the perimeter of the hut and spotted a young boy patiently waiting to render assistance. He extended his arm, palm down, waving the boy over to him. The young boy hopped to attention and the chief handed him the kava root. The boy reverently carried it off to a woman of the village who grinded it up into a fine powder.

The boy returned with the ground kava. They dumped the powder into a sock and soaked it in a large bowl of water. One man began dishing it out in half a coconut shell. They handed the first one to the chief. He drank the first bowl without any expression. Everyone clapped a few slow claps.

The man administering the kava took the bowl, filled it and handed it to the man sitting to the right of the chief. After he was given the bowl, he said, "Bula", with a deep tribal tone, and then drank the entire contents of the coconut shell. Everyone clapped after each one drank their portion. The sound they made with the clapping of their hands is only attainable if you have giant island paws.

The bowl finally came around to me and I said, "Bula," and drank it down. We sat around enjoying each other's company. Some of the men who spoke some English conversed with me about my excursion across the Pacific.

After twenty-something bowls I was ready for a pillow. I said my thanks with a slur in my voice. The chief had a couple of young girls from the village escort me back to my boat in the darkness with a flashlight. The girls of the village showed me the way back to my inflatable on the beach. I paddled back to my boat and went straight to bed.

Anchored in bliss in the lagoon of Yanuca, I spent the next few weeks surfing, spearing fish, and playing guitar. I became acquainted with most of the locals that lived on the island. There were only a handful of them. I knew some of them from my first visit, five years ago. Surprisingly, they remembered my face as well.

I met this Australian named Dangerous Dale. He lived on Yanuca and worked at one of the small surf lodges on the island. He was short with dark shaggy hair, barrel-chested, and chronic blood-shot eyes. He had a perpetual smirk of an outlaw. He also owned a sailboat that was in a harbor on the west side of Fiji.

Dale and I had a lot in common and sat around drinking Fiji Bitters at his surf lodge talking about sailing adventures, surf, and music.

My brother Corn was flying in to visit me soon. We were planning to spend some time on Yanuca together and then heading out west to another island chain in Fiji called the Mamanucas.

Chuck was taking Muzzy and I out on his motor skiff to surf the outer reef Frigates Pass. It's a cloud-break reef seven miles off the island. With no land in sight, it was strange surfing a spot out in the middle of the ocean.

The visibility underwater was incredible. There was no sand or silt from land to cloud-up the water. Surfing down the wave was mesmerizing staring at the reef speeding under your feet as though you were in a glass bottom boat.

My brother was arriving soon and I needed to sail back to the mainland of Viti Levu to pick him up. One morning I asked Dangerous Dale if he wanted to go along to show me the way through the hazardous reefs.

"Sure bro," he said. "I've been that route a hundred times."

"Great," I said. "We'll leave around noon."

"I needed to go to town anyway."

I picked up Dale in my inflatable at the surf lodge and we paddled back to the boat. I pulled in the anchor and set sail for the mainland. Things were going smooth and I was trolling a fishing line.

An hour out, we sailed over-top of a reef that was only eight feet deep. I jumped on the helm and tried to slow the boat down in case we hit bottom. I turned to Dale and angrily said, "I thought you said you'd been this route a hundred times? Is that how you earned your name?"

Dale said to me in a shaky voice, "Well, I was usually drunk."

I shook my head. We sailed back into deeper water. I carried on towards the mainland trimming the sails. Boat insurance companies don't insure boats in Fijian waters because of the uncharted reefs.

We made it to Pacific Harbor unscathed and motored up a river mouth with a few fishing boats tied to the sides of the shallow banks.

"Well, thanks for sailing in with me," I said, "even though we nearly ran aground."

Dale said, "Sorry about that one. I guess I wasn't paying attention."

"No worries, we made it."

Dale said, "Hey, there's a pub nearby. Fiji Bitters for a buck during happy hour. Wanna go?"

I was thinking to myself that the only reason he came to the mainland was to go to the bar. I said, "No thanks bro. I've got to wait for my brother, though I'll take a rain check on that one."

Dale stepped off the boat onto a dilapidated dock partially attached to the shore of the riverbank. He walked up to the main road and disappeared.

After various flights from Puerto Rico, my brother found his weary way to the *Bula*. We did all the ritual hugs and handshakes and he relayed his story of 30 hours of flying. I hauled his gear onboard, and we were off sailing back out to Yanuca. He had also been to Yanuca in the past and revered it as a magical place. He brought a couple of surfboards and his spearfishing gear.

We spent days surfing and spearing fish. We became acquainted with the owners of the surf resort where Dangerous Dale worked. We made a deal to spear fish for them for free boat rides out to the pass to surf.

The first day we speared four reef fish. One was about a 30 lb grouper that Corn nailed. The owner was impressed and invited us to eat there free for the rest of the week as long as we kept bringing in the fish.

A few days later, my brother and I were out free diving and spearing fish in the outer reefs near the surf break. The water temperature was 78 degrees with 150-foot visibility. I was down about 50 feet perched on the side of this reef when I spotted a big grouper. It popped it's head out of a cave, another ten feet below me. I had been holding my breath for a long time waiting, but descended down anyway. As I swam under the lip of an over-hang, I spotted the fish and immediately turned my gun and speared it in the head. The fish shot deep into the cave. I tried to retrieve it but I was getting dizzy from holding my breath for so long. I left it and ascended to the surface.

There were a number of sharks around that day and I flagged down my brother. I said, "I got this grouper down there, stuck in a hole with my spear gun. You think you can cover me while I pull 'em out of there."

He swam over. "How deep?" he said.

"I dunno, maybe fifty or sixty feet."

I took a few deep breathes before descending down. When I got down to the cave, I saw the spear sticking out. I spotted the fish lodged into a hole. It was dark in there. I grabbed a hold of the spear and tried to pull the fish out.

Something moving caught my eye and I glanced to my right. As my eyes adjusted to the dim light in the cave, what I saw was like a horror movie. It was the jaws of a shark opening and closing, chewing off the tail of my fish. I couldn't see the shark's body, only the head and teeth. The shark had lodged itself inside the cave and was eating my grouper.

I worked faster to pull the grouper out of the hole, burning up oxygen. Out of air, I gave up and decided to head back to the surface. As I turned around, my brother was back-to-back with me, fending off sharks with his spear gun. They were coming in at a rapid pace. He was poking them in the nose with the tip of the spear as they moved in too close. They were coming in from all directions with the blood in the water. I desperately headed for the surface.

Corn told me later that he turned around and I was gone. He then grabbed my spear and began wiggling it out of the hole with one hand and defending off the sharks with his spear gun in the other. He freed up the grouper and brought it to the surface watching for sharks. We quickly got back to the boat and out of the water.

Back on the boat I said, "Man, I got down there and was trying to pull that fish out, then I turned and all I saw were teeth."

"I turned around and you had vanished," Corn said. "I didn't know if you got sucked into the cave by that shark or what,"

"At least we got two-thirds of the fish."

The shark had sawed off the tail and about a third of its body. We slowly motored back to the island, thankful to have our limbs intact.

Back at the lodge, the Fijian cooks took the fish we speared to prepare for dinner. During dinner, some of the tourists staying at the lodge were wondering why they would serve half-a-fish in the buffet. The other guys who were on the boat told them the story. The tourist couldn't understand why in the world my brother and I would battle sharks to save a fish.

Charge it all to Ronald McDonald

My brother and I stayed at Yanuca for nearly a month. We had it too good to leave. We were living for nearly free and surfing powerful waves. We got two large swells while Corn was visiting. The best swells were the ones that evolved near Antarctica and funneled through the Tasman Sea between Australia and New Zealand. It's difficult for the ocean to create big *and* perfect surf. When the waves are huge, they are usually stormy and mixed up. However, when all the right conditions come together, it's like physics and nature concocted a phenomenon in the laboratory of liquid.

We spent a couple of hours a day spearing fish for the surf lodge, bringing back more than they could eat. Corn was getting near the end of his month's hiatus, and we thought we'd sail out to the west side to surf a couple of spots. We also wanted to visit a little party island called the Beachcomber. He had less than a week left, and it would take us two days to sail over there. I only sailed during the daylight in Fiji to spot the shallow reefs.

I was ready for a change from Yanuca. Muzzy had island fever and was already tired of his job. He decided to move on and sail west to the Beachcomber with us. He also mentioned that he had received an email from an old girlfriend who was now living in New Caledonia. She was running a topless bar in the capital. New Caledonia was on my list of islands to visit, and that gave Muzzy a slight interest to head west with me.

I needed to get the *Bula* ready for the trip to the Beachcomber with a few important things to complete. Corn and Muzzy claimed they would help. I said, "Alright, somebody needs to organize the interior, someone has to knock the barnacles off the bottom, and I've gotta work out a rigging issue. Who wants to do what?"

Corn and Muzzy looked at each other and knew it was a dirty job to scrub the bottom. Corn said to Muzzy, "Rock, paper, scissors?"

"Sudden death, or two out of three?" Muzzy said.

"Two out of three."

They went at it and Muzzy quickly lost. He had the look on his face as if he wasn't sure why he offered to help. He shrugged it off and said to me, "I see how it is, you sepos. Gimme the damn snorkel gear."

I set him up with the gear and he dove over the side disconcerted. I was working on the rigging that needed tightening. I could hear Muzzy scrubbing away under the boat. I didn't hear my brother doing much down below and happened to get a whiff of something awful.

"What is *that*?" I said. I could hear him snickering down below in the head.

"Pure health," He said.

"More like pure hell."

"Where's Muzzy right now?"

I peered over the side in the water. "Wow, hang on. He just so happens to be directly underneath the head." Before I could finish my statement, I heard the toilet pump react like a volcano. Muzzy busted through the surface screaming before he got his head out of the water.

"MAAATE. DID YOU JUST FLUSH THE HEAD? FUCKING HELL. I WAS RIGHT UNDERNE . . . BAH . . . SICK."

Corn was trying to act as if it was an accident. He quickly stuck his head out the hatch and said, "Muzzy, oh man, I seriously didn't know you were under there." Corn wasn't doing such a good job with his cover-up.

"That's it." Muzzy said. "I'm done." He kept swimming away from the sewage spill, frantically brushing himself off. I had tears streaming down my face, though I was trying to keep a little composure for poor Muzzy.

He swam it off for a few minutes and came up the swim ladder. I looked at him unsure whether he wanted to seek immediate revenge. If so, I was ready to extract them both off the boat before something got broken. Muzzy looked subdued. It seemed as though he was formulating a plan of execution. I was interested to see the balancing, but not here. We ended up calling him "Muz-turd" after the episode.

We went to shore and said goodbye to the friendly locals. We paddled back to the boat and unfastened the mooring I had set up attached to the reef. Anchoring in a live coral reef is very damaging to the reef and your anchor chain. The metal chain grinds on the delicate reef, breaking off parts of it and disrupting the marine environment. Some sailors are conscious enough to find a sandy spot to drop their anchor to protect the reef. Since there were no sandy spots off the island, I set up a mooring system. That also saved my chain from having the protective galvanization grinded off and rusting.

We pulled out of the ethereal Yanuca Island. I would return someday. We threaded our way through the dangerous reefs and out of the pass. We hoisted the sails and I set the windvane on a course for our halfway point, the Fijian Hotel. The Fijian is a hotel in Cuvu Bay about halfway to Beachcomber Island.

We had a relaxing cruise to Cuvu Bay. An hour out of the bay, we hooked into a good-sized mahi mahi. Muzzy was reeling and he told my brother to grab the gaff while I was swinging the boat into the wind. Corn didn't grab the gaff and decided to pull it into the cockpit by hand. Bad move. Our dinner fell back into the sea and swam off. Accusations and fingers all pointed at the guy who didn't grab the gaff.

We pulled into Cuvu Bay with a plan to eat at the hotel buffet after the loss of the fish.

"I'm not sure that I can afford it," Muzzy said.

My brother and I looked at each other and said in unison, "You're not going to need any cash."

Muzzy said, "No mate, I can't do that."

"What are you afraid of?" Corn said.

Muzzy began stuttering about something and I said, "Listen, all we need is a room number from the hotel. The buffet is packed, they'll never know."

"I'm not sure," Muzzy said.

"Alright," I said, "we'll walk up to the reception and find out how much the dinner buffet costs. If it's reasonable, then we'll pay."

"Fair enough mate." Muzzy half-heartedly conceded.

We anchored in the bay and rowed in to shower at the poolside facilities. I had hotels wired. I found two hot water showers and we snuck into them. That was the first hot water shower I had in months. I always used the ocean as my shower and Fijian waters were cooler than most tropical areas.

I shaved off the pirate beard and geared-up in my best hotel-mingling outfit. White paints, loud Hawaiian t-shirt and sandals. I looked like a young swinger and blended in perfectly with the rest of the sadly dressed guests. Never draw attention to yourself.

We confidently marched into the scene. As we approached the reception counter, we heard a commotion in the lobby. There was a small Fijian welcoming band. They were playing guitars and ukuleles. Five young girls, badly sunburned, danced around in a circle in front of the band. I saw a good opportunity—walked over and joined them in dancing.

Muzzy was intent on getting a price for the buffet. He walked up to the front counter. Corn just stood there watching me dance around with these girls for a few seconds, and moved in. The girls said, "Hey, where are you guys from?"

"San Diego," I said.

My brother said, "Puerto Rico."

One of them said, "We're from Melbourne, Australia and we're here with our parents."

Three of the girls were sisters and one was a friend. As we danced around, they asked us our names and we told them. One of them said, "So what room are you guys in?"

I made up some number. She stood there squinting her eyes in question. She gave up and said, "Where's that?"

I pointed in three different directions as if I couldn't remember. I said, "I don't know, somewhere over that-a-way. So what room are you girls in?"

"381," one of them said.

The other girls looked at her and one whispered, "Why did you tell them our room number?" She stood there looking dumb.

They passed it off and I jokingly said, "You better lock your doors. I'm-a-gonna climb up yo balcony later." They had a frightened, yet interested, look in their eyes.

We were about to leave when Corn said, "What are your names?" They all confusingly said their names at once. "So what are your last names?" Corn said.

"McDonald," the three sisters said in unison.

"Like Ronald?" he said. They gave him sneering smiles and fake laughter.

We said goodbye to the girls and snuck away with a room number and a last name.

Muzzy said, "The buffet is too expensive for me."

"Don't worry about that," my brother said. Muzzy shook his head in disapproval and just followed us like a mutt being dragged to the kennel.

We found the restaurant, got a table, and hit the buffet. I started on my first plate of fish and veggies. My second plate was roasted pork. I continued going back for more.

I put away six plates. My brother and Muzzy had about four apiece. The food was just above Las Vegas buffet status—quantity not quality.

The bill came and I had already scoped out an escape route through the back, just in case. My brother signed it R. McDonald, room 381. We calmly walked out, leaving the bill on the table. As we passed the security guard standing at the entrance to the restaurant, he gave us a suspicious glare. Maybe I was just paranoid.

We were 100-feet away from the restaurant, thinking we were in the clear, when we heard a loud whistle. I was one-step away from sprinting. Those humongous Fijian guys would never catch me. And there was no way I was going to jail in my gay outfit.

My brother calmly spun around and walked back to the lion's den. Muzzy and I stayed a good distance away, in case we had to run. We painfully waited for the verdict.

A couple of minutes later, Corn moseyed back to us with an easy stride and a grin on his face. He said, "They needed the whole first name on the bill. I signed it Ronald McDonald and they were happy with that." We turned and sauntered off, keeping a cool composure.

The next day we pulled anchor and set sail for the Beachcomber. It was another beautiful sunny day in the exotic South Pacific. The waters were a bluish-turquoise. The land became more arid the further west we sailed. We caught various fish along the way.

We pulled in a 15-pound yellow fin tuna. Muzzy was trying to get the hook out of its mouth as he had it pinned in the corner of the cockpit.

I said, "Muzzy, use the needle-nose pliers." He didn't listen. The tuna went berserk and somehow the hook ended up in Muzzy's hand. It was lodged deep into his palm. He was jumping up and down shouting every cuss word and multiples of them. It wasn't a small hook either. You could pull in a 300 lb marlin with that hook.

After he stopped running around the boat, we sat him down and used a syringe of Novocain to shoot up his hand. His hand was numb within minutes. Corn tried to pry the hook out with some pliers.

Ten minutes of work, and a few more shots of Novocain, it was still stuck in his hand because of the barb on the end of the hook.

Corn said, "Maybe we should push the hook all the way through, cut the barb off and pull it back out the opposite way."

Muzzy said, "Do it now before I think about it."

Corn started pushing the hook as hard as he could. It took more force than we imagined penetrating through the skin of his palm. Finally, it pierced through the skin. I pulled out my three-foot lock cutters—snipped off the stainless steel barb and Corn pulled the hook back through. Muzzy surveyed the damage.

I said, "You should've used the pliers on that fish ya nickelneck. Next time you're going end up with the hook in your mouth."

We bandaged his hand with gauze and duck tape. He kept the hook for painful memories.

As we approached Tavarua Island, the wind died. I started the engine and we motored onward, checking the surf. The surface of the ocean was like a mirror. There were perfect swell lines wrapping into the multiple passes in the area.

We motored up to the famous wave "Cloudbreak" and watched the beautiful waves peeling over the reef. I got a little too close and a large set stacked up behind the boat. I turned away from the reef and floored it to get out into deeper water. The waves rolled past us, and broke onto the shallow reef only 50 feet from the stern of the boat. My heart pumped. I kept the throttle floored until we were out of the clutches of the breaking waves.

Muzzy and my brother were both staring at me. "Yeah, we got a little too close," I said.

We continued motoring over to a good right-hander called Wilkes Pass. We anchored in the channel next to another sailboat named *Black Stallion*. I knew the young captain from Australia named Harley.

The three of us paddled out to some perfect ten-foot waves. Harley was out surfing with only a few other guys from the neighboring island, Numotu.

Harley was tall and stocky with short dark hair. He had a laid-back Aussie accent and a likable nature. He was in his late twenties and captaining this beautiful 50-foot ketch by himself.

The sea was as clear as the sky. Tropical fish swam underneath our feet weaving through the colorful reef. I felt as though I was floating on air sitting on top of my surfboard above the reef.

I said to Harley, "You guys wanna hit the Beachcomber with us tonight?"

"We just had a big one in Nadi town last night," he said. "I could be into it, but I'm not sure about the rest of the gang."

We kept surfing for hours, trading off dreamy waves as Harley was complaining about his crippling hangover. Burnt out after four hours in the water, we paddled back to the boat.

We pulled the anchor and began motoring to the Beachcomber. As we passed *Black Stallion*, I saw Harley with his dad and a few others on deck. I yelled out, "You wankers gonna make it or ya too scared?"

Harley said, "Everyone is feeling pretty rough mate, but I think we might just follow ya's over there."

"I knew you had it in ya."

You can't tempt or challenge an Aussie sailor to a night on the piss*. They'll always give in and you'll always lose.

We got word that *Easy* was anchored at a neighboring island in a bay called Musket Cove that is popular among sailors. I tried to hail them on the VHF, "*Easy, Easy*, this is *Bula*, do you copy?"

Blair answered, "*Bula*, this is *Easy*, wanna switch to 69?"

"Six-nine." We both switched channels.

"Why, hello there *Bula* boys, we missed you."

"Yeah, we've been hiding out from the party circuit and surfing for the past few months. What have you two been into?"

"After we saw you last on the open ocean tossing a bag of fish at us, we sailed up to the northern Fijian island Vanua Levu and hooked up with some mad sailors. Carson, they made us seem like amateurs and now we are quite knackered."

---

* piss = Australian slang for grog, beer, or anything that's alcohol related

I envisioned the twisted competitions among their underworld. "So, it sounds like you two are probably not up for a party run?"

Blair took a deep nasal breath like a cowboy before he takes a shot of rotgut whiskey. "What did you have in mind?"

"It looks like we've got a bandwagon heading to the Beachcomber with Harley and his crew on *Black Stallion* bringing up the rear. I got my brother on the boat and this is his last night."

"I'll talk it over with Hugh. But to tell you the truth I'm not sure we'll make it. He's in a bad state as well."

"Oh come on. One more night's not going to kill ya."

She exhaled and said, "Hugh will be back in a couple of hours and I'll run it past him, but if we don't make it, have a smashing evening. It was lovely hearing your voice again. Say hello to Muzzy for me. Bye bye."

"It was nice chatting with you Blair. Bye. This is *Bula* back to one-six."

The Beachcomber

We sailed up through the Mamanuca Islands past Treasure Island. We dropped the sails and tied up to a mooring ball 50 meters from the bar at Beachcomber Island. *Black Stallion* sailed in and anchored next to us. Around sunset, to our surprise, *Easy* arrived.

We showered over the side of the boat in the pristine waters. We got our gear on and paddled the donkey over to *Black Stallion*. After we boarded their sailboat, I introduced my brother to Harley and he introduced us to his dad Jimmy. Harley pulled out a bottle of tequila and handed it to me. "Here ya go," He said. "This'll turn ya into a legend."

I took the bottle—cannon-balled it and handed it to Jimmy. He gave me a crazy stare and sampled it.

He cringed—shoved it into the ribs of my brother and squawked, "Gawd, get that nasty sheet a-why from me."

The bottle went around the circle creating expressions of pain combined with loud hooting. We were ready to hit the scene. Hugh and Blair were going to meet us onshore.

We got to shore—pulled the donkey up onto land and had a look around as we stood on the beach. There was a big wooden bar with a thatched roof constructed on the waterfront.

We looked at each other and walked towards the place. We sauntered up to the bar and ordered a round of cocktails. I looked around and the place was dead. It was nine o'clock at night and most of the young backpackers were quietly sitting around sipping beers and playing cards.

I banged on the bar top and yelled, "WAKE UP EVERYBODY."

A large Fijian man materialized out of the back with three heavy fellows. He walked straight up to me with his pack and began waving a sausage finger at me.

"No shouting," he said.

"Right, of course," I said, "Yes very sorry, we'll keep it down sir."

They walked off without the slightest expression on their faces. I turned and said, "It seems I'll be leaving the bar with an escort this evening, and it probably isn't going to be a girl."

Shortly after the telephone-booth-boys reprimanded me, the place made a turn for the better. More people were filling into the bar.

A Fijian band began setting up on the stage in the middle of the sand dance floor. They were tuning-up their guitars and flipping switches with feedback buzzing from the rusty amplifiers.

The Beachcomber is an island that would take you about ten minutes to circle on your hands and knees. This was the method used by most after closing time. It held a maximum of 300 people. The dorm held up to eighty people. Imagine eighty smelly backpackers all smashed into one room. There were also a few smaller rooms among the palms and foliage, if you actually wanted to sleep.

By the time the band started up, there was quite the crowd forming. They played a few local favorites and then moved on to mutilate some cover song. At first, I couldn't make out what they were playing. It sounded familiar, but something wasn't right. Then I realized they were actually trying to do a cover of The Rolling Stones.

After a few more botched numbers, the band took a break. Everyone was looking around and wondering what was next. Most of our crew was ordering more drinks having never left the bar.

Then came the disco music. It started with the Village People's "YMCA" then launched into ABBA's "Dancing Queen". It gradually got worse. It was a Kmart disco. The music played on with Culture Club, Spandal Ballet, Haircut 100, and Bow Wow

Wow. I think the DJ hit the climax of bad '80s tracks when he threw on Kaja Goo Goo and everyone sang, "Too shy too shy, hush hush eye to eye."

The party escalated until the music stopped and the band got back on stage. They played a few bad cover songs and tried to get the crowd involved in a song that was the Fijian rendition of the Macarena. We heard an occasional complaint from the crowd, "Put the DJ back on." They actually preferred the Kmart disco. I did too.

The band labored through a few more and pulled off one decent rendition of "Mambo #5". They called it quits and no one asked for an encore.

The DJ started it back up with Wham. The dance floor erupted this time, and by the second round of "YMCA", one girl was up on a picnic table trying to make out the letters with her arms, but she seemed to be dyslexic.

I looked around and saw Harley flat on his back in the sand next to the bar. I walked over and said to Muzzy, "What happened to him?"

"I don't know," Muzzy said. "He got loaded really fast, and now he can't seem to stay on his feet."

Harley was wiggling around in the sand like a plump penguin waiting for someone to put him back on his feet. Most of those standing around him were oblivious to his pleas and just kicked sand on him. Some poor fool, who felt sorry for him, would pick him up and ten minutes later, he would be on his back again.

The swingers, Hugh and Blair, were drumming up an interesting drama. Hugh, a borderline pedophile by nature, was chatting up some eighteen year-olds. He was trying to get Blair in on the deal, for help of course. Blair was uninterested in the whole scene. She didn't fancy young backpackers who generally didn't know how to satisfy a woman. It looked as though Hugh might be the only one chalking up points on their demented blackboard.

I spotted my brother on the dance floor doing an Elvis jig with a Brazilian girl shaking her tail with some serious talent. She could've shined your shoes with that booty. Latinas have a motor installed in that rear-end unit. With enough of them engines, we could generate some power with asstro-electricity. Wire-up those bubble buts with some electrodes—throw on some samba and you could light up Rio during a blackout.

Just when I was thinking I should stop my over-consumption, this cute girl walked up to me with a cocktail and said, "Some of your friends at the bar bought you a drink and asked me to deliver it to you."

Muzzy had been handing me multiple cocktails all night, pushing me well over my boundaries. Now he had girls delivering them to me.

"What is it?" I asked.

"I think they said it was a Beachcomber Bloody Mary." She shrugged and handed it to me.

I took a slow sip. It was thick and pulpy with a lot of odd stuff in the mix. It was similar to a Bloody Mary but different. I took a gulp and got some more chunks on the second pull.

"How is it?" she asked.

"It's a bit weird, but not all that bad. Here have a try."

She scrunched-up her face as though she wasn't sure. She took a small sip and quickly handed it back to me. "No, baaah. Something's wrong with that drink."

I took one more gulp and she said, "No, don't drink anymore of that."

"Why, it's not that bad, is it?"

She was spitting on the floor and coughing. She tried to put her hand on the top of the cup, so I wouldn't sip anymore.

She caught her breath and said, "Look what's in the drink you dummy."

I looked into the dark concoction with all kinds of junk floating in the bottom and stirred it with my finger. Two cigarette butts floated to the surface with a whole swirl of ash. I looked at her in disgust and we both turned and looked at the bar.

Muzzy and my brother were lurking behind a wooden pillar. The girl ran to the bathroom and I just stood there with ash on my teeth. You can't feel that confident about yourself if you've never been a sucker.

Blair got tired of the juvenile gymnasium. Hughie was still fumbling at the mouth with his teenyboppers. Fed up, Blair barged out of the place heading back to the boat.

Harley was still on his back talking to random people that were standing up. His brain was still functioning but his lower half was not.

I was sitting at a bench table with Muzzy thanking him for the cocktail he had mixed up for me. The urge for retribution came over me with a certain bodily pressure. I nonchalantly whipped out my monkey under the table and began peeing on his leg with a blasé look on my face. He was telling me a story about his buddy back home. It took him more than a second to register the sensory alarm. He then looked down at his soaked leg—saw the stream of pee—looked at me in confusion and *SNAPPED*.

He spring-boarded out of his seat like Kung Fu Theater and yelled, "CARSON YOU MOTHER FUCKER. I CAN'T BELIEVE YOU JUST . . ."

The calamity gave me stage fright. I tucked it away for safety. He was storming around in circles and yelling, "I CAN NOT BELIEVE YOU PISSED ON MY LEG!"

No matter what, there's an evil piece of shit deep down inside of all of us. We're all human and we all have an ass. Be it a priest, a philanthropist or Mother Teresa; everyone wants to drop a stinking turd on someone else sooner or later.

I was just playing around, but Muzzy took it to a monumental level of mutiny. He was furiously zigzagging around in no particular direction. He barged off somewhere to sulk or bring the roof down on me.

The night carried on like a bad case of the clap. Next came the infamous stunt hour when household heroes come alive. There were some white guys trying to break-dance on the sand dance floor. It's tough enough to do that eighties gorilla dance on a regular floor, much less the sand.

An English bloke hit the floor and tried to do the worm. I felt as though I was dealing with a bunch of amateurs and thought I'd show them up. I jumped on top of the closest picnic table next to the dance floor and yelled, "LOOK OUT."

Everyone turned to see me up there with my arms outstretched and bug-eyed. The crowd quickly cleared the dance floor. I launched forward off the table into a front flip and flew through the air only rotating three-quarters of the way around landing square on my back in the middle of the hard sand. It knocked the wind out of me.

I couldn't breathe. I lay there wheezing for air. Finally able to breath, I looked up to see people staring down at me. Some were concerned. I heard an eruption of laughter from the peanut gallery and I limped off the dance floor.

I spotted Muzzy holding his sides and pointing at me. I waddled up to him and painfully whispered, "That was the stupidest thing I've ever done."

I knew my back was going to be a mess in the morning. I shuffled out of the place dragging the Muzzy with me. My brother had disappeared about an hour ago. Muzzy and I paddled the donkey back to the boat.

Humans Sailing the High Seas
is about as Natural as
a Tuna Tiptoeing across Texas

The next morning the morale on the boat was low. It was hot enough to make the devil sweat. The only thing we could do was get the boat moving to create some breeze in the stagnate heat.

I turned over the engine and untied the boat from the mooring ball. I motored away from the island of heathens and set the autopilot for the mainland of Viti Levu. My brother had to fly out that day. We sailed over to the mainland and anchored at a secluded beach close to the Nadi airport.

We said our goodbyes to my brother who was off to Puerto Rico. Every time we meet up it's like another scene from a movie. I haven't had a bad time with my bro since we were kids beating up each other.

Muzzy and I spent the day with bad hangovers provisioning the boat and getting ready for a three-day crossing to Vanuatu.

We checked out of the country the next morning and set sail. We had light winds pushing us downwind through Wilkes Passage and out into the open ocean. The day was a little rough as we sailed away from the Fijian Islands.

The night fell upon us and we spotted the lights of a fishing boat up ahead in the darkness. It was on the same southwest course as us and it was moving along at our same speed. It was only a quarter mile away most of the night. We kept an eye on it as the winds and seas increased intensity.

The fishing boat created a hazard to us all night. We actually had to stay awake during our night shift this time when we were used to sleeping through it.

The next day the winds turned more southerly, which made it more difficult to sail in the direction we needed to go. The winds increased velocity and the seas were the most unorganized I'd ever witnessed. Four swells were converging from different directions. It was extremely uncomfortable, awkwardly tossing the boat in an undulating manner.

The closer we got to Vanuatu the more Muzzy was trying to talk me into going straight to New Caledonia. The last time he checked his email, he had received another message from his old girlfriend in New Caledonia running the strip joint. She said her birthday was in a couple of days and wondered if we could sail down there in time for it. She claimed she would "set us up". I don't know if Muzzy threw in that last statement for my sake or not. He really wanted to see her, and the topless bar.

We were planning on stopping in the southern island of Vanuatu called Tana for a few days to break up the trip to New Caledonia. I was interested in seeing the live volcanoes in Vanuatu and scuba diving its world-renowned reefs. However, to get set up in New Cal, whatever that meant, didn't seem that awful. Although, I wasn't so sure about getting set up with some seedy stripper.

The next day the winds strengthened, throwing off our arrival time in Tana. I didn't want to arrive at night, but with the increased winds I calculated an arrival time at midnight. We could put out more sail, but we still wouldn't make it before sunset. We couldn't slow down either, because it made the boat sluggish and roll uncontrollably.

Muzzy looked at me and said, "Topless girls."

I thought about it for maybe three seconds, gave in and said, "Screw it; we're sailing to NEW CAL."

"Yeah mate. Her birthday is in two days. Do you think we'll make it?"

"We'll be there in a day-and-a-half at this speed."

I wanted to visit Tana, but heaving-to in rough weather all night near the island sounded miserable and even dangerous.

We sailed on through the day and caught the biggest mahi-mahi I had ever landed. It was 45 or 50 lbs and around five feet long. With the batteries topped up and the colder weather in the southern latitude, we decided to turn on the frig. We packed the refrigerator and freezer.

We were getting near the Loyalty Islands on the east side of New Cal. I thought we would spot them in the next hour and I kept an eye out for them.

Four hours later and no islands. I double-checked our position and the direction in which we should see them.

Eight miles away and still nothing. I got worried. You can usually spot a low-lying atoll with palm trees 10 or 15 miles out. We were nearly on top of them. I was wondering about my navigation equipment, the corrections of the charts and my own skills. I let Muzzy in on my ordeal. That was the second time, in all our days of sailing together, that he questioned my ability as a captain. The last time was off Samoa when I puked.

He was running around in a quandary—grabbing the binoculars and scanning the horizon. I continued to check both GPS units when I heard a snigger from Muzzy top-deck. He said, "We've got an island captain."

I ran up the stairs to the cockpit. He was pointing to the northwest. It took me a few seconds, and then I finally spotted it. It was nothing but a flat dirt mound like a hard baseball field on the moon. There wasn't a mountain or a tree on it. I recalled seeing mountainous pictures of New Caledonia and figured that these outer islands would be similar. NASA could've saved billions by flying here and fooled the world.

As we rounded the bottom of the Loyalty Islands, the sun began its final descent. We actually spotted some small mountains on the north side of the island.

A full moon rose out of the ocean after sunset. It was bright in its splendor as we sailed closer to the foreign land. We sat in the cockpit watching the moonlight glimmer off the choppy seas. Muzzy retired to the coffin and I kept the boat on course.

Welcome to New Caledonia

Just before sunrise, I spotted lights from the eastern pass. I steered the *Bula* through the Havana Passage at sunrise. The island was mountainous and rugged. However, it was more arid than the other islands I had visited in the South Pacific. It was a striking introduction. Instead of jungle and palms, there were boulders and pines.

The air and water temperature were shockingly cool. I was wearing pants, two long sleeve shirts, a jacket and a hat. Granted, it was dawn and we were at sea in 25 knots of wind. We were breathing in the moment as we neared the strange new land when *BUZZZZZZZ*.

"YOU'RE UP MATE," Muzzy yelled.

I pounced on the rod. Muzzy pulled the *Bula* into the wind. I reeled hard and steady without giving the fish an inch of play to get away. Muzzy was watching my torturous technique on the fish and said, "You're treating that fish like a whore."

"You want to give it a lollipop before I bash it over the head?"

"At least I make some sport out of it."

"I don't like losing fish. I'm sick of eating corned-beef hash."

That shut him up. I pulled the fish up alongside the boat. Muzzy gaffed it and yanked it into the cockpit. It was a 20 lb yellow-fin tuna. I got the lure back in the water and five minutes later *BUZZZZZZ*.

I offered the next one to Muzzy and he said, "Go ahead mate, I've had my share."

I reeled in another 15-lb yellow-fin and hauled it into the cockpit. I got the lure back out and another one hit. I pulled in a third 15-pounder.

In the past 12 hours, we had caught a 50 lb mahi-mahi and three 15 lb yellow-fin tuna. We had one hundred pounds of grade-A pelagic fish. We could've opened a sushi restaurant.

I pulled out the video camera. We laid the fish out on the lazarette and Muzzy turned the camera on me, mimicking a news-reporter. He said, "Three, two, one . . . you're away."

I started with, "Welcome to New Cal . . ." The rest was a mingled mess of quotes and comments.

We sailed through the extensive archipelago inside the barrier reef. High cliffs extended upward along the shoreline, rising to 300 feet. Pine forests dotted the hillsides and mystically hung over the cliffs. The wind picked up and we were flying downwind in the flat waters, tacking a serpentine route through the tight islands. It was the first time I saw seagulls and pelicans since Mexico. They were circling the boat as Muzzy filleted the fish, leaving a trail of blood in our wake.

We made our way around to the capital Noumea and sailed into the marina. I recognized many of the cruising yachts that I had seen in other parts of the Pacific over the past three years. Everyone had made their way west and was either going onward to New Zealand or Australia to hide out for the cyclone season.

As we sailed in, there was a local islander directing us into a slip for quarantine. He asked me the name of my boat over the water. I yelled, "*BULA*."

A guy standing on the deck of his boat glanced up and said, "*Bula*?" It was Cameron, the fellow I met in Tahiti on his Columbia 30' *Duet*.

"Is that you Cam-dog?" I said.

"Carson, what the heck are you doing here? I thought you were in Hawaii?"

"I was, but it's no fun being a haole in Hawaii."

"You made it here pretty fast."

"I heard it was French and I was dying for a croissant. Listen, let me get this boat in a slip—check in and then you should come over for a big fish fry. We caught a few out there."

"It's great to see ya, we'll spin by later."

We pulled the boat into the designated slip as directed. The man politely ordered us to wait for quarantine before we disembarked the vessel. The quarantine woman came to the boat, climbed aboard and inspected the filthy interior.

She said we would have to peel all our fruit and vegetables if we wanted to keep them, even the garlic. In the many years of traveling, this was the strangest request upon entering a country. I've been questioned, interrogated, fingerprinted, car-searched, strip-searched, and even checked for SARS, but I've never been asked to peel my goodies. Next, they'd be asking me to cook them a savory stir-fry. I put Muzzy to work peeling the pile of vegetables.

I said, "Sorry, but I've got to go handle the paperwork with customs." He just snarled at me and got out the peeling knife.

After all the formal paperwork, I returned to the boat and Cameron came around with his two female crewmembers.

He popped his head in the boat and said, "Great to see ya made it here."

I said, "I had a funny feeling when I left Tahiti that we would see each other again someday."

We shook hands and he said. "If you guys are cooking then we'll bring the beers."

I said, "Fair enough."

They left for the store and Muzzy said, "Alrighty then, can I finally get off this stinking boat, *captain*?"

I said, "You're free to roam, mate."

Muzzy grabbed his phone list and went to make the important phone call. It wasn't mom, dad or any worried family member. It was the strip joint.

Muzzy returned after ten minutes. He was trying hard to mask his secret smile. I said, "So how'd it go?"

He said, "Nope, no luck." He left it at that, avoiding any eye contact.

"You're full of shit. I can see it all over your face."

"Ahhh . . . IT'S ON MATE." We started giggling and letting loose our little boyish excitement.

Muzzy and his ex girlfriend Leah, who was running the strip joint, had always stayed on good terms. He said that she was on her way down to the boat with some "friends". We began cleaning up the wreckage from the crossing.

An hour later, Cameron and his crew of girls returned. I said, "Cam, what does a guy have to do to get, not one, but two girls as crew? I'll trade ya Muzzy; he's handy, and a hard worker until he gets seasick." Muzzy shot me a scowl.

Cameron introduced us to his girlfriend Trisha and his sister Lanett. Trisha was a sexy blonde from Montana. His sister Lanett was a cute brunette with a strong body. She was the outdoorsy type, wearing Patagonia gear. We all shook hands. Muzzy had his eye on Cameron's sister.

They handed us a six-pack short of a case. Cameron said, "We sampled a few on the way." I handed everyone a French beer and shoved the rest in the fridge.

Leah arrived by herself and Muzzy introduced us. She was a tall, thin, bleached-blonde with a playboy body and a head like a foot. Why does God have to play tricks on us like this?

"So where are your friends?" I said.

She said, "I asked a few of them if they wanted to come down to the boat, but most of them were busy."

I tried to hide my disappointment and went on cooking. It was better off anyway. I was safe from immoral temptations.

Muzzy and I cooked up a meal for everyone. It seemed so easy to cook with the boat sitting still. We enjoyed the security of a marina for once. This is one of the only times in a captain's life when you can relax. There's no worry of the vessel dragging anchor, getting hit by a storm, or any unforeseen mishaps, except for hurricanes. Hurricanes can dislodge entire marinas and destroy everything. But if you're going to worry about that, then don't sail to the tropics.

Everyone enjoyed the meal and we sat around drinking cheap French beer. The French make great wine, but they missed on the beer. It's worse than American beer.

Cameron said, "So Muzzy, I know Carson's brother, and I was wondering what it must've been like living on the boat with the two of them?"

Muzzy shook his head and said, "Hell mate. These sepos have been tormenting me."

Cameron said, "Oh yeah, what happened?"

I was biting my lip when Muzzy said, "Mate, these guys had me under the boat scrubbing the bottom in Fiji and his brother flushed the head while I was directly underneath it. I nearly got a mouthful."

All the girls screamed and Leah backed away from him as if he still had it on him. Everyone was looking at me in disbelief and I said, "That had nothing to do with me."

Everyone laughed and Cameron said, "Somebody should make t-shirts: I GOT FUCKED BY THE CARSON BROTHERS." Muzzy looked at me with a hateful smirk.

We choked down a few more beers and decided to hit the town. Everyone returned to their boats to throw on their best gear, something besides tattered surf-trunks and tank tops. Most everyone had at least one sufficient shirt and pair of pants to wear to a decent establishment. The five of us piled into Cameron's dingy and motored into the distant town from the marina.

Noumea is a classy French capital with typical Parisian cafés, quaint bistros and a cosmopolitan atmosphere. We found a popular bar called the Ethnic on the waterfront. It was full of sexy French girls. There's something about French girls. Even the ugly ones know how to look appealing. But good luck trying to talk to them. In the past, every time I opened my mouth and they found out I was an American, they contemptuously stared at me as though I was a cultureless baboon. I don't blame them, but at least Americans are friendly.

I decided to try my luck and walked up to a local girl. I spoke about three sentences in French and ran out of words. And

Americans wonder why they are disdainful towards us. They can speak our language, but we usually can't speak theirs.

Shockingly enough, she was very receptive and happy to talk to me. It must have been a fluke. Her English was worse than my French was. We decided on conversing in Spanish. I hung around chatting with her for awhile.

All the French girls I talked to that night were friendly. They probably hadn't met enough Americans to become biased. Most Americans haven't even heard of New Caledonia. I'm not unpatriotic, but we have been stereotyped by a number of backward representatives from certain states I'll fail to mention, because I'm from one of them.

The arrogant French girl stereotype took on a new light. Like a black guy with a small dick, it ain't all true what you hear.

We were bar hopping all night, blowing all our money. Muzzy and I ended up walking home late, unable to pay for a cab. We had lost everyone by the end of the night and we trudged onward towards the boat. We crossed through people's yards, leaped over fences and traversed fields to get back to the harbor. We used the idea that the closest distance between two points is a straight line. We finally arrived without any issues with the authorities. We found our salty domicile and passed out after crossing what seemed like the entire city.

The Strip Joint

The day started with a can of cheap beer. That was my first mistake. Then I moved on to my second mistake. That was trying to do boat maintenance with a hangover. I canned the operation and resolved myself to more beer. Muzzy joined me in the consumption.

We sat around mulling over our headaches, slowly depleting the beer stock. After the liquid motivation, we wanted to get to that strip joint by mid-afternoon. He called up Leah and she told us to come on down. I looked at Muzzy in all seriousness and said, "What am I gonna wear?" Muzzy shrugged. I only had one pair of pants and one decent shirt and I had worn them the previous night. I didn't have a wardrobe of hip gear on the boat.

I tried to spruce up my deflated outfit from the night before. I slapped it on and it reeked of smoke and booze. I said to myself, "Who cares, right?" Then I mumbled, "You'll never get laid you idiot."

We stumbled off the boat and wandered up to the main road to hitch a ride to the reputable establishment. Two rides later, we were getting close.

We hopped out of the bed of the second truck just in front of the joint. We tried to look confident as we leisurely cruised through the dark doors into the den of decadence.

Leah came out from the back and greeted us with a welcoming smile. There were graceful felines frolicking about on the makeshift stages. I stopped to look around the place, surveying the bad lighting. There were circular stages made of particleboard with various kinds of worn leather couches surrounding the stages.

I faked a nod of approval to Leah and said, "Nice place."

"Thank you," she said. "We have some lovely ladies here this evening, yes. One of the girls here tonight, is all the way from Australia. And another one is from Tonga."

I had just come from Tonga and didn't see a whole lot of slim girls there. I was afraid to see that one up on the rickety stage.

Muzzy was really into the scene and I just went along with it. I figured it was going to be interesting enough, at least to gather some new material.

We bellied up to the weathered bar. Leah said, "So, what you boys drinking?"

Muzzy said, "Gimme me a Ma-garita."

I took a deep breath to gauge my poison for the evening. With a John Wayne drawl, I said, "Whiskey for me ma'am."

"How would you like it?" Leah said.

I continued with the accent. "Straight up darling."

The male bartender got to work on our libations and returned with a crooked-toothed smile.

"Thank you," I said. Muzzy and I clinked glasses.

Leah persisted on giving us free cocktails. I began to think better of the place. Leah introduced us to each of the girls as they walked by. One was salaciously eyeing me up and down, giving me the look of the hungry donkey. I returned some of the obvious gawking and fabricated sexual fantasies in my head.

Leah got wind of the attraction and thought she would have a secret word with me. She came over and quietly said, "So Carson, it seems as though Pricilla has her eye on you."

"Yesss, it does appear so," I said.

She then switched her attitude. "Well you better stay away from that one. She's a little off." She cupped her hand next to her head shaking it as though her brain was out of kilter.

I mumbled, "Why me? Why does it always have to be the crazy one?"

"Excuse me?"

Coming out of my reverie, I said, "Oh nothing, never mind."

"Well I just wanted to warn you, so be careful."

It's as if the Devil himself sets up these little temptations for his own comic relief. I hadn't even been introduced to Pricilla yet, probably for obvious reasons.

I shied away from any more tantalizing stares and began looking at the other girls. Nevertheless, once you publicly sector out a girl in a bar in front of their friends, you can't switch. The other dancers were not remotely interested in me because I had been eyeing the crazy one.

Later in the evening, Muzzy sat down next to me at the bar. I said, "So I've been cornered by the loopy one and now I feel as though I've been banned by the rest of them."

"Ah, you're better off mate," he said. "There's nothing here but a bunch of washed up mongrels."

I resented that remark, thinking that these were some fine ladies. I vaguely remembered my first thoughts upon entering the bar were exceedingly different.

I said, "We gotta get out of here before it's too late."

He nodded in approval. We began slamming our cocktails to make a quick exit. I immediately headed for the door. Muzzy felt obligated to say goodbye to Leah, or at least give her some excuse for stepping out. I thought it was a bad move to let anyone know we were leaving. You always get talked into one more.

I said, "I'll see ya in the parking lot. If you're not there in five, I'm walking."

"Believe me," he said. "I'm out in two."

Five minutes later, I began walking when Muzzy came through the door with Leah and a new girl.

"Where do you think *you're* going?" Leah said.

I stammered, "Well, I was just ahhh . . ."

She interrupted, "Hey Carson, I want to introduce you to my friend, Melissaaaa."

I looked at Melissa up and down. She was a voodoo sex panther. She was wearing red leather hot pants and a translucent white top.

Leah added, "She's down from the UK for a month."

She didn't have to fill in the blanks. I was just wondering how this one had slipped by without catching my eye. It must've been the lighting.

Leah put an arm around Muzzy and said, "Muzzy will be staying with me, and I gave Melissa my car. She can give you a ride back to your boat or wherever *you two* wanna go."

I felt as if mom had given us her consent and let the kids out to play. Melissa was looking at me seductively.

Melissa sauntered up to me with long legs neatly packed into those hot pants. Her long black hair was hanging down inside her blouse. She slipped her hand into mine staring at me with submissive eyes. She wasn't a shy girl. I guess you can't be in that business. What startled me was her hands were rougher than mine were, and I'm a sailor. I passed it off as a dishwashing issue and thought to myself that Leah wouldn't set me up with a man, or would she. I stood back and checked the features. I started with the Adams apple and then the size of the hands. I laughed to myself, thinking that first it was the crazy lady, now it was a dude. But everything seemed to have checked out alright.

We turned and she began skipping to the car. She said in a little schoolgirl voice, "You need a ride sailor?"

We got in the car. She turned over the ignition and revved-up the engine. She backed out of the parking spot and punched it out of the parking lot. Why are strippers such reckless drivers?

She powered onward, apparently under the influence as well. I gripped the door handle and entertained thoughts of jumping out of the vehicle at the next stop light. I was having visions of police bubble lights behind us. I would be jumping out of the car running from the police, wondering if the island cops carried guns.

She said with a British accent, "What are you thinking about?"

I looked at her with a shocked stare as though she could read my mind. I said, "Oh nothing, just thinking about ahhh . . . what time it could possibly be."

"Who cares? So, Leah tells me that you sailed here all the way from California."

I tried to bring my mind back to the present. With the passing of a streetlight, I saw a flash of one of her breasts uncovered from her blouse by the wind. I looked down at those red leather pants and felt my body pulled magnetically to that luscious honey pot.

"Ahhh . . . yeah," I said. "I sailed here from San Diego."

"Wow that's a long way. Must've been scary huh?"

My mind began to change gears and I was feeling more comfortable. "Sure, it was pretty tough at times out there with some bad storms, but all in all, it was an incredible journey."

"I don't want to interrupt your story, but where's your boat?"

"I don't have the least idea. I think it's down that way and pointed towards the water."

She made the next turn. We got lost down some back road that led nowhere. She gleefully laughed and said, "We could drive around all night at this rate."

I was determined to find it. God only knew where she lived. "It's around here somewhere in the next bay, I think."

She drove on in a rambling fury, pushing the poor little French car over the edge of its mechanical boundaries. French cars are like the Rubik's cube; small, puzzling, and fun for awhile, but when it comes to getting them out of whack, good luck.

I pointed and said, "Ah ha. Here it is. Take a left."

Immediately after the last word rolled off my tongue, Melissa cranked the wheel over without braking. She barely missed the curb and we bottomed-out through the corner. We hovered onward and I looked back, then at her. How did we just make that turn unscathed? She didn't even notice. She was focused on the narrow road.

We pulled into the marina parking lot, minus the police. Exhaling for the first time since we left, I calmly said, "Well ok then, here we are." I did some math in my head before I made my next statement.

One: we were alive.

Two: no cops.

Three: she was definitely a female. No man could drive like that and get away with it.

I was confident with my next question. "Wanna see my boat?"

"Sure baby."

"Let's go."

I opened the door to the steaming mobile *car*toon and put my feet on the still pavement. I put my arm around her and we ambled to the docks.

We boarded the *Bula* and I showed her down the companionway. It was in shambles from the dinner party. There were a slew of dirty plates pilled up on the kitchen counter. A muddle of beer cans and wine bottles were strewn about on every horizontal surface of the boat.

"I take it you don't have a maid?" she said.

I searched the refrigerator for any beers. I found one left and thought to myself, how could we have missed this one earlier?

I cracked the last French beer and we shared it. At least it was cold. I put on some music and we found a semi-clean area to lounge.

After a few more sips, we locked lips and she went straight for my goodies. We continued to kiss and my head started to spin. Not good. I refrained from closing my eyes and tried to straighten up before I got sick.

I said, "Are you hot? Man I'm burning up in here. I gotta get some air." I staggered up the stairs and laid down on the poop deck. I laid there for awhile trying to get some fresh air. I ended up passing out under the stars.

I woke up the next morning top deck to the sun rising over the distant mountains. I crept down into the cabin. She had found a bed and was still snoring. A female will never fess up to snoring, even if you record them and play it back. They'll claim you doctored the tape.

I tried to recall the end of the night and vaguely remembered leaving her down below alone. Who knows if she tried to arouse me? Either way, I was glad I passed out, at least for her mother's sake, and mine.

I looked at the mess in disbelief with flies hovering around the kitchen and gnats buzzing around the beer cans. I was starving, and all we had left were things that you had to cook, so I opted for a can of roast beef hash.

As the toxic tri-product was frying up in the pan, Melissa woke up and said, "What's that horrible smell?"

"Ummm, good vittles darling. Want some?"

"Will it kill me?"

"Depends on how much alcohol you got left in ya."

"Doesn't smell like I've got enough."

She finally got up and squeezed into those hot pants for the walk of *fame*. There was no reason to be shameful. Thank god, because she had changed overnight from a 9 to a 6. The card I was holding the night before must've been upside down.

She didn't dally around for long. She gave me a kiss and exited with her hair in a bit of a tangle. She said something about having to get the car back to Leah.

I sat there in the sticky cabin with a deadly hangover. Gnats were buzzing around my head and everything was in disarray. I grinned at yet another strange chapter in my life. At least she was a girl.

Get out While You're Still Alive

Muzzy and I spent a month in New Caledonia surfing the outer islands. I was playing music with a Dutch sailor in the local cafés in Noumea on the weekends for some spare cash. Muzzy and I were living on the fish we were spearing in the outer reefs. We were on top of the world hanging out with sexy dancers on the weekends, and during the week, we were living the Bohemian lifestyle of surfing and sailing.

Then bad luck hit us. We both come down with the toxin "ciguatera". Ciguatera is a toxin in reef fish that live in the oceans close to the equator. It doesn't affect the fish itself, only the humans that eat the fish. There's very little known about this poison, therefore no one knows what is going to happen to us in the future. There have been various mortality cases. These extreme cases occurred in individuals exposed to the toxin multiple times over years.

The symptoms entail vomiting, extreme pain, sensory overload, and a strange reversal of the sense of touch. Everything that is hot to the touch seems cold, and everything that is cold seems hot. Your skin tingles all the time for no apparent reason. Once exposed to the toxin, you can't eat anything that is related to fish, fish oil, or any products thereof or you'll immediately have a relapse.

Alcohol is sadly off limits, but that didn't stop us. Immediately after I wrapped my hand around a cold beer, it felt as if it was burning my skin. I would hold the bottle as it sent little electric shocks up my arm. After five beers, my whole body turned numb.

Muzzy and I tried to make the best of our debilitated situation. We found it silly when our hands would go completely numb after one beer. Then the second beer would turn our feet numb, and so on. We were playing pranks on our own health. It wasn't the most intelligent thing, we were just trying to keep ourselves in good spirits.

It took nearly a month until we began feeling close to normal. We were ready to get out of New Cal before it finished us off between the partying and the fish poison.

We waited for a good weather window and said our farewells to all the good friends we had met. I calculated a seven-day sail to Australia and figured we should leave early in the morning. We were going to shoot for the Brisbane area, if the winds were favorable. If they weren't favorable, then we could end up as far south as Sydney.

The next morning we woke up around four a.m. in the cool pre-dawn. We weighed anchor, pulled the sails up in the dark and headed west with a nice 10-knot breeze. Seagulls and booby birds were circling the *Bula*. They were already hunting the seas for an early meal.

The sun slowly emerged and revealed a wind-swept ocean. The waves were short and choppy inside the pass. The winds had picked up to 25 knots, making it difficult to get through the outer reef pass. After tacking a few times, we managed to squeeze out of the pass and triumphantly sailed into the deep blue.

The normal procedures of settling in mentally and physically came next for another odyssey into the unknown. It's one thing to put yourself out in the elements at the mercy of Mother Nature occasionally, but continually wears on a fellow. There's no such thing as security on the high seas, even in the most bulletproof vessel. Look at the Titanic. Anything can happen, and that's what leaves you guessing. Like anything in life, you'll never get anywhere unless you take a few risks, but you don't have to go out and give the devil a wedgie everyday.

The winds were gusty and the boat was rocking along at a nagging rate. The long trips in between land in the South Pacific were grinding me down. I was personally looking forward to getting it all over.

My plan was to reach Australia and put the poor *Bula* up for sale. I hated to do it, but I was sick and tired of the long passages, the continual maintenance, and the amount of money I was pouring into the boat. I was in a constant state of entropy. Three years on a boat is somewhat like solitary confinement. I only had enough space down below to walk six steps before I hit a wall and had to spin around to do another six steps. I was pacing back and forth in my own jail cell.

If I couldn't sell her, I had to emancipate myself from the ball and chain for awhile. Anything would be better. I needed to recapture some semblance of normality, like a job, and maybe a girlfriend. It had been excessively too long since I had a woman. That's enough to drive any man insane. Maybe the Romans were right. But then again, I didn't want to sleep around with just anyone. I was thinking myself into a convoluted quandary with no beer left onboard.

After the third day out, the winds dropped to ten knots. I'll take comfort over speed. What's an extra day at sea? At least we weren't getting beat up.

The next few days tiptoed by as we crawled towards the large continent. The winds died completely, forcing us to motor-sail.

We were lounging around the cabin in the middle of the day, staring at the ceiling and Muzzy said, "You getting hungry mate?"

"Yeah, but what have we got left to eat?" I said.

The cupboard had diminished to untouched canned food from foreign countries all over the Pacific. They sat there for lack of interest or missing labels.

There was a full hierarchy of outdated supplies. Some were only a few weeks out, and others were over a year old. I would eat something that was maybe a few months out, but anything over six months was definitely off limits. However, I never threw them out in case we got lost at sea and needed them to survive.

I get oddly inventive when I'm sitting on a boat in the middle of nowhere with a lack of food. I had a friend who tore the labels off all the canned food before we embarked on a three-month road trip through Mexico. It seemed funny in the beginning, until some meals, you opened three cans of hominy. There was no dumping out precious food supplies on the trip. You get what you get.

I wasn't that daring and stuck to working with the supplies that had some form of epicurean unity. I have created some unusual concoctions in the past, some of which stuck. Most were chocked down for mere functionality.

I thought about the frozen chicken that had been in the freezer since New Cal. We turned off the refrigerator days ago to save the batteries, but I checked it anyway.

The chicken was still slightly cool and it smelled ok.

"We're in luck," I said. "Have you ever had my Jammin' Chicken?"

"No mate, never had that one. Is it some sort of Jamaican thing?"

"Nah, it's just jam and chicken."

"Ha, yeah whatever, do it up."

This invention has stuck with me through my evolution of caveman cooking. It materialized one day back in college when I was in a bind for something to put on top of some dry chicken.

Muzzy had a look on his face as though something that sounded so stupid might actually work. I pulled out the stuff and went to work.

Thankfully, the engine was running well. Otherwise, we'd be stuck at sea until the next weather system came through with some wind. There wasn't the slightest breeze and the seas were calm. We continued to motor along for days thinking the wind would return. They never did. Across the Pacific, I usually had too much wind, hoping for less. I finally got what I wished for, but wanted the old way back.

On the eighth day, we spotted Australia in the distance. It was flat, yet comforting. Three years at sea and over 20,000 miles, I was seeing a possible end of my journey. I began pondering over my entire sequential existence, wondering how a flatlander, originally from a cow town in Texas, figured out how to sail across that big puddle. A flatlander is worse than a landlubber. Not only are you stuck on land, but you're also landlocked with no sea.

We sailed into the bay and made our way to the harbor at Scarborough north of Brisbane. The sun gained intensity and the wind ironically began blowing. We were able to sail the last hour of the journey. The seagulls came to greet us. They were flying overhead wondering whether we had any food for them. We looked at them with the same sentiments. We were out of everything.

We tacked various times to reach the small harbor inside the calm bay. As we entered the channel to the harbor, I hailed the harbormaster. He directed me to the quarantine dock. He greeted us at the dock to help tie off the *Bula*. I stepped off the boat, shook the Harbormaster's hand—turned to Muzzy and honorably shook his hand to another successful trip. I stopped, looked at the sky and saluted every spirit of good or evil for allowing me to make it across the Pacific . . . ALIVE.

Bula

The Harbor Master told us we had to wait for a customs agent to come down and clear us into the country. I began hosing down the boat and Muzzy poked around appearing as if he wanted to sneak off to the closest bar. The customs agent promptly appeared at the boat. He was wearing an official shirt, grey slacks and worn dress shoes.

"Welcome to Australia," he said.

"Thank you, it's a pleasure to have made it this far," I replied.

"Oh yeah, where did you sail from?"

"Originally California."

"That's a long one mate. You still got your passport?"

"I hope so."

"Could I get your mates passport and your boat documents as well please sir."

"Sure, let me get those for you. Please come aboard." He stepped aboard and I offered him to sit down at the cluttered salon table. He had a relaxed demeanor and a friendly Australian accent.

I handed him our passports and the boat documents. He took them and pulled out some blank forms. He continued making small talk as he filled out the various forms.

After he went through the significance of the formal papers, he shook my hand, packed up his briefcase and promptly stepped off the boat. It had been a long time since anything was prompt in the South Pacific.

He said, "Once again, welcome to Australia, you gentlemen are cleared into the country. Enjoy your stay"

"Thank you sir," I replied. He walked off towards the entrance of the harbor.

After stowing everything and organizing the boat, Muzzy said, "Mate, I'm going in search of some fish & chips."

"Alright," I said. "I'm going to finish up here and maybe I'll catch up with ya in a bit." We both needed some space.

The Harbor Master Sam had asked me to come up to his office and sign a couple of forms, once I got everything squared away.

I found him upstairs in his office over-looking the harbor. He said, "Come in, come in. Can I offer you a beer?"

"Sure can," I replied.

He opened a cold Victoria Bitter and handed it to me. He then opened one for himself. Sam wasn't Australian. He had a dark complexion with dark hair. I couldn't place the accent. It was possibly from the Middle East or Turkey.

He handed me the forms for a temporary slip in the harbor. I viewed their contents and signed them. We began chatting, and he claimed he was looking for a 38 to 40 foot sailboat for his family.

"How about a 36?" I said.

He said, "You're selling your boat?"

"If I can find the right offer. If not, then I'm sailing on to Indonesia."

"She's a Columbia right?"

"Yep, 1968. Built in Southern California."

"I'm more interested in wooden boats myself, but there are none around and my wife and kids want to have a boat for sailing on the weekends."

"The boat can do more than a weekend trip."

"Yes, I'm sure of that, but I don't want to take them on a long distance trip until they've learned how to sail."

"Well, I think she's big enough for you and your family."

"How many berths are there?"

"Four berths. She sleeps six comfortably."

Sam looked out at the window at the boat, thinking.

"Let me call my wife."

He called up his wife and she sounded interested enough to come down to see the boat. He hung up the phone and said, "Our house is just around the corner. She said she would be here in ten minutes or so."

We sat around drinking the beers and Sam continued questioning me. I gave him the information in a proud yet sad manner. I was thinking about all the love and money I had put into her. Sure, I wanted to sell the boat, but it didn't hit me until someone was actually interested.

His wife Ruth arrived in a timely manner. Sam introduced us and we chatted about my trip across the Pacific.

I said, "Well, shall we?" Pointing towards the door.

They both nodded and we headed down to the docks to have a look at my girl. I had a sinking feeling as we walked down the floating docks. We came around the bend and there she was looking slightly tattered, but with a noble flare. She had endured three years across the cruel sea. Part of me wanted them to lose interest.

I stepped onto the boat and politely said, "Please, come aboard."

Sam stepped aboard and put out a hand for his wife to step onto the deck. I removed the companionway wood slates and entered the cabin down the stairs. They followed as I switched on the interior lights. The interior is the best selling point of a boat for a woman. *Bula* was still in good shape on the inside. The wood had a nice luster and the upholstery was only a few years old.

Ruth got a big smile on her face as she inspected the separate rooms and shower. Sam was indifferent and only asked integral questions, unemotionally. I was actually doing my best at selling, though answered his many question in the utmost honesty. She had some problems, like all boats, especially after the miles of torture.

Ruth said, "I love it. It's so cozy."

Sam smiled at his wife's elation and said, "Yes, the interior does have a fair amount of mahogany that's in good condition.

However, the walls on the interior of the head need to be stripped and re-varnished."

I said, "That's water damage from the shower."

Sam acknowledged, "Yes, ah huh."

The questions faded out and they both seemed pleased. I wasn't comfortable around Sam for some reason. His wife was innocent enough.

Sam said, "Would you care to take it out for a sea trial?"

I continued with my intention of selling the boat and half-heartedly said, "Sure."

"When can you go?"

"I'm free any day."

"Ok, let's pick a day with some good wind to really test it out."

"Sounds fine to me. Just let me know."

We exited the cabin and they both thanked me for letting them view the boat.

I said, "I'll be right here. Just let me know when."

Sam said, "I'm sure I can get some free time over the next couple of days."

I hid my true feelings and put on the game face. "Great. It was a pleasure to meet you both. Have a good night."

They responded, "Good night."

They say the happiest two days of a man's life is the day he buys his first boat and the day he sells it. I wasn't so happy to sell her. In fact, I felt as though I was losing a family member. She was the one who kept me afloat through the most dangerous trials. I felt as if I was betraying a girlfriend who had given me so much pleasure, but also a lot of pain. Nearly as intimate as a marriage, it brought tears to my eyes to let her go. However, I felt I had to do it in order to move on. I hoped that she would go to a good home. Sam didn't seem like a sailor to me, though he was the harbormaster after all. I just didn't trust him. Maybe it was my own defensiveness towards my baby.

Two days later, we had good wind and Sam asked me if we could go out for a sail. We took her out and she performed beautifully with 16 knots of wind. Sam was more excited now that he discovered the boat had some speed. It was probably a little faster than the traditional wooden boats he had been sailing. The more I tried to point out the good features, the more I didn't want to sell her.

An hour slipped by and we headed back to the harbor after sunset. There was some negotiating on the way into the harbor and Sam claimed he would need to haul the boat out to have a surveyor inspect the hull.

I said, "Sure, whatever you need to do, I'll be more than happy to help." I wasn't really that happy.

Over the next few days, he pulled the boat out of the water in the boatyard and everything checked out fine. We met at his house to negotiate a figure we could both live with. I was scared I was doing the wrong thing, but I knew I had already decided to go through with it.

After a nervous half an hour of going back and forth, we agreed on a number and shook hands. What a relief. Sam said he could drive me to his bank in the morning to transfer the funds.

I slept on the idea that I wasn't going to get what I wanted, but I felt as though it was fair. You never get back what you put into a boat.

Sam deposited the money into my bank account in the States and I was free to go and spend it wherever I pleased. On our way out of the bank I said, "I can make it back to the boat alone to get my things."

"Ok, well I'm glad everything went smoothly," he said. "Thank you. Now I hope the boat doesn't fall apart."

"Me too," I said sarcastically. "You got yourself a fine boat there Sam. I didn't really want to sell it, but I have to move on with my life."

"I understand."

"Good luck with the *Bula*," We shook hands one last time and I stared into his eyes. "Goodbye."

"Yes, goodbye Bryan."

I stepped out the door and began walking in no particular direction. My mind was boiling with options. As I floated down the sidewalk, I reflected upon the voyage. I walked through the fire and came out unburned. I waited for the profound element to sink in and drop some jewel of enlightenment. My mind slowly searched for that golden egg of clairvoyance that has only enlightened God, Gandhi, and umm . . . David Lee Roth. What is life all about anyway? Success? Wisdom? Creating? Giving? Or is it all about love? As humans, we strive for these pillars. But what is the root of it all? I know one thing for sure; I'm not going to waste my time worrying about it. Make as many memories as you can, so one day you can sit back and laugh at the whole thing, because nothing makes any more sense than just that.

About the Author

He's a handsome fellow. Born in the south and educated in San Diego where he wrote for the magazine "Revolt in Style". He has been traveling the world *not* looking for the meaning of life. He presently resides in Puerto Rico.

Acknowledgements

I would like to thank the following for their assistance, support and editing: Phillip Painter, Doug Maxwell, Jeanne Sinclair, Andrew King, Chris Grimes, and Thaddeus Temple for believing in my writing.